For a brief moment—and this is difficult to admit—I found myself tempted to schedule the surgery. A completely unnecessary surgery. The operation would have taken me twenty stress-free minutes, she would have gone home a few hours later, and I would have been paid close to $1,000.

I was presented with every excuse to take out this woman's gallbladder. The only problem: There was no medical reason to do so.

—from THE COST OF CUTTING

ALSO BY PAUL A. RUGGIERI, M.D.

Confessions of a Surgeon
The Good, the Bad, and the Complicated . . .
Life Behind the O.R. Doors

THE COST
OF CUTTING

A SURGEON REVEALS
THE TRUTH BEHIND A
MULTIBILLION-DOLLAR
INDUSTRY

PAUL A.
RUGGIERI, M.D.

 BERKLEY BOOKS, NEW YORK

THE BERKLEY PUBLISHING GROUP
Published by the Penguin Group
Penguin Group (USA) LLC
375 Hudson Street, New York, New York 10014

USA • Canada • UK • Ireland • Australia • New Zealand • India • South Africa • China

penguin.com

A Penguin Random House Company

This book is an original publication of The Berkley Publishing Group.

Library of Congress Cataloging-in-Publication Data

Ruggieri, Paul, 1959–
The cost of cutting : a surgeon reveals the truth behind a multibillion-dollar
industry / Paul A. Ruggieri, M.D.
pages cm
Includes bibliographical references.
ISBN 978-0-425-27231-2 (paperback)
1. Surgery—Economic aspects—United States. 2. Surgery—Decision making—Economic
aspects—United States. 3. Medical care, Cost of—United States. I. Title.
RD27.42.R84 2014
338.4'7617—dc23
2014016262

PUBLISHING HISTORY
Berkley trade paperback edition / September 2014

PRINTED IN THE UNITED STATES OF AMERICA

10 9 8 7 6 5 4 3 2

Cover photo: Asian Surgeon in Scrubs © Erproductions Ltd / Getty Images.
Cover design by Oceana Garceau.
Interior text design by Laura K. Corless.

Most Berkley Books are available at special quantity discounts for bulk purchases for sales
promotions, premiums, fund-raising, or educational use. Special books, or book excerpts, can also be
created to fit specific needs. For details, write: Special.Markets@us.penguingroup.com.

To my wife, Erin, and my three stepsons,
Matthew, Ryan, and Jack.
I will be forever grateful
for the love and inspiration
they have brought into my life.

The events described in this book are real experiences of real people and took place at real healthcare facilities. However, the author has changed people's identities, changed the names of healthcare facilities at which events took place, and in some cases, created composite characters and healthcare facilities. Any resemblance between a character in this book and a real person, or between a facility in this book and a real facility, therefore is entirely accidental.

CONTENTS

INTRODUCTION

had my first inkling that I wanted to be a surgeon before I was even accepted into medical school. Once I was there, it wasn't long before I knew surgery was my calling. That was more than twenty-five years ago and every day (well, almost every day) since then I've been able to say, *I love what I do.* As a general surgeon, using my hands, my brain, and the tools of surgery, I can make a difference in the quality of a person's life every time I step into the operating room. Sometimes I can even save a life. I'm profoundly grateful for the opportunity.

A couple of years ago I wrote a book about what goes on inside an operating room from a surgeon's perspective. I wanted to take people into that mysterious world where a day's work can ricochet from the mundane (varicose vein removal) to the sublime (repairing a torn artery before the person bleeds to death) in a matter of minutes. Those moments when something truly exceptional happens in the operating room, and even the less exciting ones, are what keep me and my colleagues doing what we do. The work itself is truly the reward—as is the gratitude of our patients.

Why, then, have I written a book about the money side of the equation? Isn't money supposed to be anathema to the high principles of the medical profession? After all, we're not stockbrokers, we're healers. Traditionally, it's been almost unseemly to mention money in the same breath as patient care.

But a new conversation is taking place in our country, and it's all about money and healthcare. None of us can get away from it, including those of us who work as physicians and surgeons. And maybe that's a good thing. I'm finding for the first time in my professional life that doctors are talking openly with each other about reimbursement, about expenses, about the challenge of running a viable practice while taking on more and more Medicare patients as the baby boom generation turns sixty-five.

As the Affordable Care Act (ACA) kicks in, the conversation about the cost of providing care in America has become even more important. And more frantic. *Who will be covered? What will it cost? How will we as a country afford it? How does all of this relate to quality—or does it?* A lot of contradictory points of view are being put forth. It's a topic worth careful consideration. And that's why I've written this book.

Currently, the United States spends more than $2.7 trillion a year on healthcare. This figure translates to more than 17 percent of gross domestic product (GDP)—and more than any other nation on earth spends on delivering medical services. A healthy piece of this $2.7 trillion pie is spent by private insurers and the federal government on reimbursement for operations and all the related expenses: surgeon fees, anesthesia fees, operating room fees, recovery room fees, hospital inpatient fees, and the "state of the art" equipment used during surgery.

Surgical procedures, more than any other aspect of health-care, generate revenue. Big revenue. Operations are the lifeblood of hospitals. And of surgeons. Surgeons do not make a living seeing patients in the office; they make a living seeing patients in the operating room. Without busy operating rooms, many hospitals would dry up, closing their doors and taking away other important (nonsurgical) services as well.

Without operating rooms full of busy surgeons, medical device companies (big international for-profit companies that produce a plethora of equipment used during surgery, such as artificial joints, mesh, robots, cardiac stents, sutures, surgical stapling devices, and laparoscopic equipment) could not survive. Nor could they face their shareholders.

With more than fifty million operations performed in this country every year, surgery is big business. Surgery is an engine that compensates surgeons performing their craft, supports hospitals promoting their surgical services, and profits medical device companies. Unfortunately, all this money carries with it power and influence. When it comes to medical decision making, power and influence are *not* what you want motivating your surgeon, your hospital, or your insurance company. I believe this taboo topic should be part of our national discussion as we shape the future of healthcare.

Historically, surgeons and hospitals have benefited financially by producing greater operating room volume, not necessarily greater quality. Surgeons know this, anesthesiologists know this, insurance companies know this, and hospital administrators especially know this. Ironically, the only ones who are unaware of the enormous amounts of money generated from their operations are the patients about to be wheeled into the operating room. It does not matter whether your heart is being bypassed, your stomach stapled, your knee scoped, your uterus removed, your spine fused, or your hernia repaired; a long line of healthcare providers, hospital administrators, insurance company executives, and medical device company big shots are profiting before, during, and after your operation. Maybe that's as it should be. Money must be made from surgery or there would be no surgical care at all. The question before the nation is, *How much is that worth?*

Over the last ten years, healthcare costs have spiraled out of control. The average person knows something is awry but not exactly what, or how to address the problem. What we *do* know is that there is a limit to the amount of federal money we are comfortable designating for medical care, and insurance companies are in business to make money. We want greater access to care and we want quality care and we want lower insurance premiums. So who's going to foot the bill for all that quality care?

The ACA means greater access to care for more of the population, but it also means even greater government scrutiny on healthcare costs, and it has already resulted in significant reductions in reimbursements to providers, including surgeons. In many ways, this scrutiny is a good thing. To remain viable, however, hospitals in every community across this country are consolidating to gain patient "market share" and buying up primary care doctors and specialists alike. This shopping spree is an attempt to control referrals to their operating rooms and retain patients in their network. *Retention* is the battle cry of hospitals today.

As a potential patient, you are affected by all this. Hospitals' attempts to control surgical referrals affect your choice of surgeon. Insurance companies are encroaching on your choices, too, with limited healthcare plans and provider networks. Sure, you can still choose your surgeon, but it will cost you sky-high deductibles if he or she is an "out of network" provider.

If you're very lucky, you may never need to see the inside of an operating room. But even if fate is that kind to you, the cost of healthcare and how it will be provided in this country is something that should matter to all of us. I don't claim to have all the answers to this puzzle, but I do hope the information and perspectives offered in this book will be enlightening. I hope you'll gain insights that will get you thinking about this topic in a new way.

Meanwhile, I look forward to getting back to what I love to do.

PAUL A. RUGGIERI, M.D., F.A.C.S.

1 FOR LOVE OR MONEY

The woman seated on the exam table was lean and fit and seemed to be enjoying perusing one of the magazines from our slightly out-of-date offerings. She looked like she was in her midforties; her chart showed her age to be fifty-two. Her face did not express any distress and when she returned my greeting she spoke in a clear, friendly tone. As I scanned her medical history, the portrait of a person in good health came into view—her lab work, blood pressure, weight: All were excellent.

Healthy and *thin* are two adjectives I do not often use to describe my patients. Why was this woman in my office?

Several weeks earlier, it turned out, her primary care physician had ordered an abdominal CT scan to investigate a nagging pain that he hadn't been able to diagnose. Eureka: The radiologist reviewing the scan noticed gallstones. Mystery solved. The patient (we'll call her Mrs. Brogan) was subsequently referred to me for a "surgical opinion," a consultation to determine whether surgery could help. As I performed the physical exam, I questioned her and soon concluded that her gallbladder was working perfectly. While some of her symptoms were vague and nonspecific, the gallstones found during the CT were what we in medicine call an *incidental finding*, nothing more. The true source of Mrs. Brogan's pain had yet to be determined.

An incidental finding happens when an apparent abnormality of some kind—unrelated to the source of the person's symptoms—is discovered during a diagnostic imaging exam. For example, if a CT scan of the abdomen is ordered to help with the diagnosis of a bowel problem and the radiologist notices a dark area, a "density," on the kidney, that information becomes part of the report and is considered an incidental finding. Similarly, if a CT scan of the chest for diagnosis of coronary artery disease reveals a nodule in the lung, that incidental finding is shared with the referring physician and, ultimately, with the patient. Let the testing (and worrying) begin.

Over the past fifteen years there has been a dramatic increase in the use of two sophisticated diagnostic imaging tools: CT and MRI scans. *CT* (often referred to as a *CAT* scan), stands for *computerized* (or *computer-aided*) *tomography*, which uses x-ray technology. *MRI*, which stands for *magnetic resonance imaging*, uses a magnetic field and radio waves. Both create incredibly detailed views of the organs and soft tissue. According to the Radiological Society of North America (RSNA), while between three and four million CT scans were performed in 1995, seventy million were done in 2010. A report published in the *Journal of the American Medical Association* (*JAMA*) in 2012 showed a 400 percent increase in the use of MRIs during this same period. It is no wonder, then, that incidental findings are becoming more common and surgery as a result of them is on the rise.

While the advance of technology has tremendous benefits in medicine, the information these tools provide can present problems as well. For example, according to the RSNA, *one-third or more* of all CT scans will reveal incidental findings, yet *fewer than 1 percent* of these abnormalities are cancer or in need of any medical treatment. *Where is the problem in that?* you may be wondering. *Knowledge is power*, is it not? The problem is that once the radiologist spots the abnormality, he or she will most likely include it in the report. (Seasoned radiologists struggle with "nonspecific" incidental findings and whether to say anything at all. Frequently, the decision to report them is heavily influenced by the ever-present shadow of a malpractice lawsuit.) This often means your doctor must share that news with you, causing you anxiety and necessitating further tests, exposing you to more radiation and often a visit to an operating room for a surgical biopsy.

By the way, the phenomenon of incidental findings is especially prevalent in the Medicare population (those age sixty-five and over). One study, published in the *American Journal of Roentgenology* in 2005, showed incidental findings to be as high as 75 percent in 259 individuals over age fifty who underwent CT scans. The reason: An aging body coupled with technology powerful enough to produce high-definition images of structures doctors have never seen before is a surefire recipe for incidental findings. Pandora's box has been opened.

There is, of course, a financial cost for all this information. Americans now spend an estimated $100 billion a year on medical imaging. But more important than the cost in dollars and cents is the cost to a person's quality of life. As H. Gilbert Welch, M.D., noted in his book, *Overdiagnosed*, "Imaging technologies are very helpful in finding the abnormalities that are making patients sick. But they are also increasingly able to find abnormalities in people who are well," a vicious cycle he refers to as "seeing more, finding more, and doing more." The studies cited in Welch's book are provocative; it's difficult to acknowledge that the number of individuals who are hurt by unnecessary medical treatment is far greater than the number helped by the advances in diagnostic imaging, but that's what the numbers show.

To take a closer look, consider another study from the journal *Health Affairs* in 2009 looking at how the increased use of MRIs can lead to potentially unnecessary surgery. This data showed that as the use of MRIs for generalized back pain increased, more spine abnormalities were detected. Whether these abnormalities were the true cause of the back pain is unclear. Yet the subsequent increase in back surgery correlates with the increase in MRI diagnostic imaging, despite the lack of definitive evidence that surgery would be beneficial. What that means is a significant number of individuals underwent major surgery on their spines (ranging from a laminectomy to spinal fusion) and yet continued to experience the pain that precipitated the MRI or, even worse, a more severe and disabling pain.

Doctors order diagnostic imaging exams for the best of reasons. The results can be definitive and lifesaving. But they can also be equivocal, unclear. What you, the prospective patient, need to understand is that in some ways your doctor is a detective searching for clues, and what's "wrong" is not always immediately clear. Incidental findings are often red herrings, diverting attention from the real problem.

———

Back to Mrs. Brogan.

I had in front of me a woman whose primary care physician had told her of the gallstones revealed on her CT scan. He had recommended that she seek a surgical opinion with me, telling his patient, "I can send you to a surgeon who will try to find any reason to operate on you. I can also send you to a surgeon who will find any excuse not to operate on you. Or I can send you to Dr. Ruggieri, who is somewhere in between." Mrs. Brogan was free of "underlying conditions" (obesity or a chronic disease such as diabetes that can cause complications during what is usually a straightforward operation). And she was willing. As a matter of fact, when I told her there was nothing wrong with her gallbladder, she said, "Why not just take the thing out? I don't need it anyway, do I?"

All that *and* she had very good health insurance. Reimbursement would not be a problem.

I had an opening in my schedule that week. . . . For a brief moment—and this is difficult to admit—I found myself tempted to schedule the surgery. A completely unnecessary surgery. The operation would have taken me twenty stress-free minutes, Mrs. Brogan would have gone home a few hours after the operation, and I would have been paid close to $1,000.

The only problem: There was no medical reason to do so.

Yes, the CT study had revealed gallstones. But they were totally asymptomatic, which is to say they were not the source of the pain she had been experiencing. Most likely, the gallstones would never in her lifetime become a problem.

Mrs. Brogan's referring primary care physician had recommended the surgery based on his extensive workup. (He also had no idea where to go next.) He was convinced the gallbladder *had* to be the source of her pain since the rest of her workup had turned up nothing. Mrs. Brogan had decided that the years of vague left-sided (sometimes right-sided) abdominal pain *must* be gallstones. All I had to do was recommend surgery. And, like so many people who consult with me, she was of the school of thought that says, *If you don't need it, remove it.* The only problem: In my mind, there was no solid medical reason to perform surgery. I was, however, not deaf to the nonmedical "reasons" to schedule the surgery—Mrs. Brogan wanted it; I wanted to please her referring physician; and as a self-employed surgeon, I needed to earn a living and resist turning away potential business. Yet . . . the gallstones discovered on the patient's CT scan were, in my judgment, strictly an incidental finding, not the cause of her abdominal pain.

Despite the report of gallstones, Mrs. Brogan's clinical history and physical exam were not consistent with gallstone pain. All of us—her primary care physician, the radiologist who read the CT scan, and I—were missing something. Something else was the source of Mrs. Brogan's pain; we just didn't know what it was. I believed her gallstones were asymptomatic, and I reassured her they were no threat. She was, as I explained, one of the millions of Americans walking around with an incidental finding. She did not need to see the overhead lights of an operating room.

According to the University of Michigan Center for Healthcare Outcomes and Policy, unnecessary surgery costs the U.S.

healthcare system over $150 billion a year. This is not a new problem. As far back as 1974, a congressional subcommittee report estimated that more than 2.4 million patients a year underwent unnecessary surgery (resulting in twelve thousand deaths). Today it's estimated that 10 to 20 percent of all operations are not needed. Of course, surgery is not the only way we waste our healthcare dollars; the Institute of Medicine uncovered $750 billion in unnecessary healthcare spending in 2009. Of this, more than $130 billion was spent on higher-cost procedures, such as operations. The cost of unnecessary surgery that *can't* be calculated is the price to the individual in lost days at home and work; emotional and physical suffering; and the risks associated with anesthesia, surgical site infection, and medication side effects—not to mention the possibility that the person will become one of the 100,000 a year seriously harmed by a medical error during a hospital stay.

Mrs. Brogan's story is not unusual in my profession. Every day I evaluate men and women who come to me with a variety of complaints, all believing they are potential candidates for surgery. Some, frankly, do not need surgery—two in four of the new patients I see should be treated in other ways. For others, the problem is obvious and treatable by an operation.

You may find this picture contradictory. Surgeons, including me, need to operate to make a living. When I perform surgery, I am reimbursed by insurance companies for the service I provide. So why would we turn away "business"? The answer lies in our commitment to "first, do no harm."

When I sit with a prospective surgical patient and recommend an operation, my decision has enormous consequences, both personal and financial, that will affect both of us. What if despite my best intentions, I am wrong in my judgment? What if I mistakenly subject that person to the unnecessary risk of surgery for no true benefit? What financial burdens will I be subjecting the patient to (not to mention the American healthcare system)? What if there is a poor outcome, with complications?

A surgeon's recommendation to take a person to the operating room should be solely influenced by medical facts, sound judgment, and experience. However, particularly today, other influences are weighing on the surgical decision-making process. Nowadays, surgeons are more pressured by "business" factors than ever before—they feel compelled to keep hospital operating rooms busy, to keep their practices going, and to maintain a living. After twenty years as a surgeon, I can say this: The line between operating for love and operating for money isn't as distinct as it once was. The reality is that some surgeons (and hospitals) are more motivated by money than by the Hippocratic oath they promised to uphold.

As a young newly minted general surgeon starting out, I was ready to operate, ready to make a living by improving lives. I was eager to conquer disease, ambitious in my desire to help all comers, and ready to take full responsibility for every person who walked through my office door. For me (and my colleagues back then), being a surgeon was not about money. We knew we were in for a nice pay raise once we left our residencies and started operating on our own, but we didn't talk about it. We knew we were going to upgrade our standard of living significantly. While the subject of making money was never openly discussed, we assumed we were going to do well. Frankly, many of us thought we deserved it, given the debt we had accumulated and the personal sacrifices we had made during training.

The saying that "doctors make poor businesspeople" has some truth to it. Even today, during medical school and training, there is little acknowledgment of the business side of a surgical practice. We don't get an insight into the costs, the profits, or how to maximize your value. Appropriately enough, the focus for interns and residents remains on becoming competent surgeons. My mentors believed that the surgical profession was one of altruism; to talk about business and reimbursement in the same breath as the best way to take out a colon cancer would have been heresy. I believe that this perspective has contributed to the shortage and dissatisfaction in my profession today. Just as sad, the failure to understand the business side of a surgical career early on negatively affects patient care.

I believe that most surgeons entering their careers are committed to a love of helping others and to practicing the highest quality of surgical care possible. I do *not* believe they are committed to their careers for the love of money. If they are, they will ultimately become hostages to it. Our focus when we are starting out is doing the best work we can; it takes a few years at least to begin to be able to earn more than a set salary. When I took my first job in a private practice, I signed a contract guaranteeing me a salary for two years as I built my referring network and patient loyalty. Because I was an employee of a private group, any monies I generated beyond my salary went to my colleagues. I was there to help cover some of their business operating expenses while reaping the benefits of practicing under the umbrella of my established colleagues. It was a fair arrangement. My group would take the risk of bringing on an untested surgeon, and I would have the security of a guaranteed wage.

After two years, if my partners found my personality, quality of work, and ability to generate business acceptable, I would be offered a full partnership. In some settings, this offer does not come cheap. It is not uncommon for a new colleague to have to "buy in" to the practice to become a partner. This buy-in can cost from $5,000 to $100,000, depending on the region of the country (and the scruples of the practice). Whatever the cost, it's a price many of us pay (often, paying over time) because the alternative—packing up and trying to reestablish a practice somewhere else—is less appealing. The "buy-in" money goes directly into the pockets of your new partners and is all perfectly legal. What you are truly buying is the ability to work as hard as your ambition drives you, and the opportunity to make as much money as you can.

As a surgeon in private practice at a community hospital, I am reimbursed directly by the patient's health insurance carrier for any operation I perform. I receive one "global" payment to cover the surgery itself plus all the care I provide afterward. If I do not have an active practice repairing hernias, removing gallbladders, cutting out colon cancers, operating on bowel obstructions, or removing cancerous thyroid tumors, I do not get paid. It's the same for all surgeons in private practice; if an orthopedic surgeon isn't busy replacing joints or repairing ligaments, he or she is not getting paid. For all of us, the busier you are (the more operations you perform), the more money you make. The fee-for-service reimbursement system for surgeons rewards quantity, not quality. Some say this system is flawed, that it encourages surgeons to operate as much as possible, perhaps even tempts them to perform unnecessary surgeries. Others point to the fee-for-service system as a major contributor to the rising cost of healthcare. I believe there is some truth to both of these concerns.

As members of an independent, private group (as of this writing), my colleagues and I are partners in a business. It is a business in which we own equal shares. We share expenses, most of which comprise employee payroll, office rent, and malpractice insurance. The diverse functions of a surgical practice mean we need to employ a staff with a variety of skills, including medical assistants, third-party billing experts, and administrative staff for filing, scheduling, and follow-up. It's expensive. As in any business, the income we generate—which is only from performing surgery—must exceed our monthly expenses or we will not remain viable.

By far, the most important business function within any private practice today is billing. The incredibly complex maze surgeons must navigate to get reimbursed for services rendered, whether from the federal government or private insurance, means a savvy billing department is crucial to a successful practice. When my senior partner started out in surgical practice more than thirty years ago, his billing system consisted of a pen, stationery, an envelope, and a stamp. After performing a surgery, he would instruct his secretary to write a letter to the insurance company on office stationery, describing the operation and how much he was charging for it. The letter would be mailed to the appropriate address, and several weeks later a check would arrive in the requested amount. It was that simple. There were no questions asked, no denying payment, no additional paperwork, and no pressure. You got full reimbursement for your services. That was the gilded age of surgical billing, and it gave surgeons a generous, uncomplicated living. Those days are long over. Today's complex system of reimbursement is very different, virtually unrecognizable to many surgeons, including me.

In order for surgeons (and all physicians) to get reimbursed for services, a specific code number (CPT code) corresponding to the service performed has to be electronically filed with the appropriate "modifier" codes and documentation. Once these are filed, it can take up to six weeks to get reimbursed. If the surgical claim gets rejected for improper coding or lack of documentation, it has to be refiled. Months could pass before any payment is approved and made.

Despite being equal partners in a surgical business, colleagues in the same practice can often earn very different salaries. For instance, in my practice, I am fourth on the income-generation chart. Several of my colleagues perform more operations than I do (by choice), and generate more income because of it. This isn't a bad thing. Some surgeons work harder at promoting themselves, advertising their unique skills and their quality work, and make themselves available day or night.

But today, "selling" surgery has become more of a necessity. Like any other service business, surgeons have clients—patients, referring physicians, hospital systems, and insurance companies— whose needs must be met. Some of these needs have nothing to do with actual patient care and are subtly eroding the ethics of my profession. The voices of hospital administrators, medical device sales reps, and insurance companies are crowding in on a surgeon's choices. That is, until I'm standing in the OR, scalpel in hand. Then, suddenly, I am alone in the decision-making process.

Mrs. Keeneland was a fifty-four-year-old woman who had been referred to me by her primary care physician because of her complaint of constant, chronic abdominal pain over the last five years. She had already been seen by an array of specialists and had undergone a battery of diagnostic imaging studies, including upper and lower endoscopy, all of which had resulted in no conclusive diagnosis. She had even swallowed a tiny camera (purposely) that had traversed through her small and large bowel, taking pictures along the way, before it exited into the toilet. Once again, nothing. Yet her pain persisted. Her primary care physician, one of my major referral sources, was at a dead end.

As I read her medical history before entering the exam room, I soon concluded that previous operations were the cause of her pain.

"Dr. Ruggieri, you need to help me," Mrs. Keeneland began before I could even say hello. "I can't live with this pain anymore." She clutched her abdomen. "I have had several operations in the last ten years, including a colon resection and multiple hernia repairs, some with mesh." I could see she knew the lingo. "My primary care doctor tells me I have scar tissue that's causing this pain. He said you can remove it, and the pain will be gone. He told me I have no other choice but surgery." She started to cry. "No one else can do anything for me. I just can't live like this anymore."

I examined Mrs. Keeneland's abdomen, covered with old surgical scars crisscrossing like train tracks. By laying my hands on a patient's abdomen, I can often discover a lot about the previous operations from the length, width, texture, and location of the surgical scars. The one fact I cannot discern is whether the operations were medically necessary. As my fingertips read her scars, like a blind person reading Braille, my mind was coming to a conclusion about Mrs. Keeneland's prognosis.

Adhesions, more commonly known as scar tissue, are an unwanted by-product of any operation. They are part of the natural healing process after surgery or any inflammatory process, such as acute appendicitis or endometriosis, and can occur anywhere in the body. Every time I venture into a patient's abdomen, I leave scar tissue behind, regardless of what I have removed. After intestine is manipulated during an operation, adhesions form, causing everything to stick together. If I reenter that patient's abdomen for another reason, the scar tissue gets worse and the risk of complications increases, especially the risk of bowel injury.

Adhesions are the most common reason for surgery of small bowel obstructions and cost the healthcare system many billions of dollars a year. Depending on the study you read, the overall treatment for adhesion-related complications has been estimated at $1.3 to $2 billion per year. Adhesions are also presumed to be one of the most common causes of chronic, intra-abdominal pain in patients today. We cannot measure them, image them, or even document their existence without another operation. It's a catch-22 situation. There is also no curative operation to remove adhesions. The ideal "treatment" is to avoid intra-abdominal surgery if at all possible. In the long run, repeat abdominal surgery to cut adhesions has not been proven to be effective, has an increased risk of complications, and is costly to the system. Only a minority of patients get relief after surgery to cut adhesions and free up the small intestine. Much of this relief is temporary at best. A study published in the journal *Lancet* in 2003 compared laparoscopic adhesiolysis (cutting of scar tissue) to diagnostic laparoscopy (no adhesiolysis) for the treatment of chronic abdominal pain. Both groups of patients had pain relief with no difference between them, suggesting that the placebo effect of diagnostic laparoscopy worked just as well as the actual adhesiolysis.

"Mrs. Keeneland," I began, "I believe your pain has many components, one possibly being adhesions inside your abdomen, scar tissue caused by multiple operations over the years." I paused, knowing she wasn't going to like what I had to say next. "Unfortunately, there is nothing I can do to make your situation any better. In my opinion, surgery is not the answer. It is too risky. A clear benefit is just not there."

She took a deep breath and dried her eyes. I continued, "There may be someone else I can have you see to manage your pain." I had barely finished speaking when Mrs. Keeneland got up and, without making eye contact, walked toward the exam room door. Before I could say another word she was gone, slamming the door behind her. She had expected me to schedule surgery, based on the optimistic conversation she'd had with her physician. She was tired and in pain, and her reaction was understandable.

Could I have operated on Mrs. Keeneland? Yes, of course. I could have explored her abdomen, cutting scar tissue to free up her intestines with the small hope of lessening her pain. I knew the scar tissue would be there. I also knew that trying to cut it out would not actually help. Exploring abdomens is what I do for a living.

Despite the real risks of bowel perforation and prolonged hospitalization, Mrs. Keeneland would have consented gladly to an operation if I had presented her chances of success with a little optimism. I could have documented specific clinical points regarding her diagnosis, enough to satisfy her insurance company to approve the surgery. For the operation itself, I would have been paid close to $1,500 (depending on her insurance) for several hours' work (depending on how bad the scar tissue was). The hospital where the surgery took place would have received ten times that amount, depending on her length of stay and whether there were any complications.

Based on my experience, the risks of operating on Mrs. Keeneland far outweighed the possible benefits despite the fact that I would be reimbursed regardless of her outcome. As I watched Mrs. Keeneland leave my exam room, I had no doubt she would find another surgeon who would "calculate" her risk differently, evaluate her chances of a "good outcome" differently, and offer her what she wanted. An operation.

"The world is gray, Jack." That line, from the movie *A Clear and Present Danger*, about why the lines between right and wrong are blurred while the outcome is crystal clear, could just as easily be taken from one of my practice's weekly meetings. In surgery, there are often clinical situations where a patient's problem falls into a "gray zone." When that happens, the decision to operate (or not) becomes somewhat arbitrary, even affected by past experiences (both good and bad). It can also be susceptible to nonclinical influences. For instance, if a patient of mine has a colon cancer, or a thyroid cancer, the problem is a very clear and present danger. In the situation of most cancers, the decision to treat with surgery is not gray. It is black-and-white, based on sound clinical outcome studies. In other disease states, however, the decision to treat with an operation is not backed by definitive data, leaving room for the surgeon to determine the best course of action. Many of these conditions are common and operations to treat them are performed on a regular basis. Mrs. Keeneland, with her pain and adhesions, falls into this category. A person with an asymptomatic inguinal hernia, incidentally found on a routine physical examination, will undoubtedly elicit different surgical recommendations from two or three different consultations. Some surgeons will want to repair it, while others will discuss the risks and benefits and urge the patient to wait and see if it becomes symptomatic.

As a surgeon in private practice, I work for myself even though I practice within a group of six surgeons under one financial roof. Within my group, I am my own independent private contractor and can offer surgical services to anyone who walks through my office door. I am not guaranteed a salary by anyone—today, next month, or next year. I am not guaranteed referrals, either. I am not guaranteed a retirement income unless I put away money every year. While I am in the business of treating surgical disease, trying to improve the quality of life of my patients with my skills as a surgeon, I am also in the business of earning an income, an income generated by carefully deciding who needs to go to the operating room and who does not. And this is where the balancing act of medical ethics comes into play.

For most surgeons, the decision to take someone to the operating room is based on knowledge, experience, ethics, and the best interest of the patient. It is a purely professional medical decision, untainted by other influences. It is unrealistic, however, not to acknowledge today's surgical workplace, where surgeons are under increasing pressure to generate income.

Surgeons are fighting to maintain their incomes in the face of declining reimbursements. For instance, fifteen years ago private insurance companies reimbursed surgeons (and gastroenterologists) close to $1,200 for a routine colonoscopy. Today, that number is under $350. Cardiac surgeons have seen their fees for heart bypass surgery decline by 200 percent over the same time period.

Now, I'll pause here to say that I understand why most of the population sees surgeons as *already* making a lot of money, maybe too much money. I suspect most would have no sympathy for a general surgeon making over $300,000 a year and crying about reimbursement rates, or an orthopedic surgeon making $500,000 a year, a neurosurgeon making $750,000, or even a cardiac surgeon making close to $1 million. *So, you doctors might be making a little less these days? So what!?!* Compared to the average American, our income makes us very rich indeed. But many of us are still fighting to remain self-employed. While we pay our high insurance premiums and plan for our retirement, we have to figure out how to do that when government and commercial health insurance companies are paying less and less for our services.

The pressure to operate can also originate from patients themselves. There are times when I know a surgery would be a fifty-fifty proposition, at best, for a successful result. In those instances, I have to say, *No, surgery is not a good idea*, despite ardent pleas from the patient—as with Mrs. Keeneland. It's not an easy conversation to have. There is also pressure from referring physicians; many expect me to use my surgical skills to "solve the problem" and make the patient completely better. And the fact is, if I am conservative too often, some referring physicians will look elsewhere for a surgeon. In the simplest terms, not scheduling surgery for a referring physician's patient means you've just put a hot potato back in his lap. He's not going to be happy about it.

Employed, salaried surgeons (especially those who work for corporate entities and hospital systems) feel constant pressure to earn enough to meet their salary and contractual quotas. Many of them are working in an environment where the threat of being replaced is real. It's a picture that resembles the cutthroat world of commercial sales more than the world of medicine. Surgical decision making has *got* to be affected, even if only a little.

The pressure to operate can also come from within surgeons themselves. Every one of us has a level of experience, a comfort zone. We know what we do well. Yet for many of us, it is difficult to admit our limitations and pass up an opportunity to operate, "giving away business," even when we should. I have observed surgeons performing operations they haven't done in years, causing minor and major complications for their unsuspecting patients. Ego, arrogance, greed? Call it what you wish. I call it criminal. It *is* difficult to acknowledge a lack of skill or experience, to oneself or a patient. It is difficult to turn down an operation (especially one that pays well) that you *probably* could perform but haven't done in the last year. It is difficult to admit to a referring physician that his patient would be better off in the hands of another surgeon. But it is the right thing to do.

Every month, I choose not to operate on a fair number of patients because I have concluded that surgery is not medically necessary. Most surgeons think the same way. Other elements that factor into my decision include the overall health of the patient and his or her ability to tolerate an operation, the risk for complications or a poor outcome, the likelihood of success, and my own experience with whatever operation the person requires. It's a multifaceted consideration. The one thing that does *not* factor in is the type of health insurance the person has. In our practice, my colleagues and I take all types of insurance, from the worst to the best payers. I (and most surgeons in practice today) am keenly aware of what each insurance plan reimburses for every operation I can perform. (Why shouldn't I be? From a business standpoint, I need to be aware of reimbursement.)

As a general surgeon, I know that my best-paying operations involve major abdominal surgery (colon resections, stomach resections). I know that laparoscopic procedures (the use of very small incisions and fiber optics) reimburse less than regular "open" surgery (larger incisions that allow the surgeon to see the entire area and organs). Reimbursement for robotic procedures is similar to that for traditional laparoscopic procedures. I have no doubt that orthopedic surgeons are aware of what they receive for joint replacements; neurosurgeons for spinal fusions; heart surgeons for bypass operations; and bariatric surgeons for stomach stapling/gastric bypass. (What is harder to pin down is what the operation will cost you and/or your insurance carrier, as Elizabeth Rosenthal, a physician-turned-journalist and *New York Times* reporter, made shockingly clear in her 2013 series about the cost of healthcare in America.)

Multiple studies, in many of the surgical subspecialties, have documented that some operations being performed today for specific diseases have outcomes no better than nonsurgical treatment. For instance, a randomized study out of Norway published in the journal *Spine* in 2003 compared lumbar spinal fusion to physical therapy in the treatment of chronic low back pain and disc degeneration. The study found no difference in pain outcomes between the two methods of treatment. The only obvious difference was the much higher cost of the spinal fusion surgery. According to the Agency for Healthcare Research and Quality, over a ten-year period (2001–2010) the number of spinal fusion operations nearly doubled to 465,000 at a cost of $12.8 billion in 2011. None of this is new information, and most surgeons are aware of such studies within their own specialty. Why, then, do these operations continue? They constitute a physical cost to the patient, as well as a financial cost to the system. Maybe surgeons are performing these operations because they truly believe they can help people, despite what the data shows. Maybe some are performing these operations because they feel subtle pressure from the political environment they practice in or the hospital system they work for. Perhaps the surgeon feels pressure to "earn" a guaranteed salary, meet quarterly benchmarks, keep patients in the community, and prevent "leakage" to other hospitals. The question that must be answered is this: Are these potentially unnecessary operations being performed for purely economic reasons?

Like every profession, surgery is not exempt from bad seeds. As difficult as it is to write this, some surgeons operate for solely economic reasons. You've read about them in the news. There was the neurosurgeon operating out of an Oregon hospital who was discovered to be performing unnecessary spinal fusion operations (a very expensive procedure) for economic reward from 2008 to 2011. He ultimately had his license suspended and faced multiple patient lawsuits. There was the cardiologist from Baltimore who, in 2009, was placing cardiac stents in patients at a clip well beyond what most cardiologists report doing. He billed Medicare over $6 million over several years. There was the orthopedic surgeon from New York who pleaded guilty to ten federal counts of Medicare/Medicaid billing fraud while performing sham operations. These well-publicized cases of rogue surgeons who were operating purely for economic reasons, completely unconcerned about the harm they were causing patients, are shocking. They are also, I'm glad to say, rare.

Recent changes in Medicare rules that are intended to improve payment transparency may help uncover more instances of fraudulent billing and unnecessary operations. A recent federal ruling removing a decades-old court injunction that prevented public access to Medicare billing information is changing the landscape, and for the better. Since 1979, the vast library of individual physicians' billing to Medicare had been hidden from view. With the Affordable Care Act, signed into law in 2010, that all changed. The thinking is that by shining the light of day on physicians' (especially surgeons') Medicare billing habits, the proclivity of some who are performing too many of one specific operation (compared to their colleagues) will send up a red flag. This kind of information (particularly if outcomes are persistently bad) could also be a fraud alert, as well as an indication of the quality and experience of individual surgeons. Medicare audits are exactly how some of the preceding examples of "unnecessary surgery" were initially discovered. While some in medicine are opposed to this trend, I believe Medicare claims billing transparency will be a helpful tool in weeding out surgeons who are in this profession for money rather than love, profiting and performing unnecessary operations on unsuspecting patients.

The greed and abuse is not restricted to surgical procedures. Other medical literature is finding data showing that patients are undergoing nonsurgical procedures they may not need. These procedures were not necessarily performed out of purely false intent but also out of a liability fear of "missing" something, or based on a "different" interpretation of existing medical guidelines. A recent study out of the University of Texas published in *JAMA* found that close to 23 percent of colonoscopies for twenty-four thousand Medicare patients age seventy and older were inappropriate based on the U.S. Preventive Services Task Force guidelines for screening colonoscopy. For individuals over age seventy-six, that number increased to 39 percent. The rates of inappropriate testing varied widely by physician. And some of the patients stated they "would not trust a doctor" who did *not* recommend the procedure, further complicating the motivation behind the numbers.

Medicare reimburses physicians approximately $260 per colonoscopy, while private insurance reimbursement approaches $350 per case. (Reimbursement for colonoscopy was once more than $1,000 per case.) As the author of the *JAMA* article stated, "Any time you have a fee-for-service system, there is a risk in over-utilizing services that get well-reimbursed for the time spent to perform them."

In the world of heart disease, coronary artery catheterization and stenting has been a common way to diagnose and treat blocked arteries and has been considered a medically sound way to avoid debilitating (and costly) cardiovascular surgery. Coronary artery stenting is also an expensive procedure, costing anywhere from

$20,000 to $50,000 per case. The treatment of cardiovascular disease, the number one killer in America, is a $12 billion market for hospitals in this country, with more than 600,000 angioplasty procedures carried out each year. The stenting business (more than 450,000 procedures per year) is not only lucrative for the heart specialist performing the procedure but also a big-ticket item for the hospital supplying the venue and equipment. A study conducted under the auspices of the American College of Cardiology, looking at more than 1,000 patients and over 500,000 procedures during a six-year period, confirmed the overuse of expensive intervention. In certain patient populations and hospitals, the inappropriate rate of coronary artery angioplasty (with or without stent placement) approached 50 percent. In some cases, a stent was placed in patients *with no symptoms at all.*

In July 2002, the *New England Journal of Medicine* published a fascinating study comparing arthroscopic knee surgery (involving lavage and debridement) to placebo surgery in patients with osteoarthritis. The study was based on a randomized controlled trial (meaning it was scientifically legitimate). Those in the arthroscopic knee surgery group had surgery, while those in the placebo group had skin incisions only, nothing more, although they believed they'd had actual surgery. When the study was published, orthopedic surgeons were performing more than 650,000 arthroscopic procedures a year at a cost of $5,000 each. The operation was a common procedure for orthopedic surgeons ten years ago; it was low-risk and easy to do, and it paid well. The study found that the arthroscopic knee lavage/debridement group had no better results than the placebo surgery group in resolving pain. Also fascinating was the news that some of the placebo surgery patients reported feeling better over time than those who had undergone the actual procedure! Since that study was published, subsequent studies have confirmed its conclusions.

The results of the study had an enormous clinical and financial impact on the practice of orthopedic surgeons, their prospective patients, and health insurance companies. Despite anecdotal success stories, insurance companies largely stopped paying for the procedure and orthopedic surgeons largely stopped performing it. The cost savings, according to follow-up studies: more than $100 million.

Surgery to repair torn meniscus cartilage is another common procedure for knee pain in this country. Close to 500,000 of these operations are performed by orthopedic surgeons each year. A *New England Journal of Medicine* study in 2008 revealed that one-third of people over age fifty experience a meniscal tear, especially those with accompanying arthritis. Surgery had been the main treatment for this problem, an operation with a cost of $5,000. Recent studies have raised new doubts as to whether all these operations are necessary. A study published in 2013 in the *New England Journal of Medicine* compared knee arthroscopy surgery to physical therapy for the treatment of meniscal tears and osteoarthritis. After six months, both the surgical and nonsurgical groups had similar results in pain reduction and functional improvement. The study questioned whether millions of patients were being taken to the operating room needlessly for a procedure whose original benefit had now come into question.

Surgery performed near the end of life must be included in a discussion of unnecessary surgery. Here's a common scenario: I am asked to see an eighty-five-year-old nursing home patient who has been admitted to the hospital with an acute intra-abdominal problem that can possibly be addressed with major surgery. The patient is frail and I know that surgery would put him at risk of complications, including infection and death. When the family wants me to "do all you can," the conversation becomes even more difficult. While I know the right thing to do is simply make the gentleman as comfortable as possible without a trip to the OR, part of me responds viscerally with an involuntary urge to do what I do best—surgery—despite the enormous odds. It's what our training drills into us. It's what I love to do. Whether the patient lives or dies, both the hospital and surgeon will be reimbursed for their efforts. But is this an example of an unnecessary surgery? Probably. It is well documented that mortality rates after major abdominal surgery rise dramatically as we age, starting at age sixty-five. Elderly nursing home patients in particular have a higher risk of dying from common abdominal procedures, such as an appendectomy or a gallbladder removal. If I take the time to thoroughly explain all the facts, most families decide not to expose their loved one to the pain and trauma of surgery when the outcome is most likely death.

One of the reasons cited for the rising costs in healthcare is the money spent in the last year of life. Close to a third of all Medicare dollars are spent during the final six months of a person's life. A study published in the British journal *Lancet* in 2011 looked at data from Medicare billing claims in elderly populations. Close to a third of Medicare patients undergo a major operation in the last year of their life, with most of those occurring within the last thirty days. In their last year of life, those who underwent surgery spent 50 percent more time in the hospital and double the amount of days in the intensive care unit.

Why do surgeons operate so often on the acutely ill elderly, especially with their much higher risk of complications and death? Financial temptations? Pressure from family to do everything possible? Pressure from the surgeon's own ego or genuine desire to help? Malpractice fears? Probably all of the above.

The reimbursement system has to be changed so that surgeons are financially rewarded for cost-efficient, quality outcomes, not just surgery in bulk. I know of two ways to change surgeons' behavior and reduce the number of unnecessary surgeries performed in this country. First: Make public our patient outcome data as it relates to cost, and pay surgeons less for poor-quality outcomes (or do not pay them at all). Second: Reduce reimbursement fees for elective operations that do not have solid medical data to support their common use, and pay surgeons less for operations that are supported only by dubious benefit data, such as spinal fusion for chronic low back pain or abdominal adhesion surgery for chronic abdominal pain.

An educated patient may also be another resource to prevent unnecessary surgeries from occurring. A 2012 study in the journal *Health Affairs* showed that patients with hip and knee problems who were educated about alternative treatments had 26 percent fewer hip replacements and 38 percent fewer knee replacements.

Every day, strangers put their blind trust in me to do what is in their best interest. They assume my decision to take them to the operating room is not tainted by self-interest, ego, money, or outside pressures. Every day I pray they are right.

2 CAN YOUR SURGEON AFFORD TO OPERATE ON YOU?

M r. Jackson, why didn't you go back to the surgeon who originally operated on you?" I was pretty sure I knew the answer but wanted to hear what the gentleman seated on the exam table had to say.

Five years earlier, another surgeon had removed part of Mr. Jackson's colon along with a cancerous tumor. Mr. Jackson had recovered well after his colon surgery and had been cancer-free ever since. Several years after the operation, though, he developed an incisional hernia that required surgery to repair it. He had gone back to his surgeon (we'll call him Dr. K) and been happy with the results. Over the past year, however, he had developed another large incisional hernia that had become increasingly painful. It needed to be repaired. Dr. K had not retired and still had an office in town. I knew he was still practicing surgery at a nearby hospital.

"I did see him, but he doesn't take my insurance now."

An incisional hernia is a split in the abdominal wall at the scar of a previous operation. Once the muscle splits, an opening is created for intestine to get strangulated in, requiring emergency surgery. The incidence of incisional hernias after abdominal surgery is close to 10 percent, and most occur within three years of that surgery. Incisional hernias occur most often in people who are obese, smoke, have diabetes, or have a surgical site infection.

As an obese, fifty-nine-year-old male with underlying medical issues—diabetes, hypertension, and a history of smoking—Mr. Jackson was at risk of complications from *any* surgery. Repairing his incisional hernia was going to take some work during and after the operation. It was also going to take a little luck to get him through it all complication-free. He was at an increased risk for any number of problems—surgical site infection, a blood clot in his leg, or a recurrence of the hernia, to name just three. The bottom line: His operation and post-op care were going to be labor-intensive. Plus, even with my best efforts, the likelihood of a good outcome was significantly lessened by his obesity and other health problems.

I now had a clear picture of why Dr. K was "not able" to help Mr. Jackson. Certainly, he was not inclined to work for the kind of reimbursement Medicaid would pay, and why in the world would he add insult to injury by taking on a patient who presented such risk? This process is called "cherry-picking." In an era of declining reimbursements and emphasis on cost-efficient patient outcomes, cherry-picking patients has forced its way back into the surgical decision-making process. More than twenty years ago when New York State publicized cardiac surgeons' outcomes, some carefully chose their operative patients in order to maximize the chances of good outcomes. Surgeons cherry-pick for reimbursement and high-risk-outcome reasons. They may also cherry-pick based on experience. Whatever the reason, I believe the current healthcare-policy climate will continue to pressure surgeons to "choose wisely" when they decide to take a patient to the operating room.

Today, health insurance companies and the federal government are looking closely at surgeons' "outcomes," trying to identify those whose complication rates are outside the norm. This is a good thing. The data can be a helpful part of "clinical transparency" and thereby contribute to improved patient care. Or so it is hoped. But this scrutiny may also influence a surgeon's decision as to which patients to take on and which ones to decline. Some (like Mr. Jackson) are not worth the risk: the ones who are almost guaranteed a poor outcome due to their state of health, not necessarily the surgeon's skill. Insurance companies' data on outcomes, however, may not reflect these finer details. And surgeons know this.

Surgeons want a record of good outcomes, with as few complications as possible, and they want to make a good living. For some among us, part of that goal is achieved with a selection process that begins in the exam room. When the prospective patient's insurance plan is low on the reimbursement scale *and* the person has underlying conditions that increase the chances of a suboptimal outcome, there are many ways a surgeon can say, "Sorry, I can't help you because . . ."

Mr. Jackson's previous surgeon "doesn't take" his insurance because Medicaid pays only twenty-nine cents on the dollar, a reimbursement Dr. K. has deemed too low. Medicaid is the worst payer for physician services in the country, well below many private payers and Medicare (the federal government-issued health insurance for those age sixty-five and older). Dr. K's decision was strictly business. He simply could not afford to operate on Mr. Jackson. I had to decide if I could.

Mr. Jackson's story is becoming more common today in private practice. Medical academic training centers—the Harvards and Johns Hopkinses of the surgical world—must operate on all comers, regardless of insurance or lack thereof. These institutions accept federal money for their training programs and do not have a choice. Surgeons in private practice do.

In a recently published study in a leading health policy journal, *Health Affairs*, nearly one-third of physicians polled (many of them surgeons) stated they would not accept new Medicaid patients. In addition, almost 20 percent stated they would not accept any new Medicare patients either. The reason: Reimbursement from both federal programs is too low. Surgeons in particular are finding that declining reimbursement rates are making it difficult to maintain an independent practice. The implications are serious. As the ranks of the Medicare-covered population grow (not to mention the increase in demand for care that enactment of the Affordable Care Act will propel), there may be a correspondingly shrinking pool of surgeons willing to provide care to these individuals. The subsequent decreased access to surgical care—for everybody, but in particular for baby boomers—would mean you might have to wait longer and travel farther to see a surgeon. You may have a difficult time getting in to see a qualified surgeon of your choice. When (and if) you do get to see one, that surgeon may not be able to afford to operate on you.

As Mr. Jackson sat in my waiting room with a problem his previous surgeon declined to address, he was oblivious to the politics and economic forces that had landed him there. He had initially been referred to Dr. K by his primary care physician, largely because both were linked financially to a larger, multi-specialty corporate entity. At the time of his operation, Mr. Jackson had carried private health insurance, one whose reimbursement fees for surgical procedures were at the upper end of the scale. In many regions, private insurance carriers can reimburse a surgeon more than $2,000 for a partial colon resection, while Medicare might pay two-thirds that amount, and Medicaid only half. Whatever the figure, it is an all-inclusive, onetime fee. It covers the work a surgeon puts in before, during, and after the surgery, regardless of how the hours or days of caring for that person add up.

Unfortunately for Mr. Jackson, two things had changed in the three years since his last visit with Dr. K, both of which brought him to my office. One: Mr. Jackson had developed another hernia at the same incision site; during a coughing fit, a hole had ripped open through his old scar. His gut stuck out like a watermelon when he stood up straight. It protruded violently, jutting out suddenly when he coughed, sat up, or stood up. The hernia had become unsightly and painful. He needed another operation to repair it, and the surgery would be difficult. Two: Soon after his second hernia appeared, Mr. Jackson lost his job and found himself without health insurance for a short period of time. Eventually, he was able to get state-issued health insurance that offered lower premiums (and less coverage). It was all he could afford. The plan allowed the bare minimum for his healthcare costs, including any surgery. The coverage and reimbursement profile of his new insurance was roughly the equivalent of the federal government's Medicaid program.

After examining Mr. Jackson, I pulled up a chair next to him. I was reviewing his operative report from his previous surgeries, buying time, gathering my thoughts. Despite being only fifty-nine years old, his body was physiologically much older. Years of smoking, lack of exercise, diabetes, and high blood pressure had taken their toll, and any one of them put him at risk for complications after a major operation. Repairing a large, repeat incisional hernia is never easy. It was going to take some work to get Mr. Jackson through the experience unscathed.

There would be intra-abdominal adhesions to deal with, old mesh to remove, and the added stress of the increased likelihood of inadvertently cutting a hole in his intestine. The new mesh I would use to repair his hernia would be at risk for infection, given his poorly controlled diabetes. Infected mesh after hernia repair is a disastrous complication. The financial cost of infected mesh after it has been placed surgically has been estimated, based on a study presented at the American College of Surgeons 2013 Clinical Congress, to be more than $100,000 the year after initial surgery. It also adds two and a half inpatient hospital days to a patient's stay. With this complication, everybody loses: The patient loses precious months, the healthcare system loses money, and the surgeon loses patience. Mr. Jackson's operation would take a good three hours. He could be in the hospital for several days, barring any complications. There was no guarantee of a good outcome or that his new hernia repair would be long-lasting. The bottom line: His operation and care were going to be labor-intensive, requiring many hours, vigilance, and worry. In addition to all this, his current state-issued health insurance would reimburse the surgeon willing to take a chance on Mr. Jackson about a third of what his previous private insurance would have.

"Mr. Jackson," I said, "you have a large recurrent hernia that only major surgery can address."

He nodded. "Okay. Let's do it." He was ready. He was tired of living in his current state. Tired of wearing loose clothing to hide the growing bulge coming from his abdomen. Tired of having to "adjust" his stomach and push his gut back in when he sat down.

I had to ask the question again. "And you did go back to the surgeon who performed your first two operations? I believe he is still practicing in town." I paused. I knew Dr. K was quite capable of working on Mr. Jackson again.

"I did see him. He told me he couldn't do the surgery because he no longer takes my insurance." Mr. Jackson seemed a little embarrassed. "He didn't even want to examine me."

I later learned that Dr. K had left private practice to work for a large for-profit hospital chain. He had gone from working for himself to working as a salaried employee under contract to produce, cover his salary and expenses, and meet bonus quotas. When he turned away Mr. Jackson, he was making a conscious decision to maximize his work efforts by accepting only patients with better-paying health insurance. He could (and would) avoid the poor payers.

I had suspected this was the case all along. This was the real reason Mr. Jackson was sitting in my exam room now. Five years ago, he had needed a colon cancer operation. Two years ago he had needed a hernia operation. In both instances, Dr. K had been happy to help. Now Dr. K had turned him away not because of the complexity of the operation or a lack of experience. Dr. K's decision not to operate on Mr. Jackson was not clinical. It was purely a business decision, based on financial considerations.

Mr. Jackson believed his original surgeon could not operate on him now because he "did not take his insurance." I had seen this before, and in my experience the reality of the situation was something else completely and, in my view, devoid of any loyalty to the patient. Dr. K had done the math and concluded it would be cost-prohibitive to take this patient to the operating room: low reimbursement, the physical work involved, and the risk of a poor outcome meant that by the time he got through the effort of operating on Mr. Jackson and nursing him out of the hospital complication-free, the reimbursement received would not even cover overhead.

Many state-offered health insurance plans pay surgeons on the same level as Medicaid: twenty-nine cents for every dollar billed. If I bill Medicaid $1,000 for removing a gangrenous gallbladder—using minimally invasive techniques without damaging the person's common bile duct, getting the patient out of the hospital several days earlier than with a more invasive "open" procedure, and save the system tens of thousands of dollars in the process—I receive $290. Medicare pays close to thirty-eight cents on the dollar. Private insurance plans might approach sixty cents on the dollar, often reimbursing surgeons twice as much as Medicaid.

If you add up the time and resources spent on the actual surgery, postoperative care in and out of the hospital, and office overhead trying to collect from state-issued health insurance, you can see why some surgeons might decide Mr. Jackson's case is not worth it.

In addition to removing cancerous tumors, repairing hernias, and performing emergency appendectomies (sometimes even saving lives), surgeons in private practice are also running a business, with overhead approaching 40 percent (not including the cost of malpractice insurance). Then there's the added cost of appealing rejected billing claims; one out of seven Medicare claims is rejected, requiring additional staff hours to resubmit. Maybe it is not surprising that surgeons like Dr. K are thinking twice about operating on complicated patients with only Medicaid or Medicare.

In contrast, overhead expenses for primary care physician practices can approach 60 to 70 percent of revenue because processing reimbursement for their patients in the current complex bureaucracy of fee collection is even more labor-intensive. From a strictly business standpoint, many primary care practices are deciding to close their office doors to new patients covered only by Medicare or Medicaid. These physicians have found that delivering primary care services (and the overhead of billing) is simply not worth the reimbursement.

A study published in the journal *Health Affairs* in 2011 found that physicians in the United States spend an average of $61,000 more per year on office expenses involving interacting with health insurance companies than physicians in Canada do. The study further found that the costs of dealing with health insurance companies on payment issues in this country averaged $83,000 per physician per year, nearly four times the cost for Canadian physicians. Overall, the study found that the overhead cost of dealing with insurance companies was $27 billion more in the United States than in Canada. How could that be? For one thing, office staffs in the United States spend *eight times* as many hours each week per physician dealing with financial issues as their Canadian counterparts do.

It was within Dr. K's right to decide not to take Mr. Jackson's case (and his insurance), despite operating on him the first time. Surgeons in private practice can pick and choose elective cases. Salaried surgeons employed by teaching hospitals are obliged to see all patients. Teaching institutions receive federal money to support the training of the next generation of doctors and surgeons and therefore must take all patients, regardless of insurance or any other consideration. Salaried surgeons employed by private hospital systems, as was the case for Dr. K, are not obligated to do so; they can (and do) choose their patients. Despite this, surgeons like Dr. K are under constant pressure to efficiently use their time to generate revenue. This pressure is affecting patient access to surgical care.

Today in the United States, some surgeons have a bit of latitude when it comes to determining for whom they will provide care. Is this ethical? Depends on whom you ask. A young surgeon starting out, eager to build a practice, might be more willing to take on any patient. For one thing, newly minted surgeons want to start earning a living; they have education debt and, usually, a family to support. Plus, they tend to have a more altruistic perspective, a belief that it is their mission to help anyone who needs their services. They still feel invincible, too, believing they can tackle difficult cases with impunity. The stress of having to take personal responsibility for bad outcomes (or the scarlet letter of a malpractice lawsuit) has not yet made its mark on their psyches. Experience has not yet forced them to face their own clinical limitations.

If you ask a surgeon well into his or her career, or a surgeon with a highly specialized skill, you will get a different answer. These doctors are more comfortable financially and don't feel as pressured to take on every potential patient who comes to their offices. They are at a point in their career where they have the luxury of thinking carefully about whether operating on a complex patient is worth the risk for the likely reimbursement. Experienced surgeons are more comfortable admitting their clinical limitations, too, having learned the hard way that some patients are better served by the skills of another surgeon.

Still, despite the disturbing trend of doctors declining to see patients covered only by Medicare or Medicaid, most surgical practices in this country continue to take individuals regardless of their health insurance. My practice is one of them.

As I looked over Mr. Jackson's medical records, I was trying to decide if I could afford to operate on him. Unlike Dr. K, however, I was evaluating Mr. Jackson from an entirely different perspective. It did not matter to me what type of insurance he had. As long as he had something, he was a potential patient. Without any insurance, an elective operation was out of the question; the hospital would not allow me to schedule it. Unless he could pay out of his own pocket, starting with a payment to the hospital in advance, he would never see the operating room. He also needed to pay a deposit to my office. Once this was done, a payment plan for both the hospital and my services would need to be established. Only then would his surgical procedure be scheduled. This is the nature of our business. Elective surgery is not free.

Patients without insurance who decide to self-pay are often, unknowingly, charged top-tier rates for their hospitalization and surgery, in line with what the better-paying insurance plans offer, or even higher. The charges are well above what Medicaid and Medicare pay. It's a reflection of our free-market economy. Charging self-pay patients more than standard public health insurance rates is legal; whether it is unethical is often the question. If an individual is willing to pay without negotiating or getting a second or third financial opinion, he or she might be paying too much.

Is this way of doing surgical business ethical? I don't believe it is. For one thing, those self-pay patients who want to negotiate a lower fee don't have a reliable source of information to turn to. Fees for the costs of surgical operations and subsequent hospitalizations are all over the map. There is no organized, public transparency that patients can make sense out of. The irony is that if these same individuals *had* health insurance (of *any* kind), the charges would be much lower because *those* reimbursements are nonnegotiable. Without the buffer of an insurance plan to protect them, patients are at the mercy of hospitals and surgeons.

In addition to the uninsured, patients with high deductibles may have difficulty getting into a surgeon's office. High-deductible plans are becoming popular with employers because they keep premiums down. The flip side is that while employees may make a smaller contribution to their employer-issued health insurance coverage, they will pay a high price when surgery is needed. Surgeons know that under a high-deductible plan most of their fees must come directly from the patient's pocket. Anyone can default on a surgeon's bill, or pay only a portion of it, and the cost of trying to collect the fee can be an expensive exercise in diminishing returns. This is why many surgeons request a partial payment up front when the person has a high-deductible plan. Traditionally, plastic surgeons have been the only ones to collect a fee from a patient *before* any service has been provided. It is the nature of their business; their customers are not surprised by this scenario. Since nearly all plastic surgery is elective and not covered by insurance plans, these surgeons have almost never had to deal with insurance companies. They can enjoy the ease of operating on a cash-only basis. Virtually all other surgical specialties rely on insurance companies for payment and could never survive as cash-only practices.

The hospital is in direct competition with the surgeon for the patient's dollars when the person's coverage is a high-deductible plan. For that reason, most hospitals want a payment up front, before surgery. After the patient is discharged, the hospital will bill the patient's insurance company for the rest of the fee. Hospitals have the resources to find out how much the person with a high deductible has left to pay before the deductible limit is reached. Most independent surgeons' offices are also competing for this deductible number in order to stay competitive. Historically, many surgeons have felt uncomfortable asking for payment up front before scheduling an operation, except plastic surgeons. In the past, it was only when a patient returned to the surgeon's office for a follow-up appointment that the billing process to the insurance company began. The problem with doing business this way is that the insurance company will subtract whatever balance is left on the patient's deductible (if any) from the surgeon's charges. It will reimburse only the difference, forcing the surgeon to bill the patient directly for the rest. Historically, surgeons' offices have had a difficult time collecting these fees. Patients are reluctant to pay more out of pocket, believing their insurance plan should have covered the costs. Some simply do not have the cash. Surgeons are reluctant to pressure a patient to pay the rest of the deductible in the face of a bad outcome, fearing the threat of legal action. Whatever the reason, surgeons trying to collect fees after an operation on patients with high-deductible plans often are not successful. And for these reasons, without money up front, surgeons are finding they may not be able to afford to operate on patients with high-deductible plans.

At the opposite end of the spectrum are "worker's compensation" patients, individuals who require surgery because of an injury on the job. This unique category of insurance is often a top payer for surgeons' services. In these cases, the surgeon's fee is negotiated at the highest end of reimbursement. Surgeons have leverage when negotiating with employers because they are not bound by contracts with other third-party payers. Most employers are willing to pay the higher fee to expedite care of the employee; the sooner the surgery is done, the faster the employee can return to work.

"Concierge medicine" is another unique way of doing business in the delivery of healthcare, and one that's becoming increasingly common. The concept originated out of physicians' frustration over the hassles of dealing with the bureaucracy of insurance companies. Today, some doctors (mainly primary care) use this model to tailor their services to those who can afford them. Concierge physicians take a hefty cash (or credit card) payment in advance in return for providing virtually twenty-four-hour access for the year. For those who can afford it, concierge medicine means no waiting days or weeks for an appointment, no spending two hours in the waiting room, no seeing a physician assistant rather than the doctor, and no rushed five-minute visits. Instead, you will see the doctor and your visit will feel leisurely, lasting an hour if that's what it takes. In addition, you will likely have the doctor's cell phone number for off-hours questions or concerns. Unreturned phone calls, no openings for an appointment for weeks, waiting forever for your test results—not going to happen in concierge medicine. This "boutique" approach to healthcare works especially well for primary care physicians; their services are needed throughout every stage of life, so they can count on long-term commitments. These boutique-practice doctors—usually qualified, conscientious board-certified physicians—can enjoy a good living while completely bypassing the exasperating billing maze created by the insurance companies.

Concierge care is becoming popular in major metropolitan areas, where the population is large enough to support it. At first glance, it may appear that concierge medicine is just another example of free-market consumer choice, and we usually view choice as a good thing. There's a downside, though. This business model removes a number of quality primary care physicians from the finite pool of doctors available to the rest of us. Most working people cannot afford concierge medicine. Any drain on the number of primary care physicians means your access to healthcare is further limited. With the aging of the baby boomers and their subsequent increased need for medical care, and the growing number of Americans of any age who will have access to healthcare under the Affordable Care Act, a shrinking number of doctors would mean longer waits for appointments, and even traveling longer distances to see a doctor.

Concierge care doesn't apply to surgeons. Yet. What I offer as a surgeon is help when needed. I am a general surgeon, a specialist, and treat one specific problem at a time. I intervene only when called on. I perform the surgery, take care of you afterward, and usually see you for a couple of follow-up appointments. There is no long-term contract I can offer for preventive care during your lifetime. I do not charge a maintenance fee. I am reimbursed for my work in the operating room. Period. This is how the system is set up for surgeons.

In some ways, I am practicing a variation on concierge medicine (without the direct financial benefits) by selecting whom I take to the operating room for elective surgery. Mr. Jackson is a prime example of this. By all indications, his original surgeon decided he could not (from a financial standpoint) afford to operate on him. I was deciding that I could not afford to operate on him from an outcome standpoint.

As I mentioned, my current surgical practice has a history of taking all comers, regardless of the type of health insurance the person has. My partners and I believe in this approach and live by it. Yet I was concluding that I might not want to operate on Mr. Jackson. It was not, however, for financial reasons.

"Mr. Jackson, you have a large, recurrent incisional hernia," I began. "Repairing it would entail a long, difficult operation. I would have to deal with a significant amount of scar tissue and could run into problems removing the mesh from your first hernia operation. Because of your other health issues, you are at risk for complications." He listened intently.

"The mesh you already have puts you at risk for a bowel perforation. Because you are a smoker, the surgery would put you at risk for pneumonia, and because of your diabetes, any surgery puts you at risk for a wound infection or blood clots—potentially serious complications." He nodded.

I continued to explain the risks. "Even if I successfully repaired the hernia you have now, you could develop another one later, which would also require surgery. If the surgery to repair the hernia is not done right the first time, a second operation automatically lessens your chances for success. You would be in the hospital for several days, which could expose you to further risks such as a hospital-acquired infection."

I paused before finishing. "The bottom line, Mr. Jackson, is that you are at a higher risk for an imperfect outcome for several reasons, the first being that this would be a repeat hernia operation."

I wanted to be blunt with him. There was clearly a great risk he would not have a good outcome. And given his underlying medical problems and previous surgeries, his likelihood of a recurrent hernia after the second repair was as high as 30 percent.

Today, fortunately, when a surgeon sits down for a consultation with a prospective patient, greater emphasis is placed on measured clinical outcomes. There is recognition that this conversation is an important factor in practicing quality surgical care. Clinical outcomes after surgery have always been important to surgeons, but in years past our discussion of such matters did not include the public. These conversations took place behind closed doors as surgeons practiced the balancing act of building a good reputation while maintaining the ability to make a living.

In the past, we have been guilty of not policing our outcomes with adequate transparency. This tradition, thankfully, is changing under the weight of out-of-control healthcare costs. Clinical outcomes are no longer important just for surgeons; today they are everybody's business, because poor outcomes are not representative of quality care *and* they cost the system money. Hospitals are vigilantly monitoring surgeons' outcomes. Insurance companies are keenly aware of surgeons' outcomes because they are still obligated to pay for poor ones. Even the federal government's Centers for Medicare & Medicaid Services (CMS) is monitoring our outcomes, and for the same reasons. Measuring outcomes is key to clinical quality and improved transparency, and it is one way to use healthcare dollars more wisely.

Mr. Jackson's potential for complications and a poor outcome were clearly on my mind when I was deciding whether to operate on him. I was not looking forward to the physical work it would take to attempt to correct another surgeon's poor outcome. I also winced at the mental toll I would be under as I worked to get him out of the hospital safely. I was aware of the many eyes that would be watching—eyes that monitor surgical patient clinical outcomes. In the end, it would not have mattered what type of health insurance Mr. Jackson had. His operation was just too much for me to tackle.

The time is coming when the quality and cost of my outcomes will decide which operations I can perform and on whom I can operate. The time is coming soon when I will be reimbursed based on how well my patients do and, conversely, penalized for complications. I welcome this future. I believe all surgeons should have to prove their clinical merit before they step into the operating room to perform an operation.

Mr. Jackson was still waiting for me to finish speaking. I think he had already surmised how this meeting would end. He had sensed I was not eager to take him to the operating room from the beginning of our conversation.

"Mr. Jackson," I said with a slight sigh, "I am sorry but I am unable to repair your hernia here at this hospital." I could see the disappointment in his eyes. "As I've said, your operation is going to be very difficult to perform without you developing a complication. Each time any surgeon goes into the abdomen to repair a repeat hernia, the chances of a good outcome go down considerably. That said, there are surgeons in another city with more experience at this particular procedure than I. You'll be better served by seeing someone else and I'm happy to find a qualified surgeon for you." It was the least I could do and did.

The seeds of Mr. Jackson's problem were initially sown by the failure of his first operation and the surgeon who performed it. Conveniently for Dr. K, this time around he refused to operate on Mr. Jackson under the guise of "not taking his insurance." I'm quite certain he would have scheduled the surgery if the money had been right. My reasons for not wanting to operate were based on knowing that the outcome, at best, would not be ideal. Mr. Jackson needed a surgeon with experience in redoing abdominal wall hernia operations. I was not that surgeon.

Second, he needed to be at a teaching hospital, where many surgeons (including residents) would be involved in his daily care, not just one surgeon (me). My hospital was not the right hospital for Mr. Jackson. Third, if he did have a poor outcome, the responsibility for that outcome could be absorbed a lot more easily by a surgeon "protected" by the prestige of a larger academic, teaching institution. I am in private practice. My only protection is the name on my office door. Absorbing poor outcomes does not come easy for any surgeon, especially those in an office-based private practice setting. I could not afford to operate on Mr. Jackson because the professional cost to me was too high.

Poor outcomes are being closely monitored these days, as well they should to ultimately improve the quality of care. This high scrutiny, however, may lead to the unintended consequence of limited patient choice and access to care.

—————

Jeremy was a twenty-three-year-old college-educated bartender, brought to the emergency room early one morning after crashing his motorcycle into a tree. He was lucky. His helmet saved his life, protecting him from serious head trauma. The rest of his body wasn't so lucky. The tree he hit at forty-five miles per hour did not move when he crashed his left upper flank directly into it. Once he was inside the trauma room, a CT scan revealed a ruptured spleen and blood pooling in his abdomen. Jeremy was hemorrhaging inside his abdominal cavity, or more specifically his intraperitoneal space. This is a large, saclike space holding in most of the intra-abdominal organs. In addition to your liver, spleen, stomach, and intestines, there is also a lot of empty space that can accommodate other things, such as free blood.

An average adult's blood volume is anywhere from five to six liters, or 5.5 to 6.5 quarts. Jeremy's intraperitoneal space could accommodate much of this from his injured, bleeding spleen. Ultimately, though, the blood flow to his heart, brain, and other organs would dry up. Hypovolemic shock would ensue. It would all end in cardiac arrest and death within a short time if the bleeding was not stopped.

I was "on call" for the emergency room that night, meaning I was obligated to perform emergency general surgery as needed. That made it my job to remove Jeremy's damaged spleen right away, that night, not the next morning. Taking emergency room "call," coming in to operate on critically ill patients in the middle of the night, has always been part of any surgeon's job description. We all know this when we enter the profession. We may not like it at times, but we have to accept it. If you want to be a doctor who doesn't have to get up in the night and come in for emergencies, you become a pathologist. There are no living emergencies in pathology. Every patient you examine is dead and on ice. They can wait until the morning.

Covering the emergency room has been a component of any surgical practice, in any hospital, for decades. Hospitals often make it mandatory to take emergency room call when you apply for full operating privileges. The hospitals benefit from linking elective operating privileges to emergency room coverage, particularly when being on call is not compensated—a wacky situation that was common for decades and is still true in some places. Being on call means not enjoying a glass of wine with your dinner or a glass of whiskey before it, passing on an invitation to a concert or play or party, staying home and going to bed with one eye open and the phone ringer volume on high, mentally prepared to hop out of bed at one o'clock in the morning and rush to the hospital to care for a critically injured or ill stranger. And when call ends at seven A.M., you still have a full day at the office or in the OR ahead of you. It takes a toll.

Jeremy's operation went well. I removed a badly mangled spleen at 2:10 A.M. He spent several days in the intensive care unit (ICU), leaving the hospital alive and intact a week later. The day before his discharge, I was reading a note in his chart from social services. Jeremy had no insurance, no way to directly pay for the care he received from me, no way to pay for the week's stay in the ICU. In order for me to get reimbursed for my services after the fact, I would have to get it directly from Jeremy in the form of some mutually agreed-on payment plan. This path is usually unrealistic and uncomfortable for surgeons. Patients like Jeremy are frequently just written off, their cost absorbed by the surgical practice. Hospitals, on the other hand, can collect monies from other sources when the patient can't or won't pay. In the state of Massachusetts, where I practice, the number of uninsured people decreased from 8 percent to less than 2 percent of the adult population ever since Gov. Mitt Romney signed his healthcare bill into law in 2006. While close to 98 percent of the state's population has coverage today, a little over one-sixth of them are covered by public plans akin to Medicaid. It is a well-known fact that Medicaid offers the lowest rate of reimbursements for physician services. With the rolling out of the federal Affordable Care Act, the ranks of the uninsured are supposed to drop from roughly fifty million people to under twenty million, depending on which study you read or which political party you are affiliated with.

For me, as I reviewed Jeremy's chart, these were moot points. Jeremy, I had discovered, was one of the uninsured.

Hospitals and health centers continue to get reimbursed for the services they provide for the uninsured and poorly insured. They do not receive top dollar, but they do get something. Their payment comes from what is called the *uncompensated care pool*. For instance, the year before Romneycare was signed into law, the uncompensated care pool (also called the *free care pool*) in Massachusetts was well over $1 billion. This pool was funded by contributions from insurance providers, hospitals, and state and federal sources. Nowhere in this pool are the funds earmarked for payments to physicians and surgeons who care for uninsured patients. This is true in other states as well. Why? Maybe hospital lobbyists are more influential on a state and federal level than the lobbyists representing the medical profession. Maybe the fact that physicians are forbidden to unionize and cannot speak with one voice places them in a weak position to bargain for monetary rights. Physicians cannot strike. Surgeons cannot hold the emergency room of a hospital hostage. Or can they?

Traditionally, surgeons have been reluctant to speak up about compensation inequity, possibly because of their perceived "status" in society. Maybe surgeons have been afraid to seem "greedy" or have feared the loss of business from referring physicians employed by the hospital. Maybe independent surgeons have feared that hospitals would simply purchase their own surgeons if they ever balked at covering the emergency room without compensation for being on call.

Today we are in a new era. Surgeons taking night and weekend call for emergencies are compensated. Their expertise and availability to cover a hospital emergency room and operate on critically ill patients is no longer free. In a 2012 Medical Group Management Association (MGMA) survey, the overall percentage of physicians paid to take call had increased from 60 percent to 70 percent. For surgeons (especially general and orthopedic), more than 80 percent are paid to cover emergency rooms. For neurosurgeons, this number is even higher. Call pay varies, ranging from $900 to $3,000 a night, which the surgeon is paid whether or not he or she is called in.

What has changed over the last ten years? Why now are more surgeons getting reimbursed for taking call, the same job they had been doing for decades without pay? Two words: supply and demand. The supply of quality general surgeons has been dwindling, while the demand has increased. The same can be said for other surgical subspecialties as well. Surgeons are finally realizing they have the leverage (if they have the courage) to negotiate a fee for their services when on call.

The surgeon shortage is real, with no end in sight. The shortage may already be making inroads that affect patient care. A U.S. study published in *Annals of Surgery* in 2013 revealed a higher incidence of ruptured appendices in rural communities compared to more populated areas. Since the shortage of surgeons already exists in rural areas, patients with acute appendicitis have to travel farther and wait longer before they can be operated on. This delay is thought to be the cause of the increased incidence of rupture. Why does any of this matter? A person with a ruptured appendix will be in the hospital longer, is at higher risk for complications, and adds tens of thousands of dollars to the national health bill.

Several dynamics are at play in the shrinking number of new surgeons leaving residency programs. One is that medical students are no longer going into surgery, especially general surgery. Surveys indicate that medical students view a surgeon's lifestyle as "very unappealing" because of declining reimbursement fees, long hours, the high rate of burnout, malpractice costs, and an ever-increasing bureaucracy. In addition, today half of graduating medical students are women. Surveys show that many of them find the long training period for surgeons and the subsequent lifestyle sacrifices unattractive. Some of the nonsurgical specialties are more lucrative than surgical specialties and offer a better quality of life. Dermatology, for example, is today one of the hardest residencies to get into because of the lucrative reimbursements and manageable lifestyle. The competition for those slots is fierce.

The second dynamic affecting the ranks is the number of surgeons who are retiring. Just like the rest of the world, we get older. Surgery is physically and mentally demanding, and as more of our energy is required to chase reimbursement, burnout pushes some of us to early retirement. The challenge of running a financially viable practice is real. Some surgeons have simply had enough of taking care of older, sicker patients while watching their fees drop year after year.

Being on call can be counted as another factor in our declining numbers. It is a real detriment to running a practice. If I am up all night operating on patients (many of whom have little or no insurance, by the way), I may be forced to cancel the next day's surgery schedule (for patients who all have health insurance). Fatigue from being on call may also force me to cancel my next day's office visits, losing potential business.

Mr. Jackson was not an emergency case, and his plight was not unique. Today, many physicians and surgeons are closing their doors to Medicare or new patients altogether, regardless of their health insurance. In a report by the Medicare Payment Advisory Commission, which advises Congress on Medicare reimbursement to physicians, adults age fifty to sixty-four are having trouble getting in to see a new physician. Close to 30 percent of privately insured patients looking for a new primary care doctor are having difficulty finding one. It is a disturbing trend.

Mr. Jackson will wait longer and travel farther to see a

surgeon. When he does finally get in to see one, there is no guarantee he will have his hernia repaired again, given its complexity and risk. There is also no guarantee that the surgeon will have the experience to perform the operation. If Mr. Jackson waits too long, his problem may flare up and force him to an emergency room one night for treatment. When he arrives, there is no guarantee he will be met in the operating room by a qualified surgeon. There is no guarantee he will ever see that surgeon again after his operation. There will be no guarantee because today financial circumstances and business arrangements are dictating who your surgeon is going to be.

As the federal government's Affordable Care Act rounds the first turn and gets into the back stretch, some thirty million people are expected to have health insurance for the first time over the next five years. This is the good news. The bad news is that many of these newly insured who require surgery will have a difficult time getting into a qualified surgeon's office of choice. The problem is complex, but the main component is the conscious decision of many surgeons in practice *not* to operate on these newly insured because they simply cannot afford to do so. A growing shortage of surgeons plus a larger number of people with access to healthcare equals limited patient choice of and access to care.

When a patient like Mr. Jackson walks into my office, I may not be able to operate on him because of the complexity of his condition. Unfortunately for Mr. Jackson and others like him, for many surgeons the decision will be based solely on money.

3 A DYING BREED

Rest in peace, independent practitioner. Regardless of which study you read, this seems to be the sentiment today. The independent physician in private practice, both primary care physician and surgeon alike—operating a small business, delivering personalized care to patients, and historically immune to outside market forces—is a dying breed. He or she is a dinosaur, an aging relic from a different era.

I am that dinosaur. As of this writing, I am that independent surgeon working for myself. The statistics are beginning to favor this fact. Today, the majority of practicing physicians are employed by either large private groups or hospital systems. Since 2000, the number of physicians employed by hospital systems has increased dramatically. Currently, the estimates are that roughly 50 percent of all physicians are employed by hospitals. Many of these employed physicians are in primary care and its subspecialties, such as cardiology. Over the course of the last five years, surgeons have begun to follow the herd and join the ranks of the employed physician.

Historically, surgeons in community practice (where most surgery is still performed in this country) have been an independent breed. They have been reluctant to work for any entity but themselves. They have been resistant to the changing pressures of referral forces. Because of the revenue-generating service they provide to hospitals, surgeons have also been immune to the political pressures hospitals have exerted on other specialties. Because of their ability to generate revenue freely for themselves, surgeons have been protected from many of the economic pressures other specialists have been experiencing for years. That, however, is all changing. In a recent survey published in 2013 in *JAMA Surgery*, 68 percent of surgeons identified themselves as employed, no longer in business for themselves. Between 2006 and 2012, the number of surgeons employed full-time by hospitals increased 32 percent. This trend of the "employed" surgeon is even capturing those coming out of residency. In survey after survey, most view it as inevitable that they will enter their professional practice as a salaried surgeon working for a hospital system.

The self-employed surgeon running a private practice is gradually morphing into the employed surgeon wearing a group or corporate logo. The surgeon previously committed only to himself or herself is now often financially committed to a larger entity.

Why is this significant? Will the delivery and quality of healthcare change because of this dramatic shift in the surgical workplace? Will it affect your access to care or your ability to choose your own surgeon? It did for Mr. Chase.

———————————

"What a mess in here," I mumbled into my surgical mask.

I was painstakingly cutting through Mr. Chase's adhesions, webs of scar tissue tethered to his small intestine, twisting it into a web of knots. His bowels were kinked like a backyard water hose. This was his third hospital admission with a bowel obstruction caused by scar tissue from his original operation five years ago. This time his bowel obstruction did not respond to medical management, continued to get worse, and forced him to seek surgery. His initial operation five years ago had been billed as a simple "outpatient laparoscopic procedure"—a cholecystectomy, removal of his gallbladder. The problem was that it had been anything but simple for Mr. Chase. Complications from this simple outpatient procedure almost led to his demise.

Five years earlier, Mr. Chase had gone to his primary care physician complaining of the intermittent pain he had been experiencing for several months. His problem was easily diagnosed: gallstones. Solution: surgery to remove his gallbladder. Surgeons have been performing laparoscopic cholecystectomies since 1987. It is a routine operation for any surgeon with the appropriate experience. As with any operation, though, complications can occur during the procedure. But for most experienced surgeons, they are infrequent and can usually be dealt with successfully before the patient leaves the OR.

Once the diagnosis of symptomatic gallstones was made,

Mr. Chase's primary care physician sent him to see a surgeon. He did not, however, refer him to just any surgeon. He referred him to a fellow employee, a surgeon he was linked to professionally and financially. There were several surgical groups in town, each with their own degree of expertise and reputation. Some were independent and some were employed by the hospital. Mr. Chase's primary care physician had been in practice in the community for more than ten years. He was aware of the reputations of all the surgeons and could have referred his patient to any one of them. Despite this, he referred Mr. Chase to a surgeon we'll call Dr. T, who had been hired recently by the hospital in an attempt to increase the surgical business in its operating rooms.

When he arrived, Dr. T signed a contract, guaranteeing him a base salary for several years with the opportunity to earn more via quarterly production bonuses. This is how it works when surgeons are salaried employees of a hospital system: guaranteed salaries, the opportunity to earn more based on the number of cases, and none of the pressures that go with running a private practice business. Those pressures—personnel changes, billing, compliance, running the daily operations of an office, negotiating with insurance companies, refiling rejected billing claims, and paying for malpractice—all disappear when a surgeon becomes employed. Despite this, employed surgeons do have financial responsibilities. They must *at least* earn their salary or risk being paid less, or let go, when their contract is up for renewal. And as a member of a larger organization, most employed surgeons automatically have an "administrative fee" deducted from their yearly salary. This fee is applied to cover the administrative expenses the surgeon employee generates within the organization. It can range from 5 to 20 percent and is deducted right off the top of monthly paychecks. Where this money actually ends up is anyone's guess.

In addition, hospital- or system-employed surgeons may not feel the need to be as physically or mentally available twenty-four hours a day as their independent colleagues. More and more, surgeons coming out of training see themselves being employed by a large group or hospital system, working shift hours, unlike their private practice colleagues who have a history of being available night and day for their patients. The difference in professional mentality can be explained by a generational training gap; many of the newly minted surgeons come from a residency experience that fosters the "shift" mentality. Since 2003, surgical interns and residents have been limited by law to work only eighty hours per week. They cannot go one minute over this limit, regardless of what they are doing or whom they are caring for. Once their "shift" is up, they must leave the hospital. The goal behind this dramatic workplace change is improved patient safety and a reduction in the number of medical errors resulting from sleep-deprived residents working around the clock. Despite good intentions, however, hourly workplace restrictions may have resulted in negative consequences. Surgeons with a time-clock mentality may not have as strong a commitment to their patients as their older colleagues do. The habit of clocking out to the incoming resident once a shift is up also degrades continuity of care for patients. For many young surgeons, entering practice as salaried surgeons employed by hospital systems, the time-clock model is all they know.

Surgeons who trained before 2003 worked under no such restrictions. They worked as long and as hard as their mentors wanted them to. This had positive and negative consequences. Obviously, there were safety issues; extreme fatigue can lead to mistakes. There were also benefits to patients that one shouldn't lose sight of: Before 2003, you were involved in a patient's care from the beginning to the end, regardless of your fatigue, blood, sweat, and tears. You worked longer hours, spent more time in the operating room than today's trainees, and reaped the benefits in clinical experience. There was no break, no nap (another requirement today).

I trained in this era. This intense experience fostered a unique bond between me and my patients—a deeply personal bond that, I believe, conditioned my mind to think I *had* to be available for my patients twenty-four hours a day. Signing off to a colleague was reserved for those occasions when I was out of town. Maybe this dog-with-a-bone attitude stems from my type A personality. Maybe it is a by-product of the need to be in control—classic surgeon mentality. I and many of my colleagues who trained before 2003 carried this bond of constant commitment and availability into our community practices. We were infused with a sense of honor by the trust our patients placed in us, and we considered their essential submission of their very lives into our hands a sacred privilege.

From a business standpoint, independent surgeons feel like they *have* to be available twenty-four hours a day to create a successful practice. In the past, surgeons starting out used to hang around emergency rooms, looking for work opportunities. As in any other start-up business, availability leads to growth opportunities. As a surgeon in private practice, I do not generate income unless I operate. My salary is not guaranteed; what I make in a month depends on how many surgical cases I take on.

I am still reimbursed in a fee-for-service business model, which gives me incentive to work harder. The more productive I am, the more I benefit financially. I also have to be available to referring physicians as much as possible in order to maximize my business and keep it strong.

I am not surprised to read studies like the MGMA industry survey published in 2011 that show that once primary care physicians become salaried employees for hospitals, with a guaranteed income, their clinical productivity decreases. Does the security of a guaranteed paycheck subdue the business incentive, the entrepreneur's flame that fuels a desire to work harder? Does knowing that at the end of the month a check will be there, no matter what, have a negative influence on the desire to be available for patients, to be more diligent, to work harder? I think it does. Will the quality of surgical care be affected as more surgeons join the ranks of the employed? While it has not yet been documented, the growing ranks of employed surgeons may not be able to escape this phenomenon of human nature.

In addition to relieving surgeons of the pressures of running a business, the built-in referral system is a tremendous benefit for surgeons who are employed by a large multispecialty group or hospital system. Surgeons, as specialists, have always relied on referrals from primary care physicians to generate business. This voluntary referral arrangement puts them in the vulnerable position of having to rely on the recommendations of other physicians to get patients. In the past, this referral system was based on one's hard-earned professional reputation, the familiarity that arises from long-standing working relationships and personal collegiality. Most patients trust that their primary care physician will refer them to a surgeon based solely on the expertise

and competency of that surgeon. Why would they think otherwise? With a referral to a particular surgeon, the trust and reputation of the primary care physician is on the line. Who would
imagine there could be any quid pro quo, any financial motives
associated with it? Mr. Chase didn't. In the days when I was
establishing my reputation as a surgeon in private practice, the
equation was simple: Surgeons who performed quality work,
treated patients compassionately, and had normal personalities
were rewarded with more referrals. It was as simple as that.
Today, simplicity is not the norm.

Employed, salaried surgeons today enter into business arrangements with the groups or hospital systems they work for.
The most important professional benefits from these arrangements is short-term financial security and an instant referral
base once the contract is signed. As an employed surgeon, you
don't need to toil for years, building a reputation of quality outcomes for your referrals. You do not necessarily have to be available to solicit business. As part of a hospital system, all employees
share common professional and financial goals. Professionally,
all physicians strive to practice quality medicine and surgery.
Financially, the employed physicians and administrative leaders
want to generate revenue, earn a profit, and grow. By capturing
patients within their business system, multispecialty groups and
hospitals maximize their earning capabilities—from the beginning of healthcare use until the very end.

From a business standpoint, it was only natural for Mr.
Chase's primary care physician to refer him to the surgeon who
had recently joined his team, the hospital's team. This is what he
is supposed to do. When he refers Mr. Chase to a surgeon
employed by the hospital system, the revenue stream will be cap-

tured by the hospital. From a professional standpoint, there were independent surgeons in town who had more experience and were more competent than the one Mr. Chase was referred to. The problem was that those surgeons had no employee-employer relationship with the hospital, so it could not influence or benefit financially from their behavior.

Are you surprised by this picture? It's perfectly legal. Hospitals grow their bottom line by preventing patients from "leaking" out of their system. In order to prevent leakage, they first must gain control by owning the primary care physicians. Amazingly, a *New England Journal of Medicine* article published in 2011 concluded that despite losing up to $250,000 per employed physician for the first three years, hospitals and healthcare systems willingly take on the losses in order to control the flow of referrals to specialists and surgeons. A hospital industry survey published in *Medical Economics* in 2013 showed that, as a general surgeon, I can generate close to $2 million a year in total revenue for the hospital for which I choose to work. For orthopedic and neurosurgeons, this figure is even higher. No wonder hospitals are willing to eat the losses incurred from primary care physician practices as long as they have their own surgeons on the payroll.

Should Mr. Chase's primary care physician have disclosed his business connection with the surgeon he recommended? Did Mr. Chase have a choice of surgeons or was his fate preordained? Most important, is the quality of a patient's surgical care influenced when financial motives play a role in an employed surgeon's ability to receive patient referrals?

Despite four hours on the operating room table, two days in the intensive care unit on a ventilator, and a total of nine days in the hospital, Mr. Chase was able to go home and recover. The reason his abdomen was now full of thick, dense scar tissue encasing his intestines could be traced back to his first simple laparoscopic cholecystectomy operation. It was during this surgery that Mr. Chase's intestines were accidentally punctured by one of the laparoscopic instruments. This complication, called an enterotomy, is well known in the laparoscopic literature. It can occur, like many laparoscopic complications, if a surgeon is not experienced enough or is inadvertently careless during an operation. It occurs in 2 out of 100 procedures; if it is recognized and repaired at the time it occurs, patients do well. If the injury to the intestines is not recognized, patients quickly succumb to infection from fecal spillage and can die. Unfortunately for Mr. Chase, his surgeon had not recognized the injury in time. Mr. Chase became septic from infection and had to be re-operated on after being transferred to a larger medical center. Luckily, he survived the ordeal. The acute infection in his abdomen, however, caused scar tissue to flourish, scar tissue that fixed his intestine in one place. Although he had survived, Mr. Chase acquired a risk for intestinal obstructions because of the scar tissue. Today, that risk had come to fruition.

Did Mr. Chase's primary care physician know anything about his referring surgeon's outcomes, or did he just know that they shared an employer, the hospital? Did he have an obligation to know more? Could he have referred him to a more experienced surgeon in the community, one not employed by the hospital, based on his knowledge of outcomes? Of course he could have. But it would not have been the "correct" business decision. His surgeon of choice was the hospital-employed surgeon. This was where his patients were supposed to go based on the pressures of a business model that demands patient retention in hospital systems. This is how it works today. Hospital-employed primary care physicians refer to hospital-employed specialists/surgeons or else their personal compensation bonuses may suffer in the end. Mr. Chase's referral was preordained because of a business arrangement. He was not given a choice of a surgeon. And, unfortunately for Mr. Chase, the surgeon chosen for him was less experienced than others in the community and that inexperience is what led to a perforated intestine, intestinal obstruction, and another trip to the operating room.

Surgeons coming out of training prefer to be employed by hospitals or larger groups rather than going into independent practice. More and more, surgeons in established independent private practice are selling their services to hospitals. The reason: the Patient Protection and Affordable Care Act signed by President Obama in 2010. Either by accident or by intent, the signing of this act changed the business model of how physicians will practice medicine in the future. When the Affordable Care Act became law, the mandates (discussed in more depth in Chapter 9) and guidelines created a business platform for the future delivery of healthcare, including payments to hospitals and healthcare providers and cost-cutting strategies. Because of these mandates and the finite number of federal (Medicare and Medicaid) healthcare dollars available, hospitals were encouraged to consolidate and circle the wagons. Hospital systems also felt the need to protect and expand their local market share of patients. They felt the need to find ways to profit from the changes mandated by the Affordable Care Act. With this expansion, hospitals proceeded to buy up physician practices, specifically primary care practices, since they control the flow of patients entering the system. What better way is there for hospitals to keep control of the flow of patients and expand their financial base than to employ the primary care physicians who control them? With direct employment, hospitals theoretically have control over patients from the time they see a primary care physician to the time they need surgery. With direct employment, a hospital can control all the revenue generated as a patient goes through its system.

In all fairness to the Affordable Care Act, this phenomenon has its roots in the 1990s with the onset of managed care. At the time, hospitals were encouraged to buy up primary care physician practices so they could control patient populations, control costs, and increase the bottom line. That experiment failed because hospitals ultimately lost money from the practices they purchased. One big reason they lost money was that the productivity of their newly employed physicians decreased over time once under the umbrella of a guaranteed salary. In addition, the perception that it led to the rationing of care by delaying surgical procedures so money could be saved was unacceptable to most Americans. Patients revolted. Managed care also did nothing to control costs, and it did not have the backing of the federal government. In addition, during the managed care experiment, hospital systems did not work to employ specialists and surgeons, the high earners that might have made the model financially viable.

Today, hospitals need to employ specialists, especially surgeons, in order to capture all available patient-care business and maximize revenue streams. Hospitals have also recognized the need to expand surgical "service lines" to keep healthcare dollars under one corporate roof. If a hospital did not employ neurosurgeons to provide neurosurgical services to patients in the community, it would go out and purchase them. If cardiac surgery was not being done at your community hospital, its administrators would find a way to employ cardiac surgeons and start a program. The bottom line: When the Affordable Care Act hit, hospital systems and large multispecialty groups felt the need to go shopping for their own surgeons. They felt the need to expand their operating room services in anticipation of what was to come. It was a buyer's *and* seller's market. A surgeon's potential to generate revenue for a hospital system can only be maximized when that surgeon is employed by that hospital system.

For established surgeons in private practice, this climate change could not have come at a worse time. A perfect storm of practice conditions has placed independent surgeons in a vulnerable negotiating position with the hospital systems looking to employ surgeons. First of all, the growing shortage of surgeons has put a strain on many established community practices. With dwindling supply, common sense would suggest that surgeons are in a position of strength when hospitals come calling. This is not the case. The shortage of surgeons has led to an increase in burnout for practicing surgeons; longer hours, early retirements, and difficulty in recruiting new surgeons into private practice have taken a toll. This difficulty has been exacerbated by the high salary market created by surgeons coming out of training with a desire (and expectation) to have a better quality of life than their predecessors. To most in established practices, "better quality of life" is a euphemism for signing off after hours and taking less call.

In addition, many established surgeons in community practice believe, rightly or wrongly, that new surgeons coming out of training are not as qualified as they should be. There may be some credence to this: A recent study in *JAMA Surgery* documented a 26 percent decrease in the number of operations surgical interns were exposed to at ten U.S. training programs compared to those who trained before 2003, when duty hour restrictions were implemented. Surgical trainees today are just not getting enough operating room experience because of the restrictions on work hours. In a 2014 *Annals of Surgery* review of fifteen training programs, residents and program directors in twelve were concerned training had been compromised. Along with this, many more newly minted fully trained surgeons are failing their board examinations than ever before. This lack of clinical exposure throughout training eventually spills out into the community.

Coupled with the shortage, surgeon reimbursement has been declining over the last decade as the costs (including malpractice insurance and the mandated use of electronic health records) and bureaucracy of private practice have been rising. Hospitals, because of their relationships with insurance companies, have always negotiated better reimbursement rates for operations performed by their surgeons versus those in private practice. These rates are just another factor hospitals dangle to entice surgeons to join their team. "Join us and you will be reimbursed 25 percent more than your competition down the street for each hernia repair you perform, regardless of your outcomes." The problem with this business model is that quality is not even factored into the reimbursement equation. Studies have continued to show there is no correlation between higher reimbursements and better outcomes in surgery. Higher costs do not equate to better quality. As an independent surgeon in private practice, I'm paid less for each operation regardless of outcomes.

The Affordable Care Act has also added the extra cost of bureaucracy and paperwork to a surgeon's practice. This expense cannot be absorbed as easily by surgeons in private practice as it can by those who work for a larger corporate entity. The financial cushion is just not there. Along with all this, the emotional and physical pressures of running a viable business while trying to practice quality surgical care are making hospital employment look more attractive than ever.

Still, the primary reason that established independent surgeons are becoming hospital employees is that they are being pressured by hospitals to do so. As the late Speaker of the House Thomas "Tip" O'Neill once said, "All politics is local." The political pressure being exerted on private practice community surgeons today is local and mounting. In every community, hospitals control most of the primary care physicians, who, in turn, control the patients. If independently practicing surgeons are reluctant to become employed and join a hospital team, their practice may be at risk. Hospital systems understand they are in a position of strength to negotiate contracts; if no agreement is reached, they will go out to the larger market and purchase other surgeons. This is easier said than done, given the current shortage of surgeons. Independent surgical groups cannot afford the salaries being given to newly trained surgeons today. Yet because they have the money, and because they have control over patient populations, hospitals are succeeding in their acquisitions plans. Agreements with employed primary care physicians allow big systems to cut off referrals to independent surgeons once the new "help" has arrived. Do hospital administrators care that they are discarding years of loyalty and quality surgical care from independent surgeons? Evidently not. It is strictly a business decision, a decision to maximize control and revenue streams.

Now, to be fair, hospital system administrators may not see it this way. They justify their decisions to employ surgeons at the expense of quality private surgeons in the community by crying about the need to control costs and improve quality. The truth is that hospital systems *will* have an easier time controlling their costs when they control surgeons by employment. Hospitals will increase their revenue by benefiting from their surgeons' clinical production. Quality outcomes? Hospitals will have an easier time standardizing their "version" of quality when *their* surgeons are doing the lion's share of the operations.

At the moment, the market for surgeons is still both a buyer's and seller's market. On paper, it can appear to be a seller's market because of the shortage of surgeons. In reality, though, because of the overwhelming resources hospital systems can bring to bear, it is more of a buyer's market. Through it all, hospitals are feeding on a surgeon's worst emotions: fear and greed. By employing surgeons and controlling the referral base, hospital systems know that competing private practice surgeons will fear the loss of future business, essentially the loss of their ability to earn what they are accustomed to earning (some call this professional blackmail). This fear is real, runs deep, and is a big distraction to private practice surgeons negotiating with hospitals. The other emotion surgeons experience when their livelihood is threatened is greed. With fear fueling them, some surgeons allow the greed of short-term guaranteed financial security to cloud their decision process. Hospital administrators are well tuned to these emotions and have the resources to take advantage of them.

And so it's no surprise that more and more newly trained surgeons seek hospital employment when looking for their first job. When you add in uncertainties about the effect the Affordable Care Act will have on private practice profit margins, hospital employment becomes even more attractive. Many new docs carry significant debt from their education; reports from the American Association of Medical Colleges show the average educational debt of new physicians approaching $160,000. These young doctors want to get paid what they think they're worth. Many also have families and want to establish financial security sooner rather than later. They do not want to start out as an associate, sharing expenses, building up a practice, and waiting two to five years to become a full partner with full benefits. Why should they take on the pressures of trying to run a business when they could do well working for a system? Today's new surgeons want a better quality of life than their established colleagues may have. They don't want twenty-four-hour call. Newly trained surgeons want to practice surgery during the day and go home at night. To be honest with you, I don't blame them. Being employed by hospital systems, with all their resources, can offer newly trained surgeons many benefits a smaller private practice group simply cannot.

Large multispecialty groups or hospital systems can afford to offer salary packages that smaller, independent surgical groups cannot. Instant, guaranteed money for several years. Most employment contracts offered by hospital systems offer a guaranteed salary comparable to market value. For instance, because of the shortage, many national recruiting firms offer starting salaries for general surgeons between $300,000 and $400,000. Often, this pay is guaranteed for two to four years, plus an opportunity to earn more in "production bonuses" at the end of the year. There are no expenses, no malpractice insurance to pay, and no hiring or firing of office personnel, and there is free ancillary help in the form of nurse practitioners or surgical physician assistants. Private practice groups often cannot compete with any of this. It all seems too good to be true and in some ways it is. Yes, there is financial security, but it is not forever. When the contract ends, if surgical production has not generated enough revenue to cover the employed surgeon's salary, he or she may make less. The guaranteed salary is no longer guaranteed.

As a surgeon in private practice, I view caring for my patients as a twenty-four-hour-a-day responsibility, a continuum of attention. I have always believed in making my clinical services available whenever needed. I also view running a business as a twenty-four-hour-a-day responsibility, and I know that if I work hard, I should see my business grow. I am not guaranteed anything unless I work for it.

Will the guaranteed financial security that employment brings to surgeons remove some of their motivation to work hard, decrease the time they make themselves available to patients, and affect the continuity of care? There are two schools of thought on this. What if, after being guaranteed a salary, a surgeon's production begins to slowly decrease because the fire fueled by the personal incentives of running a practice is muffled? Fewer operations are performed, patients wait longer to have elective surgery, and access to timely surgical care is compromised. On the positive side, it could reduce costs by eliminating the desire to perform unnecessary surgery. Hospitals would not welcome this because fewer operations mean less revenue.

What if a shift mentality sets in for surgeons? What if your surgeon's desire to be personally available for his or her patients after office hours is diminished because it is not necessary? There is another employed surgeon on call to take over. What if your surgeon starts to be less enthusiastic about taking night emergency room call and having to come in to operate in the middle of the night? In the past, emergency rooms were a fertile ground for growing a private practice and reputation. Could this shift mentality eventually erode the quality of care delivered? What if a surgeon gets a call at one o'clock in the morning about a patient with acute appendicitis in the emergency room and decides not to come in, leaving it for the surgeon coming on duty at seven A.M. to perform the operation? What if that patient's appendix ruptures during the delay, causing a complication when it is finally removed, and a prolonged hospitalization? I worry about scenarios like this. Human behavior is affected by a multitude of motivations; when there is less of a personal incentive in the game for surgeons, their behavior will reflect that reality.

An employed surgeon's behavior inside the operating room can be influenced as well by decisions made in a hospital's administration, finance, and purchasing departments. While far removed from direct patient care, these departments are affecting the quality of care every day. Here's an example: As a laparoscopic surgeon, I use a device called a trocar to enter a patient's abdomen. A trocar is a six-inch-long tubelike device, five to twelve millimeters thick, that comes to a point at one end. Trocars are used to provide ports for cameras and thin laparoscopic instruments that are used during laparoscopic (also known as minimally invasive) surgery. Trocar sales are big business for medical device companies because they are used so frequently by so many surgeons. Different companies produce trocars for a range of prices. I practice surgery at two hospitals; one is a for-profit hospital and the other is a nonprofit corporate entity. One day, my colleagues and I were notified that the for-profit hospital was changing trocar companies. We did not think much about it until we realized they were switching to a cheaper device, one that many of us had rejected several years earlier at the nonprofit hospital. We rejected it because it was wider than advertised, wider than what we were using. The wider the trocar, the greater the chance of hitting a blood vessel as it goes through the abdominal wall. It could potentially also result in more post-op pain for the patient than the ones we were using. But it was much, much cheaper, which is very appealing to purchasing departments and chief financial officers (CFOs). Despite what I considered to be a sham "trial use" of the cheaper trocar in the operating room and despite our protests, the decision was made to switch suppliers. Cost ruled the day and the surgeons in the operating room had no choice but to use the cheaper trocars or go elsewhere. The surgeons employed at that hospital could not go elsewhere because of their financial ties and contractual obligations. As an independent surgeon in private practice, I could.

Will the pressures on employed surgeons—to be productive, earn the guaranteed salary, and meet production bonuses—affect the quality of patient care? I believe they will. I don't have difficulty imagining that an employed surgeon facing a contract renewal *could* feel sufficient financial pressure to potentially schedule unnecessary surgery; just think back to the example of Mrs. Brogan's case, from Chapter 1. A renewed contract with a reduced salary and more production incentives could pressure surgeons into the operating room. The threat of losing one's job because of low volume (fewer surgical cases) is yet another pressure that could affect decision making. All of this pressure can push surgeons to go beyond their clinical comfort zone, including performing operations they might not have much experience in doing. When surgeons perform operations they do not carry out frequently, inexperience often leads to complications and poor outcomes. I have observed this in private practice as well. The difference, however, is that employed surgeons are supported by resources that can absorb the negative impact of a bad outcome much more than can the surgeon in independent practice. Hospitals have big financial stakes in their surgeon employees and more incentive to carry them through the negative wake of a bad outcome. In addition, the built-in referral system for employed surgeons in large systems keeps business flowing. Contract referrals can keep business flowing until the number of poor outcomes reaches critical mass. On the other hand, independent surgeons have only their reputation to carry them through the pain of a bad patient outcome. Their independence means they have more to lose financially, too. The saying "practice makes perfect" is true for many endeavors in life, including performing surgery, as well-documented statistics show. Five years ago, had Mr. Chase's surgeon performed an operation in which he did not have much experience? If so, why? I think Mr. Chase would have wanted to know. If he had, he might have chosen another surgeon.

There are personal implications to the surgeon once he or she decides to leave the world of private practice and become employed by a hospital system. The first, I believe, is psychological. Older surgeons, in the latter half of their careers, can find it difficult to accept the fact that they have a boss, a hospital CEO (chief executive officer), someone (usually) without an M.D. after his or her name. As long as anyone can remember, there has always existed a contentious (while respectful on the surface) relationship between the physicians in practice at community hospitals and the administrators who run these hospitals. Each group has strong egos and particular points of view regarding the other's value. Many physicians view hospital administrators as having no understanding of what it takes to practice quality medicine, while administrators stereotype physicians as lacking in business acumen and vision. Traditionally, physicians have felt that they alone are the guardians and deliverers of healthcare in their local community. They often believed that without their expertise and patients, the hospitals would not survive. Without physicians and their patients, hospitals would just be buildings with empty beds, administrators without jobs. On the other hand, hospital administrators have often believed it is a privilege for any physician in the community to have the opportunity to use their hospital. Both groups think they know what is best for patient care, and those viewpoints don't always match. Because of this tension, the relationship between practicing physicians and hospital administration has always been one of mutual need rather than love.

Despite the contentiousness of this relationship, independent practicing physicians have had leverage because they have controlled patient flow. Historically, surgeons often had the most leverage because their services generated substantial income for hospitals. If two competing hospitals in a community were vying for a surgeon's patients, this leverage would become even more significant. Changes in the balance of power, however, mean this leverage has all but disappeared. Independent surgeons, once in a dominant position to dictate workplace terms to hospital administrators, are now having those terms dictated to them. Established surgeons can have a difficult time accepting the fact they are working for the very corporate administration types they have long despised.

How this psychological capitulation will affect not only the surgeons on a personal level but also the quality of surgical care they deliver is an important question. I suspect most surgeons will reluctantly kiss their independence good-bye and succumb to the economic and political pressures pushing them into signing a contract. I suspect most will not find happiness despite the short-term financial security because they know, deep down, they are selling their high-priced souls. They may also understand but not want to acknowledge that contracts do not last forever. In the end, I believe most surgeons will lose whatever professional zest is left inside when they sign. I also suspect new surgeons will not perceive themselves as entering a profession their older colleagues still view as a special calling, a lifelong dedication to patients. Instead, surgeons may just want to do their jobs, collect their paycheck, and go home, completely shutting out their workplace after hours. The personalized package of surgical care offered during "the good old days" may become impersonal. (Eventually, the surgeon holding the scalpel blade may not even be human; "he" could even be a robot.) Will this change of mentality influence the surgeon who is about to remove your uterus, repair your hernia, replace your hip, or operate on your spine? Will this change affect the overall quality of care you receive after any one of these operations? I guess we are going to find out.

I believe physicians coming out of surgical residencies will have an easier time accepting their roles as employed surgeons because they are more pliable, are not yet set in their ways, and have no history as independent practitioners to haunt them. Academic surgeons, the ones who train our surgeons of the future, have always practiced in an employer-employee business environment. The surgeons on staff at medical training centers have always worked for the institutions and never for themselves. Traditionally, they have been paid a salary for their duties, with the potential to earn more with production and teaching incentives. Young surgeons are eager to maximize their net worth now and strike a balance between working and family life. Guaranteed employment offered by hospital systems can allow a new surgeon to achieve both—right out of training.

Another effect of employment for longtime self-employed surgeons is an uneasy feeling of loss of control, on many fronts. The first is losing control over the operations of your office (billing, personnel, and the decision to implement electronic medical records). Many also lose control over the process of hiring new surgical colleagues. Hospitals often hire a new surgeon without consulting those already employed. One day you might find yourself sharing office space with a newly employed surgeon without having had any input into why that surgeon was hired or the qualifications attached to that surgeon. And, as an employee, you may have no choice but to trust your patients' care to that new surgeon when you are not working. In addition, surgeons lose control over where they can operate. A 2013 article in *JAMA Surgery* summed it up succinctly, noting, "Direct employment also gives hospitals the freedom to impose additional requirements on the physician, such as requiring employed physicians to refer to the hospital's service lines instead of other entities." For surgeons, this means you are restricted as to where you can perform surgery and therefore restricted in the hospital choices you can offer your patients, choices that are based on employment, not necessarily quality. Much of this restriction is in the name of maximizing revenue and controlling costs. Once surgeons are employed, hospitals can reduce costs by controlling their practice options. Hospitals can also decrease costs by limiting the choices of equipment used by surgeons in their operating rooms and by buying the least expensive devices, rather than the ones most desired by the surgeons.

In addition to losing personal and professional control as an employed surgeon, I believe you lose control over your job description. Often, newly employed surgeons are asked to take on clinical and administrative responsibilities in order to justify their salaries. Once a hospital has you under contract, you may be asked to go to other hospitals in their system to see patients and cover the emergency room. You may be asked to set up an office in a neighboring town, in addition to seeing patients in the community in which you practice. All this equates to more travel time and the stress of trying to be in more places in less time. Sometimes surgeons are asked to move into administrative positions, which can be uncomfortable. For instance, a surgeon I know well recently made the jump from private practice to employed surgeon for a for-profit hospital. In addition to his clinical duties, he is expected to be on the board of a committee that tightly monitors where the system's patients are being operated on. Part of the job is to meet with the private surgeons left in the community and make them aware that he is watching their numbers. He is charged with convincing the independent surgeons that it is in their best interest to use *his* hospital when their patients need surgery. At one of these meetings, I could clearly see his discomfort in carrying out his new job on behalf of the administration. He had no choice, though, now that the system was paying his salary.

I also believe employed surgeons will see a slow erosion of their job security, despite the promises of guaranteed money and referrals. Once the guaranteed salary contract has expired, hospitals will have these surgeons in a vulnerable position. If you have produced surgery numbers well beyond the expectations, all is well. If you haven't lived up to your production numbers enough to pay your salary, there are two options. The first is renegotiating a new, shorter-term contract for much less money and production incentive bonuses.

The second option for the hospital or system whose employed surgeon's patient volume has not met quota is not renewing the contract. If the hospital system has plans to replace you with another surgeon, all it has to do is make the salary terms of a new contract so undesirable that you cannot afford to sign it. The problem is, where do surgeons go once they have left employment in a hospital system? They do not have a practice to fall back on, and they may have to move to another city to find a job. Many just end up working part-time or retiring. The bottom line is that once you become a surgeon employee of a hospital system, they have you.

Another potential casualty of employment in a hospital system may be the ability to openly disagree with the organization.

Will surgeons, as highly paid employees, be confident enough to speak up against hospital policies affecting patient care without worrying about corporate retaliation? Will employed surgeons be able to speak out against hospital cost-cutting measures that infringe on patient care without being labeled whistleblowers or troublemakers? Can they voice their displeasure without worrying about the security of their job? If you are branded "not a team player," referrals may dry up. Or, you may suddenly be "asked" to take more emergency room call. You may also be asked to travel farther to see patients and generate surgical business in another town. You may be replaced. You could end up as a surgeon without a practice. If let go, you may discover that the clause in your contract prohibiting you from practicing within the area drives you out of town.

Will employed surgeons be able to openly highlight waste and fraud without fear of losing their jobs? As highly paid employees, surgeons risk much if they criticize the organization that employs them, even when the intent is improved patient care. Knowing the economic stakes of speaking against the corporate team, I suspect many may choose to be silent.

Now that more surgeons are giving up their independence and joining the ranks of the employed, will they have the ability to unionize? Historically, surgeons have been an extremely independent breed of physician, perhaps too independent for their own good. For whatever reasons—ego, stubbornness, a view of themselves as well above the average working stiff, money, competitive juices—surgeons have never been able to use their local muscle to influence hospital behavior. Instead of being able to unionize freely decades ago, surgeons may now be forced to in order to survive.

Will unionized surgeons be given collective bargaining rights when negotiating with their employers? Will surgeons be able to strike if they feel the hospital systems they work for are not negotiating salaries or working conditions in good faith? Can you see it now, a Teamster walking the picket line in solidarity with a white-coated surgeon over improving health benefits? Will there be appeal boards to contest unfair firings? As employees, will surgeons be able to negotiate for vacations, sick time, or family leave?

The writing is on the wall for all surgeons, including me. The era of the independent surgeon is drawing to a close. More and more patients will be cared for by surgeons whose economic and surgical lives are directly influenced by the corporate entities that employ them. What, if any, impact will this dramatic shift in the surgeon's professional world have on the access to and quality of surgery practiced in the future? It remains to be seen, but there *is* a reason the American Medical Association (AMA) specifically addressed this shift in 2012 with new guidelines for physicians selling their practices. Tellingly, the AMA stated that "patients should be told whenever a hospital provides financial incentives that encourage, discourage, or restrict referrals or treatment options." The AMA statement continued: "Physicians should always make treatment and referral decisions based on the interests of their patients." Isn't this how physicians and surgeons already practice, and have for hundreds of years? Or is it?

As a patient, should you know who your surgeon works for before agreeing to an operation? If you're interested in a dinosaur's perspective, the answer is "Yes!"

4 | TURF WARS

A re you kidding me?" I could not believe what I was hearing. I put the scalpel down on the Mayo stand and walked over to the phone where the circulating nurse was on the line with a hospital across town. "Are they serious? You mean to tell me they refuse to send over the mesh I need? I know they have it. I used it last week." I forced myself to lower my voice. "I have a patient on the table, under anesthesia, and they are refusing to help?"

I was in the middle of repairing Mr. Jacker's inguinal hernia when I learned that the mesh I needed was not available. After a frantic search in the OR's central supply, I was informed our hospital no longer carried it. I took full responsibility for the situation; I had made the mistake of *assuming* it was on the shelf.

Over the years, there had been times when I would ask for an item in the middle of an operation, such as mesh or a surgical stapler, only to be told it could not be found. These occasions were rare and, fortunately, a phone call to the hospital across town was all it took to remedy the problem. The item would arrive within minutes, no questions asked. In the past, both community hospitals had been happy to help each other out when asked. In the past, the two hospitals had worked together as needed on a variety of levels—and always in the interest of patient care—to supplement each other's clinical needs or fill a deficiency in a service. There was never any financial exploitation of the situation. It was a friendly working relationship. Sure, there was competition between the two, but it always took a backseat to patient care and the needs of the community. Physicians associated with each hospital covered both emergency rooms willingly, admitting patients based on patient preference, not financial edicts. In the past, a mutual respect had existed between the two hospitals. Unfortunately, that was then.

Now, my patient, Mr. Jacker, was under general anesthesia with three idle laparoscopic instruments sticking out of his insufflated lower abdomen. I didn't have the mesh to complete his operation, and it appeared I was not going to get it. Clearly, the rivalry between the two community hospitals I had operated out of for the last fifteen years had reached a sorry state.

The competition between the two community hospitals had been escalating for a few years. The breaking point came when one of the hospitals decided to start its own cancer program. For years there had been a gentlemen's agreement between the two hospitals over cardiac and cancer care. One had the facilities for comprehensive cardiac care, including angioplasty and heart surgery, while the other had a long history of comprehensive cancer care. Each complemented the other's services well for the good of the community. From a patient-care standpoint, needs were being met at both hospitals. From a business standpoint, no one complained or got greedy. Both hospitals were making plenty of money. Unfortunately, that had all changed. The potential revenue generated from the lifelong treatment of cancer patients was too tempting to be ignored any longer by the hospital lacking in those services. As soon as the first neighborhood house was purchased and torn down to break ground for the new cancer center, all hell broke loose. The two hospitals were in an all-out war. With the cancer line crossed, direct competition between the two hospitals had morphed into an ugly land grab for physician practices, real estate, and patient business. Each was trying to protect its turf while poaching on the other's.

While my colleagues and I were well aware of these machinations, the competition's resistance to supply the mesh I needed to complete my operation was shocking. The relationship between the two hospitals had reached a new low, and it looked like my patient was going to pay a price because of it.

"Who are you talking to?" I gestured to the circulating nurse to place the phone to my ear. I was trying not to take out my rising anger on her.

"I've been talking with the operating room at Tavers Hospital." She sounded exasperated.

"I'm going to talk to them myself. This has gone too far. Enough of this bullshit 'kill or be killed' competition crap." I exploded out of my gown and gloves, leaving a torn piece of gown stuck on my right arm. "Get the head of their operating room on the phone."

Grabbing the phone, I shouted, "Who the hell am I speaking to?" The voice was muffled on the other end and I did not recognize it. I was so angry I wasn't hearing anything anyway. "Listen,

I have a patient, *open*, on the table *right now* and need that mesh to complete his surgery. If you don't want to hand it over to the courier we send, I will personally come over there and rip it from you myself." The person on the other end was saying something unintelligible; all I could make out was, "This has been a misunderstanding . . ." Before I hung up the phone, the mesh was on its way. It was all I needed to know. Once it arrived, I completed the operation quickly and sent the patient home. Mr. Jacker had no idea what had transpired. He had no knowledge of the turf war erupting between the two hospitals or how it almost affected the quality of his surgical care that day. Fortunately, he never had a reason to find out.

This mesh story is just another episode in the raging war between two hospital systems positioning themselves for the dramatic healthcare reimbursement changes coming down the road. It is emblematic of a war that is rumbling across the nation. The two hospitals involved could be anywhere, in any community, in any state. It is a war aimed at protecting an established economic position in the community while simultaneously trying to make inroads into additional, revenue-producing clinical service lines. It is a war where generously paid hospital administrators are flexing their spending muscles, firing off missiles to improve market share.

Unfortunately, it is a war where physicians are conscripted into service, forced to choose sides, leave behind years of loyalties, and, at times, battle each other for patients. This war is turning physician colleagues—professionals who have worked together for years covering each other's patients—into adversaries.

It is a war where, ultimately, patients are the casualties, the collateral damage as hospitals vie for every possible healthcare dollar.

As a surgeon practicing in the community for fifteen years, I have seen a dramatic shift in the relationship between the two hospital systems and how they do business. I suspect I am not the only surgeon making this observation because it is common in every community today. I believe one of the driving forces accelerating this shift originates from the mandates written into the Affordable Care Act of 2010, mandates that will significantly change the way physicians and hospitals are reimbursed. While the full effects of these mandates are just beginning to have an impact, community hospitals are in a "Wild West" phase of expansion, trying to increase market share now. The Affordable Care Act's looming shadow added fuel to the already burning fire of fierce competition, pushing hospital systems to freely go at it. It is a survival-of-the-fittest approach. It is also a "bigger-is-better" mentality, regardless of cost, because of the finite pool of federal and private healthcare money available in the future. It is a mentality pushing hospital administrators to expand their medical/surgical services and broaden their brands. In the short term, this mentality costs money by investing in technology and physicians. In the long run, hospitals may make money by controlling their costs and their physicians, and limiting competition. Bigger does not necessarily mean better-quality healthcare. It just means the bigger the hospital system, the better chance of getting more federal money when Medicare starts allotting "block money or bundled payments" for the treatment of diseases based on patient lives. It boils down to a numbers game. The more physicians a hospital has under its umbrella, the more patient lives counted by the federal government, hence the potential for more federal money allotted. The bigger you are, the more leverage you have as a system to negotiate fee contracts with private insurers. The bigger you are, the more leverage you have to influence specialists, such as surgeons who rely solely on referrals, to steer business to your operating rooms.

Surgeons are not accustomed to this mentality. It is a mentality furthered by the Affordable Care Act's roughly $700 billion Medicare payment cuts to hospitals (and specialists) over the next ten years, cuts hospitals are already trying to make up for by buying up surgeons to guarantee a busy operating room, expanding surgical services, and locking in potential valuable healthcare real estate. Nonprofit and for-profit hospitals alike are in a feeding frenzy, spending money to compete with one another to position themselves for future healthcare dollars. Both are buying up physician practices, in the hopes of cementing patients into their systems. Because I am an independent practicing surgeon, the road I now travel to each hospital's operating room has become hazardous. Checkpoints are posted along the way, interspersed between political land mines—checkpoints that have everything to do with the business of surgery and nothing to do with patient care.

As a prime example of the ongoing hospital turf wars, in Pittsburgh the acrimonious battle between Highmark, the region's most powerful health insurer, and UPMC (University of Pittsburgh Medical Center), the dominant healthcare provider, is drawing national attention. The outcome may well serve as a test case on the impact of consolidation in the healthcare industry. At the heart of the dispute is Highmark's effort to acquire a financially troubled local hospital group.

The battle has become unusually bitter, according to the *Wall Street Journal*, spearheaded by the two companies' chief executives: UPMC's Jeffrey A. Romoff and Highmark's Kenneth Melani. Mr. Romoff, who has built UPMC into a $9 billion juggernaut and put its initials on the tallest skyscraper in the city, calls Highmark a "monopoly." Dr. Melani uses the same term in warnings about UPMC's power and has referred to Mr. Romoff in an interview published in a local newspaper as "trying to rape the commercial marketplace to build his empire."

Their fight has played out through advertising campaigns, a legal battle, and lobbying over bills. Doctors are being pressed to choose sides and fear losing patients no matter which one they align with. The struggle in Pittsburgh has roots that go back decades. UPMC, a nonprofit, has grown to $9 billion in annual revenue with 58 percent of market share in Allegheny County. By 2011, the nonprofit Highmark had annual revenue of $14.8 billion, and was sitting on reserves of about $4.1 billion.

The *Wall Street Journal* has continued to cover the war between the two giant hospital systems in Pittsburgh, and in an article in March 2012 it quoted a primary care physician who said he tells his worried patients that "all of us are pawns in this fight." Since then, a judge has settled the dispute by allowing Highmark to complete its hospital purchases, develop its own medical system, and employ its own physicians to compete with UPMC. Despite the settlement, the damage to the city's physicians and patients was irreversible.

The case was, and still is, reflective of what is going on in the delivery of healthcare in every community today. Hospitals are battling over physicians, especially surgeons, who generate revenue for their operating rooms. It is a battle about money and control. In the end, the lawyers are the winners and patients are the losers. Unfortunately, for the moment, the physicians are caught in the middle.

I understand the need to control healthcare costs, the need to make the delivery of healthcare more efficient, the need to increase access to care and improve quality. Some argue that the consolidation in healthcare today will help reduce overall costs, make the delivery of healthcare more efficient, and improve quality. In the short term, however, hospital systems are not focused on lowering costs. Their interest in improving quality quietly takes a backseat to their appetite for maximizing market share. The true focus on cost control and improving real quality will come later. It will come once the spending to expand stops. It will come once all the physicians are employed under one collective roof. It will come later, once the federal Medicare/Medicaid "block money" gets distributed as the Affordable Care Act's reimbursement mandates start to take shape.

What really is at stake here? Why are hospitals consolidating, buying physician practices (both primary care and specialists), and falling all over each other to fence in every last patient? It is quite simple. It is the more than 17 percent of gross domestic product (GDP; increase that to 20 percent by 2020) currently being spent on the delivery of healthcare that's at stake. Of this $2.7 trillion, roughly 31 percent (over $800 billion) is spent on hospital services and 21 percent (over $500 billion) on physician services. Of the hundreds of billions spent by the federal government's Medicare program, roughly one-quarter goes to hospital services. Of the roughly $400 billion spent by Medicaid, 60 percent goes to pay hospitals for their services. Both spending totals are expected to increase, with Medicare increasing 7.3 percent yearly because of aging baby boomers and Medicaid 20 percent yearly because of state expansion. By 2020, some projections show government healthcare spending as high as 50 percent of all the money spent nationally. The stakes are obvious as competing hospitals fire shots at each other in an effort to preserve their own turf and expand into others: billions of healthcare dollars.

A lot of that money is generated by operating rooms. According to the Centers for Disease Control and Prevention (CDC), more than fifty million surgical procedures are performed each year. The estimated cost of the most common inpatient operations performed is north of $200 billion. Since hospitals receive 60 to 80 percent of this, the financial incentive to lure patients into a particular hospital's operating rooms is high. The surgical treatment of disease is big business for hospitals on many levels. Today, hospitals are trying to infiltrate every surgical disease market with their own surgeons. If they cannot employ their own, they will go after the private groups in town, making them offers they cannot refuse. They are not bashful about whom they infuriate, buy out, or step over. Why would they be?

According to the CDC, the market for spinal fusion surgery in this country is over $12 billion a year. Surgical procedures such as spinal fusion are big revenue producers for hospital operating rooms and, for many, are the top surgical service line. The average annual salary for spine surgeons is three-quarters of a million dollars, based on the latest MGMA physician-compensation survey. I have no problem with this level of compensation, given the years of sacrifice necessary to become a competent spine surgeon. Actually, because the work is so highly specialized, a good neurosurgeon's worth is probably much greater. A 2010 hospital revenue survey by Merritt Hawkins (a leading physician staffing company) concluded that a single neurosurgeon can generate over two and a half million dollars in revenue a year for the hospital he or she chooses to take patients to. If I were a hospital CEO, why wouldn't I go out and lock up my own neurosurgeons in order to direct patients to my operating rooms?

For years, it did not matter who employed the surgeons or who signed their checks at the end of the month. Neurosurgeons have always been a scarce commodity, and even today many communities are lacking adequate neurosurgical services. Consequently, best efforts were made, even by competing hospitals, to have emergencies covered throughout the community by having surgeons, particularly neurosurgeons, cover all emergency rooms. This arrangement was all about the interest of patient care, pure and simple. There were no financial motives behind this tradition, for surgeon or hospital. This goodwill arrangement was never pressured until recent market forces forced hospital CEOs to look for every opportunity to generate revenue and stifle the competition. Today, many surgeons, particularly neurosurgeons, are valuable bargaining chips when it comes to competing hospitals. Hospital CEOs understand their financial worth and their ability to generate revenue in the operating room.

In this brave new world, the days of having all surgeons cover the emergency rooms of all hospitals in a community, regardless of employment, are long gone. Now hospital CEOs are telling the competition across town to pay up for use of their employed surgeons' emergency room coverage. Pay, or get your own. The hospitals with the resources couldn't care less if their competition cannot provide emergency room surgical coverage. "Either pay up or I am pulling my surgeons out" is a remark (a threat, really) that I have come across in my recent travels. Not once in this new dialogue have I heard, "in the best interest of patient care." Not once have I heard regret about forcing patients to go from one local hospital emergency room to another, no acknowledgment of the inconvenience this "transfer" causes to the ill individual or the family members. What patients don't know is that surgeons *are* available, just not to you at your hospital if they are employed by the competing hospital.

These changes, and many like them, are strictly business decisions, made in the best interest of a hospital's balance sheet. Employed surgeons have little say in any of these business decisions, despite a history of working together to care for all patients in a community. They are forced to take sides, knowing full well it could hurt their own business and, ultimately, hurt patients. Hospital-employed surgeons have to do what is in the best interest of the hospital, not themselves, even if their employer's decision may not be in the best interest of patient care.

In addition to spinal surgery, according to the CDC, joint replacement is another lucrative surgical market for hospitals. The costs of knee replacement surgery alone exceed $10 billion a year. Orthopedic surgeons are highly sought after by hospitals because of the revenue their talents can generate. A single orthopedic surgeon can generate a substantial amount of money for a hospital each year—nearly $2.5 million. As with neurosurgeons, orthopedic surgeons are also needed to cover emergency rooms in every community. Some community hospitals who employ their own orthopedic surgeons are telling the competition to "pay up or get your own." Sharing is no longer an option. The business need to fill one's operating room with orthopedic surgical procedures far outweighs the community's need for accessible orthopedic care.

Some hospital systems are even bringing in outside companies who provide their own orthopedic surgeons, coming into communities and providing emergency room coverage for hospitals for a fee. I call this the "carpetbagger" business model. These companies, hired by a hospital, make available their own employed orthopedic surgeons so emergencies can be operated on at that hospital. Practically speaking, your hip may be replaced on a Sunday by a journeyman surgeon with no community reputation; he or she may be someone you meet ten minutes before the anesthesia drugs start taking effect. Once your surgery is over, the first face you see Monday morning may not even be a surgeon's face but that of an employed physician assistant or even a hospitalist internist hired by the hospital. The surgeon who replaced your hip is probably long gone. When your orthopedic surgeon does make rounds on Monday, his or her face may not be the face of the surgeon who performed your surgery the night before. When you are discharged, you probably will be introduced to a brand-new orthopedic face, or you might see the physician assistant again. When you go for a follow-up appointment, I'm not really sure whom you will see. I do not mean to pick on orthopedic surgeons because this scenario is applicable to all surgeons, including general surgeons like me. Whatever the specialty, the "carpetbagger" business model of patient surgical care is, at the very least, impersonal and disruptive to the continuity of care. At the very worst, it lends an added potential for medical errors because of the multiple handoffs that must occur when a new surgeon takes over your care.

Part of the reason this new business model is growing in popularity for orthopedic procedures is the diminishing number of orthopedic surgeons. Along with the growing shortage, many are opting out of emergency room call. Orthopedic surgeons, and all community private practice surgeons for that matter, are deciding not to be available after hours. Surgeons are realizing that they can make a decent living *and* enjoy a quality life without needing the Medicaid and Medicare business that emergency rooms generate. For many community surgeons, emergency operations on patients can be challenging and stressful. They can take longer, disrupt regular office hours, and disrupt life in general if done in the middle of the night. Often patients needing an emergency operation are sicker going into surgery. And after surgery, these patients can monopolize the surgeon's time and still end in bad outcomes because of the acuteness of their disease. Frankly, in the era of decreasing reimbursements and surgeon shortage, community surgeons are deciding to separate themselves from emergency room call because it is just not worth the stress, the added malpractice risk, or the reimbursement.

As a consequence, community hospitals are experiencing an urgent need to fill a surgical void while simultaneously looking for new ways to capture the revenue generated from emergency surgery. The field of acute care surgery has been evolving over the last decade in an attempt to improve the surgical care of critically ill trauma and burn patients. Its essence involves hospitals dedicating teams of their own employed surgeons of all specialties to cover all emergency surgery, trauma surgery, and critical care. The concept has worked well at university teaching hospitals because the surgeons involved, including the residents, are employed by the university and are dedicated only to the treatment of the critically ill patient. For a university, there is no room for private practice surgeons to be a part of this model.

In addition to the obvious clinical benefits of having a dedicated acute care surgery team available twenty-four hours a day, large private community hospital systems are aware of the financial benefits as well. This business model may allow hospitals to monopolize the surgical market share in any community by getting access to patients first, right from the emergency room. It may be a way for hospitals to gradually push out the local private competition who are unwilling to capitulate to hospital demands, join the team, or be bought out. It starts in the emergency room, where patients are first seen by ER physicians contracted out by the hospital. These front-line physicians will have pressure on them to refer not only the critically ill but also the not-so-critically-ill—the ones who will require elective surgery later—to the hospital-employed acute care surgeons. They will feel pressured to feed these surgeons cases at the expense of possibly more experienced, more competent, unaffiliated community surgeons. Private practice surgeons will, at times of their own volition, be purposely cut out of the loop of surgical business generated by a busy hospital emergency room.

As this clinical business scenario continues to play out in communities across the country, how will patient care be affected? What worries me is that in the rush to protect their own clinical and financial turf by hiring surgeons, hospital systems may not be focusing on the quality of the employed surgeon as much as the contract terms. With the shortage of surgeons getting worse every year, coupled with the urgent need to hire and compete, will hospitals compromise on the quality of whom they hire for the sake of keeping their operating rooms open for all business right now? Where are these new surgeon hires suddenly coming from? Will these hired-gun surgeons be part of the local medical community, or will they be carpetbaggers? If the latter, will patient care be compromised by "part-time" surgeons hired by hospitals to come in, compete with the hospital across town, and be pressured to generate business to pay for their guaranteed contracts and potential productivity bonuses? Two of the biggest clinical consequences of two competing community hospitals duplicating surgical services, in a fixed community population, with each trying to maintain a stranglehold on their patients, are restriction of patient choice and the creation of an adversarial practicing environment for physicians. A big financial consequence of a turf war or consolidation is higher costs due to the lack of competition. Patient choice is restricted because internists are forced to refer their patients to their own specialists for care and surgeons for surgery, despite the potential existence of better-quality ones across town. For physicians, especially surgeons because of the income they generate, old-school collegiality is gone when hospital administrators are constantly monitoring your operating room "production."

"Dr. Ruggieri," my secretary shouted down the corridor. She knew my office door was open. "Dr. Scapa is on the phone. He wants to speak to you."

"Shoot," I mumbled. I was filling out paperwork and did not want to be interrupted. "Just put him through."

Dr. Ryan Scapa was a well-known internist and leader of a large medical group in town. His group carried a lot of clout with specialists, particularly surgeons. They controlled a substantial number of patients in the community, patients that could generate a lot of business for surgeons when the time came for an operation. In addition, Dr. Scapa's group also generated a lot of revenue for Balblair Hospital, his "home" hospital, and kept patients away from the competition, Tavers Hospital.

Both hospitals belonged to large corporate systems, with each owning several hospitals throughout the region. With the financial support of the parent systems, Balblair and Tavers were buying up physician practices with abandon in an effort to gain market dominance. Both hospitals were spending more than a million dollars a year on marketing campaigns, determined to gain market share in the multibillion-dollar business of cancer and cardiovascular care. In addition to practicing medicine, Dr. Scapa's other paying job was to make sure the patients he referred to me were operated on at "his" hospital, Balblair, and not the competition across town. He counted the monthly operations and tracked where his group's referrals to me and my partners were admitted for surgery.

The last time I had heard from Dr. Scapa was two months earlier. He had called, pissed off that I had operated on one of his patients at Tavers Hospital, the competition. The truth was, Dr. Scapa's patient did not *want* to go to Balblair because of a relative's bad experience there and had said no. I had privileges at both.

"Paul, Ryan here." His voice was a monotone. "Paul, when I refer a patient to you for surgery, I want you to use Tavers Hospital."

Odd. "Last time we spoke you were twisting my arm to bring your patients to Balblair Hospital. What's changed?" I had heard rumors but wanted to hear it from him.

"Our group was recently purchased by Tavers Hospital," he continued. "It was in the best interest of our group to make the change." He paused. "You need to explain to any future patients I send you that Tavers is the better hospital, the hospital I prefer." He chose his words carefully, knowing full well I understood their meaning.

"Ryan"—I had put aside the paperwork and was giving the conversation my full attention—"do I or my patients have any say in this?"

There was a long pause on his end. "I send all my patients there for surgery. Let's say it is in your best interest, Paul, for my patients to have any surgery they need at Tavers Hospital." He said those last three words slowly and deliberately. I could tell the conversation was over.

I wasn't ready to hang up. "What if they refuse to go to your hospital, Ryan? What do you want me to do? Do you want me to force them to have an operation at a hospital they're not comfortable with? Do you want me to *lie* trying to change their mind?" No answer. There was silence for several long seconds.

"Paul, I know you will do the best you can." He coughed right into my ear. "You know how the game is played. If we don't see improvement in your numbers we'll have no choice but to deselect you as a referring surgeon." The conversation was now over. I was left listening to the dial tone. Another lesson I never learned in medical school.

Cardiovascular disease, the number one cause of death in this country, is an enormous source of revenue for hospital operating rooms. According to the American Heart Association, the current financial cost to treat cardiovascular disease in this country approaches $300 billion. By 2030, the AHA predicts this number will reach $800 billion. Coronary artery bypass grafting surgery (CABG) is one of the most common heart operations performed today, with well over 200,000 procedures carried out in operating rooms across the country every year. According to the American Heart Association, the *average* cost of this operation is roughly $117,000 (the range is from $80,000 to $250,000), not including the surgeon's fee. Heart surgery programs can generate millions of dollars in revenue each year for a hospital.

In addition to heart surgery, cardiac catheterization and balloon angioplasty (with or without stent placement) generate enormous amounts of money for hospital systems and the cardiologists who perform them. Both procedures are performed in a hospital setting, with the goal of opening up blocked heart arteries and avoiding major heart surgery. The cardiac stent business is a multibillion-dollar business for medical device companies, hospitals, and cardiologists. With over one million procedures performed each year, hospitals are scrambling to open up "cardiovascular care centers" they can call their own and buying up cardiology practices like candy for the explicit purpose of benefiting from the revenue generated by the stent business. Cardiologists, in turn, are accepting offers to be bought out because they see the writing on the wall. They see decreasing reimbursements for their services and vulnerability in their reliance on referrals from hospital-employed primary care physicians.

Cardiologists offer hospitals a number of ways to enhance their bottom line. In addition to placing stents, cardiologists perform echocardiograms, nuclear stress tests, and other procedures that hospitals can bill for once the cardiac docs are under employment. The problem is that hospitals charge more (sometimes four times as much) for a procedure that would have cost much less if done in a private cardiologist's office. Procedures carried out by hospital-employed cardiologists are billed as hospital-based, not office-based, hence the bigger reimbursement because of previously negotiated contracts. Hospitals are well aware of this billing advantage and are rushing to entice cardiologists into employment. In addition, other specialists who perform procedures, such as gastroenterologists, receive more money for procedures as hospital-based employees. Why wouldn't hospitals employ their own gastroenterologists and charge insurance companies 20 to 40 percent more for a colonoscopy because the procedure is done by a "hospital-based" gastroenterologist? As an independent surgeon, I am often reimbursed 20 percent less than a hospital-employed surgeon (with an office ten minutes away) for the same operation, regardless of the outcome.

If community hospitals are unable to employ their own interventional cardiologists, they will find a way to align themselves with a university hospital and lease them just to get into the lucrative cardiac cath business. A Duke University study presented at the American Heart Association conference in 2012 analyzed the billing data of over eighteen thousand patients who underwent elective balloon angioplasty. The average cumulative cost for each procedure was close to $24,000. Hospitals are also looking to employ their own interventional cardiologists in order to close the revenue circle and keep patients within their systems. By employing the primary care physicians who initially see patients with heart disease in the office, hospitals have control of the referrals from the beginning. Hospital-employed primary care physicians refer heart patients to hospital-employed cardiologists for balloon angioplasty and stent placement. If surgery is needed, the employed cardiac surgeons step into the referral loop and keep all the business in the confines of four walls. By employing all the players in the game, in addition to owning the stadium, hospitals maximize their revenue-generating capacity at the expense of patient choice.

In addition to making money by treating heart disease, hospitals have an enormous financial opportunity in the business of treating cancer. Cancer is the number two cause of death in this country. The National Institutes of Health has estimated the total amount spent on cancer treatment will be well over $150 billion a year by 2020. Of this total, about a third of the money will be spent on direct medical costs, such as surgery, chemotherapy drugs, radiation therapy, and laboratory and imaging services. As with the explosion in cardiac catheterization labs, community hospitals are rushing to build their own "comprehensive cancer care centers," regardless of whether the need exists. They are willing to spend enormous amounts of money bringing in their own cancer surgeons, radiation oncologists, and medical oncologists in order to minimize the leakage of patients out of the community. Radiation oncologists are particularly valuable because radiation therapy is being used more and more to treat a variety of cancers. In addition to spending on the physicians, hospitals are willing to invest in the expensive capital equipment necessary to deliver radiation treatments. The bottom line (if you ask any hospital chief financial officer) is all about the potential revenue from the treatment of cancer with radiation therapy because of its growing market share and generous reimbursement.

Along with the treatment of cardiovascular disease and cancer, the expanding market for the surgical treatment of obesity has hospital CEOs licking their chops. Today, two-thirds of people in this country are considered obese. A Johns Hopkins School of Public Health study estimated that close to $170 billion will be spent on the treatment of obesity and obesity-related health conditions this year. Hospital systems are keenly aware of this potential for revenue and are eager to tap into the surgical treatment side of this growing market. The surgical treatment for obesity (called bariatric surgery—the so-called gastric bypass operation) actually consists of several different types of procedures.

The clinical benefits in treating obesity with bariatric surgery and reducing the long-term health hazards it can cause (such as diabetes) have been well documented. The notion that spending money on bariatric procedures *now* to reduce the cost of *future* healthcare for obesity-related diseases, however, has recently come under fire. The thinking has been that paying for bariatric surgery will clinically improve a patient's health in the long run by lessening the effects of several chronic diseases affiliated with obesity such as diabetes, hypertension, and the risk of certain cancers. This improvement, in turn, will ultimately save healthcare dollars by lessening the costs to treat those chronic diseases, which the weight loss can eliminate. Sounds good, but is it so?

The same Johns Hopkins School of Public Health study recently looked at a six-year follow-up of patients who had undergone bariatric surgery. More than 29,000 patients were followed. The study analyzed the short- and long-term costs and savings associated with bariatric surgery. Based on their analysis, the authors concluded that bariatric surgery did *not* reduce the overall healthcare costs in the long term, as one would assume. The study also concluded that the ability of bariatric surgical procedures to reduce costs over the long term is unclear. In addition, the short-term savings from laparoscopic bariatric procedures may not be sustainable in the long run. But to hospitals, it does not matter whether it is a laparoscopic gastric bypass operation, a lap band procedure, or a lap gastric sleeve procedure. It does not matter whether there are questions regarding the long-term cost savings of bariatric surgery. Yes, there are recent short-term studies (NEJM.org in March 2014) showing bariatric surgery to be superior to medical treatment in treating diabetes. This study and others like it are promising in possibly reducing the long-term medical costs of treating obese patients. Hospitals are not waiting for definitive, long-term answers. What matters most to hospitals now is that these operations need to be done in their operating rooms. With over 220,000 bariatric procedures performed annually at an average cost of $29,500 (range of $18,000 to $35,000), hospitals are doing whatever it takes to start their own bariatric surgery programs. The battle to lure bariatric surgeons, at a salary approaching a million dollars a year, is serious. Surgeon reimbursement for a single bariatric operation can approach $5,000. Like neurosurgeons performing spinal surgery, experienced bariatric surgeons are a valued commodity to hospitals. Not only do their patients bring in revenue from their surgery and postoperative care, they require long-term follow-up, blood work, and other services, all of which generate future revenue streams for hospitals.

In addition to the cardiac, cancer, and bariatric surgery markets, ambitious community hospital systems are attempting to set up certified trauma centers in order to capture revenue generated from surgically treating trauma patients. The growing acute care surgery business model mentioned earlier in this chapter has ignited a keen interest in this previously untapped market. Traditionally, academic teaching centers were the focus of treating trauma patients because they had the resources, including staff. In addition, they had no choice because these institutions received federal dollars to fund their teaching programs. Until recently, community hospitals have avoided treating critically ill patients injured in traumatic accidents because their operating rooms and intensive care units were ill-equipped for it. If a trauma patient (such as a car accident or gunshot victim) happened to be brought to a local community hospital emergency room, they would nearly always be immediately transferred to a university hospital close by. In addition to the hospitals being unequipped to deal with trauma patients, often the surgical staff was not in favor of taking them. Trauma patients traditionally did not reimburse surgeons well and, to add injury to insult, increased their workload and contributed to a nightly disruption of their lives. For both hospitals and surgeons, the financial reward was just not worth the investment.

Times have changed. One study out of the University of Michigan revealed that the surgical treatment of trauma patients *does* pay in the short term—and it can pay even more in the long term. This study looked at more than three thousand trauma patients cared for over a two-year time frame and found that substantial revenue was generated by these patients for both hospital and surgeon. Money was initially made during their acute hospitalization and, once they were discharged, in follow-up services (office visits, labs, and imaging studies). The bottom line: Today hospitals see the surgical treatment of trauma patients as another business market to enter.

Are there any limits to what community hospitals will go through to guard their existing turf, expand into new turf, or encroach on a competing hospital's turf? In today's land grab, probably not. In Sumter, South Carolina, Tuomey Hospital was found guilty in May 2013 of violating federal laws against conflicts of interest (called the Stark Laws) and filing false Medicare claims by secretly paying a group of surgeons in the community so they would bring their patients to Tuomey for surgery and not a competing surgery center.

Because of the increasingly competitive environment, competing community hospitals are rushing to open up their own comprehensive breast care centers, wound clinics, minimally invasive surgery centers, and any other type of "center of excellence" you can think of. It does not matter whether these hospitals are duplicating services already offered in the community by another hospital or surgical group. Competing hospitals want to control their own surgical service destiny, despite the short-term costs. They want to make available every surgical service known to humankind so they can keep patients in their system and maximize the revenue generated from their care. "Retention and minimized leakage" is the new gospel that hospital administrators are preaching to their employee physicians and surgeons. These same administrators expect the system to retain a percentage of patients from the population that their employed primary care physicians control. It is a percentage that ultimately translates into revenue for the hospital and performance bonuses for both employed physician/surgeon and administrator alike.

Today, every hospital is tracking every patient under its insurance roof from the day they see their primary care doctor to the day they step into the operating room. As an independent practicing surgeon, if I do not steer the patients I see to their "home" hospitals, I might receive a phone call that week to explain myself. I surely will receive a phone call at the end of the quarter from a hospital administrator crunching the numbers. The caller may also be an employed physician wearing another hat that day, in charge of keeping the patient herd from straying. This call will usually be very businesslike, stressing the need for me to achieve a specific retention percentage with the patients referred to me by that hospital's employed physicians. There will be no threats, but the subliminal message comes across loud and clear. This is a numbers game. I have yet to hear the word *quality* or *outcomes* mentioned during these phone calls about surgery numbers or retention percentages.

Mrs. Jones was a relatively healthy sixty-five-year-old grandmother of ten, referred to me for colon surgery. Her primary care physician expected me to schedule her surgery at his employer's hospital so she would be retained within the system. The problem: She refused to go there. She wanted her surgery performed at what was (unbeknownst to her) the "competing" hospital. I always try to accommodate a patient's preferences for surgery, even when I know I will take flack about it later. Without hesitation, I scheduled Mrs. Jones's surgery at the hospital of her choice and left it at that.

Several days later, I received a frantic call from Mrs. Jones.

"Dr. Ruggieri, I'm sorry to bother you but my primary care physician called me at home today." He voice was trembling. "He said I will *owe* more money if my surgery is not done at his hospital." I didn't interrupt, wanting to hear the rationale. "He was adamant that I have it done at his hospital. He said I'd be 'out of network' and it would cost me more."

Wow, I thought, *this is a first*. I had never heard of a physician calling a patient, trying to change her mind about where to have surgery. In addition, the argument he made was flawed since her insurance (Medicare) would charge her the same amount no matter where she had her surgery. "What else did he say, Mrs. Jones?"

"That was pretty much it." Her voice cracked. "Is it true?" Before I could answer, she said, "You know, I really don't care. If I have to, I *will* pay more. He can't force me to go to that hospital."

In the end, I assuaged Mrs. Jones's fears, reassuring her that she would not have to pay more out of her own pocket. I performed her colon surgery at the hospital she requested, and after her recovery she fired her primary care physician for lying to her. The other shocker: Mrs. Jones's former primary care physician was someone she had known for years.

Who will be the winners and losers when these hospital turf wars end? I believe the biggest losers will be the patients and potentially the quality of care they receive because of choice restriction. Patients will lose because their ability to choose their physician and surgeon will be severely restricted. Once hospital systems gain control over all providers of surgical care, the door will close. Patient choice will be restricted because their employed primary care physicians will be financially pressured to keep them from straying off the reservation. It will also be restricted by the financial penalties of going outside the system. Patients will be forced to pay more out of pocket to see "out of network" surgeons two blocks away who have more operative experience than the ones employed in their hospital's network. The other casualty, which may or may not affect patient care, will be the professional independence of the physicians and surgeons providing that care.

Yes, hospitals need the services surgeons provide. But surgeons are replaceable, and if we refuse to capitulate to the administrators, we will be replaced. If our clinical practice habits or business production do not conform to what the hospital corporate culture dictates, we're out. We are replaceable if the cost-cutting hammer knocks on our office door because some administrator has decided we have outlived our usefulness. The reality of working for a hospital system, no matter our unique expertise, is that we are considered a commodity—like oil, corn, or orange juice. Surgeons may be special commodities, able to cure disease with their hands, but like any other commodity we can be purchased, consumed, and even sold as a result of decisions made by an administrator, in an office miles away from the operating room.

What about hospitals? I believe hospitals, at least in the short term, are the financial winners in this ongoing war. They are winners because the revenue opportunities in the business of healthcare today are numerous and growing. Large hospital systems have the money in the bank and they will spend it, buying up primary care physicians and specialists. As hospitals increase their physician payroll, they gain more leverage for reimbursements with private payers and the federal government. The key is controlling physician behavior first in order to influence the way they practice. Hospital systems have the resources to capture their local piece of the money spent in this country on healthcare. The stronger hospital systems continue to increase their market share, while the weaker ones get swallowed up. It will be survival of the fittest. The stronger hospital systems continue to expand their services, almost to the point of monopolizing local community care, at the expense of the private practice system. Invariably, monopolizing a service industry leads to less competition and higher costs. Healthcare is such an industry.

I believe, however, that many hospitals will end up losing in the end. As the lessons of the managed care era of the 1990s taught us, many hospitals ended up losing money over the years after buying up primary care physician practices. Once the current buying and building frenzy stops, some hospitals may find themselves employing surgeons who cannot generate the revenue needed to pay their salaries. With hospitals wanting it all, the duplication of surgical services in communities may lead to a change in the supply and demand curve. There may not be enough patients to fill all the operating rooms. Faced with fewer patients and declining reimbursements for surgical procedures, hospital systems may find that they are overpaying surgeons who are unable to meet expectations.

When the hospital turf wars subside and surgeons acquiesce to their roles in the new "physician-integrated hospital system" model, the practice of surgery will be changed forever. The competition for healthcare dollars forces independent surgeons to take sides and infringes on a patient's ability to choose. Ultimately, you and your surgeon are the big casualties in this ongoing hospital turf war.

I had finished reviewing Mrs. Johnson's records and decided she did need to have her thyroid gland removed. "Mrs. Johnson, the biopsy on your thyroid nodule came back positive for cancer. You have thyroid cancer and will need surgery."

She remained silent, looking down at her feet. Hearing the words *You have cancer* stops everything. The word *cancer* is such a sudden emotional burden that most people initially collapse under its weight.

"The good news," I continued, "is that most thyroid cancers are curable with surgery. Most people live a long and happy life after they are treated. If you had to have cancer, this is one of the better ones to have." With those words, I could see her spirit lift. The light returned to her face. After going over the risks with her, I was ready to schedule her thyroid surgery.

"I'll have my assistant schedule your operation at Balblair Hospital, and she'll call you with the date and the preadmission testing information you'll need." Her referring physician and health insurance dictated that she go to Balblair for medical services, including surgery.

She looked at me and said quickly, "I don't want to have my surgery there." I stopped writing in her chart. "My cousin had a horrible experience and I definitely do *not* want to be operated on there." She had made herself clear.

Now what was I supposed to do? I had just finished telling

this woman she had cancer; now I had to strong-arm her into getting operated on at a hospital not of her choosing? Not only would it be against her clearly stated desires but I would be taking on added risk: If a problem *did* occur during her care at Balblair Hospital, she could point to me as the one who had pressured her to go there. Her referring physician wanted her to go to there because of his relationship with the hospital. I would have preferred to take her case there just to keep the administrative number counters off my back. The problem was, she did not want to go. In the end, she agreed to go to Balblair Hospital because she trusted my unbiased judgment.

Mrs. Johnson's surgery went well and the cancer was completely removed. The problem came the night after her operation. She tried to get out of bed to go to the bathroom, slipped, fell to the floor, and fractured her hip. She had to go back to surgery the next day to repair her hip fracture and ended up spending several more days in a hospital she never wanted to be at in the first place. I was shaken by the news.

I had operated on Mrs. Johnson at Balblair Hospital because she trusted my judgment. My judgment, however, had been swayed by irrelevant, petty issues—an ongoing turf war. It hadn't felt good at the time, and it felt even worse now. I had succumbed to the pressure to please a referring colleague, to go along with the new world order of healthcare delivery. I had let down my patient. Not an easy thing to admit, but facing our own flaws never is.

5 THE HUMAN COST OF QUALITY

could smell his infection from the hallway as I approached his hospital room. The aged-cheese odor of pus percolating through his abdominal staples was unmistakable. I dreaded facing the man, but he was my patient.

I stood at the side of his bed and looked him in the eye. "Mr. Frazier, your surgical site is infected." I was well aware of the physical and financial burdens his infection would cause him. "I will need to remove some staples and open up your wound. The pus needs to escape. This is the best way to treat the infection."

He was not happy with this news, and neither was I.

Each year, close to two million hospitalized patients experience surgical site infections after surgery. In addition to adding extra days to a hospital stay, these infections cost the nation $5 billion a year. Worse than that, surgical site infections (SSIs) are related to ninety thousand deaths in hospitals every year. I was hoping to keep Mr. Frazier from being part of that sobering statistic.

Four days earlier Mr. Frazier had endured a major colon resection for recurrent diverticulitis, an operation that removed a foot-long section of his colon. The surgery had gone well and he had been hoping to go home tomorrow. His wound, however, had developed an infection, and a serious one at that. He would be in the hospital several more days, each hour exposing him to the risk of even more problems, particularly the potentially deadly hospital-acquired complications. When it was all said and done, his infection would add tens of thousands of dollars to his hospital bill.

To heal properly, his abdominal wound would need to be washed out and packed with gauze on a daily basis. Intravenous antibiotics needed to be started right away to treat his surgical site infection. While on antibiotics, he would be at an increased risk of developing another infection, called C. *difficile* colitis ("c-diff" for short). This infection (caused by the very antibiotics he needed) eats away at the lining of the colon. It can lead to more surgery or even death. Unfortunately, this was exactly what had happened to Mr. Frazier's roommate two days prior. He developed C. *difficile* colitis from antibiotics given to him to prevent infection after an elective knee replacement. The c-diff infection did not respond to treatment, and he was dying as the infection began to consume other organs. As a last resort, I had to emergently remove his infected colon, leaving him with a permanent ileostomy. The gentleman *did* recover—but not before spending a comatose week in the intensive care unit on a ventilator. He had walked into the hospital for an elective knee replacement, expecting to spend two or three days there. As a result of a postsurgical infection, he left the hospital thirty days later with a new knee, no colon, a permanent ileostomy, several weeks of rehab ahead, and a bill totaling hundreds of thousands of dollars.

Mr. Frazier's surgical site infection meant his recovery would take longer, which would cost him more time out of work. His insurance company would have to pay for the additional care he would need once he left the hospital. Because of this single surgical site infection, he would be predisposed to develop an incisional hernia later in life, requiring additional surgery to repair. With additional surgery comes the potential for complications, another hospital stay, more sick leave, and additional fees, maybe in the tens of thousands of dollars. Mr. Frazier is living proof of how one surgical complication (unintended) can result in a cascade of negative events that come with enormous financial cost and, even worse, can lead to permanent disability.

Hospitals are keenly aware of their surgical site infection rates and the surgeons' hands attached to them. With today's push for transparency in medicine, SSIs are just one of many measurable clinical benchmarks being used to define quality patient care. Using measurable benchmarks that define quality in the delivery of healthcare has become a national priority. And that's a good thing. The urgency to identify best practices and the processes that can ensure their use is fueled by the multitude of studies revealing the insidious physical cost of imperfect care in our current healthcare system. Using benchmarks has also become a priority because of the growing financial cost attached to imperfect care, estimated to be more than $100 billion annually. With fifty million surgical procedures in this country costing close to a total of $400 billion a year, the price of imperfection (complications and surgical errors such as wrong-site surgery) is significant. Sadly, it's on the increase. Overall, complication rates for surgery range from 3 to 17 percent. A single surgical error or bad outcome can add tens of thousands of dollars to any hospital bill. With this backdrop, you can see why hospitals are being held accountable for imperfect surgical care and why the pressure being applied is financial. As in any other business, money provides a powerful incentive to pay attention. Today, Medicare guidelines affect reimbursement; they will result in financial rewards for good care and financial punishment for hospitals whose care doesn't measure up to established quality standards. Meeting legitimate quality surgical benchmarks *does* improve patient care—the first priority—but it also reduces costs, creating a "win-win" situation as hospital administrators like to say. In this era of hospital accountability and competition, hospitals want to do whatever it takes to stay one step ahead of the Centers for Medicare & Medicaid Services' guidelines.

But despite a renewed vigor to meet clinical quality benchmarks and become more transparent to the public, hospitals are not always eager to focus on their own in-house quality measures or publicize them. For one thing, improving quality in hospitals costs money that could otherwise be earmarked for new operating rooms or capital equipment, bringing in more surgery, increasing market share, and improving revenue opportunities. Hospitals have never been in a rush to volunteer their own surgical quality data. Operating rooms are sacred cows to hospitals because they generate revenue. Lots of it. If you don't have to publish surgical quality outcomes data, why would you? You'd just be giving marketing ammunition to your competition.

In the past, hospitals have not made serious efforts to improve surgical care for two simple reasons. First, no publically vocal entity has held them accountable to improve clinical measures that would reduce surgical complications, surgical infection rates, or "never" events (wrong-site surgery or retained surgical sponges). The second reason (and probably the one with a greater influence, sadly) is that no legitimate entity has held them accountable for their reluctance to publish outcomes, to be transparent. Until now, hospitals have had no incentive to prove quality and be more transparent about it. Today there is: money. Poor-quality care, measured by outcomes, will not be fully reimbursed by Medicare (and the private carriers are not far behind); the days of *here's-your-check, no-questions-asked* reimbursement are over for hospitals. On the other hand, there has been no incentive for *surgeons* to focus on their own quality benchmarks and become more transparent. The system of payment we've all grown accustomed to, hospitals and surgeons alike, has rewarded us for quantity, not quality. It is a setup that feeds imperfection.

A recent study out of Harvard University, published in *JAMA*, looked at financial data related to surgical complications at a large hospital system in the southern United States. Over a five-year period, more than thirty-four thousand surgical discharges were analyzed to see what effect surgical complications had on the hospital's revenue stream. Nine different types of operations were reviewed and patients with any type of health insurance (private, Medicare, Medicaid) were included. Hospital revenue was compared between patients who experienced complications and those who did not. The authors concluded that complications pay, and handsomely. While the consequences to patients are painful when surgical complications occur, hospitals benefit—financially. The study concluded that for those with private insurance the per-patient benefit for complications was more than $39,000 compared to those without complications. Medicare patients with complications represented a *benefit to the hospital* of more than $1,700 per patient versus those who did not experience complications. When averaging in all patients' insurance types, the bottom line was a benefit of $8,000 per patient after costs for those with complications when compared to those without.

Other studies have looked at the financial benefits of surgical complications to a hospital's bottom line and have reached the same conclusions. One study, published in *Annals of Surgery* in 2012, analyzed national Medicare claims data out of the University of Michigan over a three-year period. The authors looked at the financial gains hospitals experience for complications after coronary bypass surgery, hip replacement, abdominal aortic aneurysm repair, and colon resections. In its conclusion, the study found that hospitals with higher complication rates were paid the most by Medicare. This study did not specify actual complication costs per patient. However, hospitals tend to find creative ways to pass along the extra costs of complications to patients and payers. In a study published in *Health Affairs* in October 2012, the impact of reducing surgical complications on a hospital's bottom line was analyzed. Reducing surgical complications is vital for quality patient care, but the study found that for hospitals with a stagnant surgical volume, reducing complications resulted in a loss of revenue. Even for hospitals with a growing surgical volume, reducing complications negatively influenced their bottom line. You can see why hospital administrators feel stuck between a rock and a hard place. They are willing to improve patient care by implementing programs that can reduce surgical complications, but they do not want to lose revenue by doing so. If hospitals had a choice, from a patient-care standpoint, of course they would rather not have the complications occur at all. In a perfect world, this would be the case. Unfortunately, within the imperfect world I live in, complications do occur. Within the current imperfect reimbursement system, hospitals continue to get reimbursed for their costs.

The results of the Michigan study along with the Harvard study are not surprising given the current system of reimbursement. What's the incentive for a hospital, or a surgeon for that matter, to devote resources to improving surgical quality and transparency? Hospitals and surgeons have always had clinical incentives to improve patient care by reducing infection rates and complication rates. These incentives, however, have obviously not been enough to light a fire under anyone. Since the landmark study *To Err Is Human* was published in 1999, revealing the staggering number of deaths in hospitals due to medical errors, hospitals and surgeons have had the motivation and time to focus on quality. But until recently, not much had truly changed. What *has* finally ignited the fire of quality improvement is the threat of reduced (or withheld altogether) reimbursement. When money talks, hospitals listen.

In 2008, the Centers for Medicare and Medicaid Services (CMS) stopped paying for certain hospital-acquired complications (including infections) that it deemed preventable. Included in this list are catheter-associated urinary tract infections, retained surgical items, air embolisms, severe decubitus ulcers (bedsores) from lying in a hospital bed, surgical site infections after coronary bypass graft surgery and placement of cardiac implantable electronic devices, vascular catheter-associated infections, complications from falling out of a hospital bed, and blood transfusion incompatibility mistakes. CMS went even further in 2009 and added surgical site infections after bariatric and orthopedic surgery, blood clots in leg veins and lungs after joint replacement surgery, complications from poor glucose control in diabetics, and physician-induced pneumothorax (collapsed lung) after venous cauterization placement.

If, after having her appendix removed, my grandmother falls out of bed on postoperative day three, breaks her hip, and requires surgery, Medicare will not reimburse the hospital for *any* care associated with this "preventable" complication. The hospital has no choice but to absorb the expenses associated with complications from the fall. The orthopedic surgeon who repairs her fractured hip will, however, be reimbursed because he or she should not be punished for quality of care that led to the fall and fracture. If my grandmother develops a urinary tract infection because her bladder catheter was left in too long, Medicare will not reimburse the hospital for the cost of treating that infection. If, the day before she is about to leave the hospital, pus starts to ooze from her hip fracture repair incision, the cost of treating this infection will not be covered by Medicare. There are no Medicare payments for surgical site infections after joint surgery. The list goes on and on. In addition to what is already decreed, Medicare is planning to withhold reimbursement for more preventable surgical complications in the future. Under the Affordable Care Act's emphasis on controlling costs and improving quality, the list of preventable surgical complications slated for "no reimbursement" will continue to expand.

With intravenous antibiotics and intense local wound care, Mr. Frazier's infected surgical wound was beginning to improve. He was becoming more optimistic; I was becoming more anxious with each extra day he stayed in the hospital. One morning, after four days of antibiotics, I removed his bandage, inspected his incision, and got sick to my stomach. To my horror, I could see a loop of Mr. Frazier's small intestine staring at me through two abdominal wall sutures that had broken apart. The infection at his surgical site had eaten through a part of his fascia that I had sutured back together after opening him up for his initial operation. The opening in the fascia was a window into his abdomen, a window full of intestine. This complication is called a dehiscence, an unexpected separation of fascia. It is a costly complication, often guaranteeing a return trip to the operating room to reclose it and a prolonged hospital stay. I reluctantly took Mr. Frazier back to the operating room to repair his dehiscence. After another week in the hospital (and tens of thousands of dollars in costs), he was finally able to leave the hospital for a rehabilitation facility to recover from his operation and subsequent complications.

Eventually, Medicare is not going reimburse me for what it deems preventable complications that occur inside hospital walls, complications like Mr. Frazier's. It may even try to claw back a percentage of the fee it reimbursed me for his original surgery.

The story of Mr. Frazier is not unique; complications after surgery occur in every hospital. The unfortunate part of his story is that he had to return to the operating room for repair of an additional complication that resulted from his first surgical site infection. Because Mr. Frazier's complication occurred while he was an inpatient, the hospital had no choice but to account for it. It became part of a report in the quality improvement department. It also was added to the cases of surgical site infections that must be publicly reported. I had to account for it by explaining myself at a department of surgery meeting reviewing postoperative complications. That, however, was where my accountability stopped. Which is why, despite what every hospital in this country reports on its website as its rate of surgical site infections, the public numbers are only half the truth.

The surgical site infection rate numbers posted for public consumption are grossly underreported. To get the real story, you'd have to look in surgeons' offices and emergency rooms across the country. In January 2013, the American College of Surgeons National Surgical Quality Improvement Program released findings from a large study of complication rates after surgery. Over a five-year period, more than 550,000 patient cases were reviewed. Within thirty days of surgery, 17 percent of patients had experienced complications. Of those, 42 percent occurred after discharge, and most of them (75 percent) happened within the first two weeks after discharge. The authors concluded that complications after discharge "account for a significant burden of postoperative complications and are an important avenue for quality improvement in inpatient general surgery." For the patients in this study, surgical site infections and venous blood clots in the legs and lungs made up 91 percent of all complications *after* discharge. Surgeons have known for a long time that surgical site infections can begin in the hospital but go undetected, not recognized until the patient ends up in the surgeon's office for a follow-up visit. Many are often brewing inside the body as the discharge orders are being processed.

"If hospitals only look at what happens during the index hospital stay, they're missing a big part of the picture," said Dr. Mary Hawn, chief of gastrointestinal surgery at the University of Alabama–Birmingham and coauthor of a similar study looking at the incidence of complications from surgery occurring after a patient is discharged home. This study, presented at the American College of Surgeons Clinical Congress meeting in 2012, found that a third of all complications in sixty thousand operations occurred after discharge. Of these, more than half were surgical site infections. What is so significant about these numbers is that these complications will *not* show up in the data on a hospital's website.

Many of these infections can be successfully treated in a surgeon's office. Hospitals do not actively pursue this data from surgeons, so the truth rarely makes it back to the hospital's public ledger. Not surprisingly, surgeons themselves do not volunteer the existence of these problems—they probably don't even know their own numbers. So, there is no way for the public to know surgeon-specific surgical site infection rates. Currently, there is no entity pressuring surgeons to be transparent with their surgical site infection rates. There is no financial pressure on surgeons to be transparent about their complication rates as a whole.

In Mr. Frazier's case, the hospital had no choice but to add his surgical site infection to its publicly reportable numbers because it occurred while he was still an inpatient. As for quality outcome data on practicing surgeons, the public continues to be left entirely in the dark. Remember this when you read of a hospital that proudly boasts of its low surgical site infection rate, particularly if it is using this data to compare its quality to its competition. I would take such data with a grain of salt.

The question of who *can* define surgical quality, without bias, and *how* it is defined, remains, at the very least, controversial. It also is confusing, as illustrated recently in the wake of two well-known quality rating entities announcements. In 2013, *U.S. News and World Report* came out with its list of the "Best Hospitals" in the country. It ranked Johns Hopkins Hospital number one, followed by Massachusetts General Hospital and the Mayo Clinic. Given their reputation, these rankings were not surprising. The confusion began several months later when *Consumer Reports* came out with its ratings of more than 2,400 U.S. hospitals based on the quality of surgical care. The top three best hospitals listed in *U.S. News and World Report* (Johns Hopkins, Mass General, Mayo Clinic) were ranked in the "worst" category for surgical quality overall in the *Consumer Reports* survey. I realize that one rating looked at overall hospital quality while the other focused on quality surgical care only. But the discrepancy in ratings for those three hospitals, on the surface, does not make sense. How can one hospital be the best overall yet the worst for surgical care, especially when surgical care is a big component of each hospital's patient volume? If you were a person about to have your hip replaced or heart bypassed in Baltimore, Boston, or Minnesota, which rating would carry the most weight? Based on the conclusions of *U.S. News and World Report* and *Consumer Reports*, I would get a second opinion. In a recent *Consumer Reports* survey of more than 2,500 hospitals, overall patient-safety scores (1 to 100) were all over the map. The bottom line of this survey concluded that patients in "top-rated hospitals" were 34 percent more likely to die after an operation than those in hospitals rated on the low end of the survey.

One final question to ask regarding the search for quality surgical care is, Do past quality performance ratings in hospitals accurately predict future quality? Unfortunately, this question sounds very familiar to the legal statement made by financial institutions across the country wanting to invest your money: "Yes, we are good, but past performance does not guarantee future returns." Although the aforementioned question has yet to be definitively answered for overall hospital surgical quality, there are some recent studies showing past quality can predict future quality outcomes in obesity surgery.

What is even more confusing is the numerous rating agencies out there giving their blessings to hospitals as the "best" in this type of surgery or "number one" in the region for treatment of a specific disease. This rating game reminds me of the state of professional boxing today. As the different "world title" belts proliferated over the years in boxing, the legitimacy each belt signified became diluted. Many of these boxing world title belts were a result of organizations taking advantage of a growing market share, not interested in the quality of their product. Whether the rating is an "excellence award" or a "center of distinction" designation for a specific type of surgery, it is difficult to know the legitimacy of any of this. For instance, my partner and I did a double take at a large poster advertising an award at a community hospital we both operate out of. The colorful poster named the hospital as the only one in the region ranked in the top 5 percent in the nation for the treatment of stroke. After seeing this, we turned to one another, shook our heads, and smiled. "I had no idea they even treated stroke patients here." With almost every hospital advertising that it is in the top 5 percent in *something*, the public is left confused. My sense is that hospitals are guided by the agencies giving out the awards to help them fit their data into a narrow scope of practice in order to claim a prize. In addition, if a hospital is fortunate to be chosen as a "top hospital," it may come at a financial cost. Some of these rating agencies charge a licensing fee to hospitals if they want to advertise their top rating to the public. So, are hospitals actually paying for the privilege of being rated "the best" in whatever disease category they advertise?

Welcome to the confusing world of trying to define quality surgical care. Who is actually in charge of defining the benchmarks representative of quality surgical care for hospitals and surgeons? The ultimate entity defining quality surgical care today, particularly in the Medicare/Medicaid population, is the federal government. The main reason the Centers for Medicare & Medicaid Services (CMS) have final control over quality benchmarks is that they hold the reimbursement checkbook. CMS, under the Affordable Care Act, has enormous power to dictate quality benchmark policy to hospitals. The organization will continue to create quality benchmarks for hospitals to meet, and the hospitals will find themselves paying a financial penalty for failure to do so.

Much of what CMS creates as policy is rooted in data from scientific studies, data used to improve patient care and reduce costs. Its policy is also influenced by studies developed by non-profit healthcare organizations, such as the Leapfrog Group (leapfroggroup.org). Organizations like this one are dedicated to improving healthcare and reducing costs. Another organization strictly dedicated to improving surgical outcomes in hospitals is called the National Surgical Quality Improvement Program (NSQIP). NSQIP is a product of the American College of Surgeons and hospitals can use it, for a cost, to examine their own surgical outcomes data and find ways to improve patient care.

For instance, urinary tract infections (UTIs) are a leading cause of infection in hospitalized patients, especially after surgery because many have urinary catheters in place to monitor urinary output. The longer a catheter stays in, the higher the risk of developing an infection. Patients who develop a UTI may require a prolonged hospital stay, adding thousands of dollars to a hospital bill. The length of time a urinary catheter is in place is the single most important risk factor in postoperative patients for developing a UTI. CMS has set quality benchmarks for hospitals to meet regarding UTI rates; hospitals that don't meet these benchmarks won't be paid when UTIs occur. As a result, hospitals are falling over themselves to develop practical policies, urging surgeons to remove a urinary catheter twenty-four hours after an operation. Some are developing new policies to bypass uncooperative physicians altogether in the decision-making process by allowing nurses to remove a catheter if criteria are met.

As a result of the federal government's ability to define surgical quality and reimburse accordingly, hospitals are keenly aware of their own quality data. In addition, hospitals are privy to practical quality benchmark data for every surgeon using their operating rooms. The big difference here is that the CMS quality data on hospitals is available for the public; the quality surgical data that hospitals track about themselves and their surgeons is not. It's unfortunate, because much of this surgeon data (such as the number of operations performed yearly, surgeon-specific infection rates, overall complication rates, rates of return to the operating room, and even death rates) could be very helpful to the public and be part of an individual's reason to choose a specific surgeon. It does not seem fair that hospitals should be privy to important information while prospective patients, whose health could be influenced by it, are not. As the Affordable Care Act unfolds, more quality benchmarks will be rolled out for hospitals and surgeons to meet in the continued effort to improve patient care and lower costs. Whether greater transparency will accompany that effort remains to be seen.

I noticed Mr. Frazier's name on my list of office patients coming in for follow-up visits and it made me a little nervous. I had not heard from him, or his visiting nurse, since he left the hospital a week ago. I wasn't sure if this was a good thing or a bad thing, given what had happened to him in the hospital. It would not have surprised me if I had received a call from his nurse soon after discharge, letting me know that his infection was getting worse. That hadn't happened, though, and now it was time to see how things looked.

"Mr. Frazier." I ushered him into one of the exam rooms. "How are you feeling?" I was anxious to remove his dressing and take a look.

"I was doing okay up until yesterday, when the nurse who comes in to change my dressing noticed a different color drainage coming out of the wound." He started to peel off his bandage. "It had a green color and a little bit of an odor." He paused. "For the life of me, I thought I saw one of the pills I took the day before stuck to the dressing when my nurse changed it. It looked like the blue pill I take for my blood pressure."

Now I *was* nervous. I did not want to say anything until I

saw the wound for myself. I slowly peeled off the bandages. Suddenly, my worst fears were confirmed. At the base of his incision was a small opening stained with bilious drainage. I paused to carefully gather my thoughts.

"Mr. Frazier, you have developed a small bowel fistula at the bottom of your incision." I had difficulty looking him in the eye.

"A what?"

"A fistula, a small hole in your small intestine, has eroded up into your incision. This is the source of the green-colored drainage." I could not believe my eyes. His bad luck would not end.

"What does this mean, Dr. Ruggieri?" There was a bit of an edge to his voice now that hadn't been there when our conversation began.

"I am sorry, Mr. Frazier, but I will have to readmit you to the hospital to get this under control." I could feel the acid churning in my stomach. A fistula is an abnormal connection between two organs, in this case between Mr. Frazier's small bowel and the skin of his unhealed, open wound. It is a connection that can lead to persistent infections, malnutrition, and a prolonged hospital stay if not addressed quickly and properly. Most often it is treated successfully without surgery, but patients must be admitted to the hospital for treatment. In Mr. Frazier's case, his fistula was human-made, probably by something that occurred during his surgery several weeks ago. I may have accidentally nicked his intestine during his surgery, the probable source of his wound infection immediately after surgery. The fistula was most likely smoldering, undetected, while he was still in the hospital. It did not develop into a full-blown entity until after he had left the hospital.

"I do *not* want to go back into the hospital. Please . . ." He looked at me, dazed. "I knew they sent me home too soon, I just knew it." He shook his head. "Isn't there some other way to deal with this, outside the hospital?"

"I am afraid not," I answered, feeling as low as he did.

In addition to surgical site infections, another clinical quality benchmark being closely monitored these days by CMS and marked for a "no reimbursement" policy is hospital readmission rates. The number of individuals being readmitted to the hospital within thirty days of a previous discharge is rising and costing the healthcare system billions of dollars a year. In a 2009 *New England Journal of Medicine* article, it was estimated that one in seven Medicare patients is readmitted within thirty days of his or her discharge, costing Medicare close to $18 billion annually. A 2013 follow-up study published in the same journal found that 13 percent of patients were readmitted within thirty days after having a major operation.

One of the goals of the Affordable Care Act of 2010 is to hold hospitals accountable for readmissions that occur within thirty days of discharge. The ACA directed CMS to create the Hospital Readmissions Reduction Program (HRRP). When initially developed, this program focused on three major medical diseases with high readmission rates: congestive heart failure, acute myocardial infarction (heart attack), and pneumonia. Starting in 2013, hospitals were penalized 1 percent of their base Medicare payments if they did not meet the thirty-day readmission rate benchmarks set forth by CMS. In 2014, this financial penalty increased to 2 percent, and it will increase to 3 percent in 2015. In addition to these conditions, in 2015 CMS will commence a policy to penalize hospitals for high readmission rates after certain elective surgical procedures. Financial incentives seem to be working, given the fact that thirty-day readmission rates for Medicare patients decreased in 2013.

Patients who are readmitted within thirty days after surgery are a burden on the financial health of hospitals and the nation as a whole. One study in the *Journal of the American College of Surgeons* in 2013 evaluating readmissions after colorectal surgery found that an 8 to 12 percent readmission rate added $300 million in extra costs per year. Hospitals and surgeons today are under increasing pressure to prevent patients from returning within thirty days of their operation, primarily because of cost. On the surface, higher thirty-day readmission rates can also represent inferior care, reflecting poorly on both hospital and surgeon.

Eventually, thirty-day readmission rates after specific elective operations may be used as a benchmark to determine quality of care among hospitals and surgeons. In a 2012 study published in the *Journal of the American College of Surgeons*, the authors looked at more than 1,400 patients who had undergone a general surgery operation during a two-year period. Of these 1,400 patients, 11 percent (163) were readmitted to the hospital within thirty days. Upon analysis of the data, the single most significant independent risk factor for readmission was found to be the presence of postoperative complications. If a patient had one or more complications after surgery, he or she was four times as likely to return to the hospital within thirty days. Postoperative complications appear to be the main reason patients are being readmitted after surgery. By knowing the thirty-day readmission rates for specific operations for both the hospital and surgeon, the prospective patient can make better decisions about where to have surgery, and by whom. Eventually, this quality benchmark for specific operations will be tied to reimbursements for hospitals just as surgical site infection rates are.

When hospitals claim low readmission rates as evidence of superior care, you should know that the numbers may not be telling the whole story. Because of the reimbursement penalty, hospitals are doing whatever they can to prevent you from being readmitted to the hospital within thirty days of your operation and having to report it. If the hospital can keep you out until the thirty-first day, it will not be obligated to report the readmission; it will also not have to absorb the cost of your care. If the hospital *can't* keep you out within that thirty-day window, you may be cared for as an "observation" patient, a status that doesn't count as a readmission—even if you are in the hospital for *days*. And if, after your stay as an observation patient, you are discharged from the hospital to a nursing facility before you can go home, you will find that Medicare won't cover that cost because you were never "admitted" to the hospital. The motivation behind the guidelines to use thirty-day readmission rates as a quality benchmark is well intended; a hospital's compliance doesn't always look so good in the bright light of day.

For years, better outcomes have been linked to surgeons with more experience in a specific operation. In many ways, surgical quality boils down to numbers. The more operations you do, the better you become. As your skills (and confidence) improve, your patients' risk of complications and death after major surgery diminishes. These statements have been consistently supported by the surgical literature for years. In 2003, a *New England Journal of Medicine* study analyzed outcomes data for eight major cardiac and cancer operations from more than 474,000 Medicare patients over a one-year period. The study concluded that a higher risk of dying was associated with "low-volume" surgeons than "high-volume" surgeons. What is also interesting is that it did not matter how many operations were performed at any specific hospital. For most of the operations reviewed, the risk of dying among patients operated on by a low-volume surgeon was higher than for a high-volume surgeon *regardless* of the experience of that hospital. It may be more advantageous to find an experienced surgeon with adequate volume numbers, and not necessarily an experienced hospital, to minimize your risk of complications or death in the operating room.

As interesting as this study is, it did not tell the entire truth. In a more recent report published in the *Journal of the American College of Surgeons* in 2013, which looked at all studies in the surgical literature evaluating the relationship between surgical outcomes and high-volume hospitals, a slightly different conclusion was reached. This study concluded that high-volume hospitals *did* have better outcomes for operations such as colorectal cancer surgery, abdominal aortic aneurysm repair, coronary artery bypass grafting, pancreatic surgery, bariatric surgery, esophageal cancer surgery, lung cancer surgery, and prostate cancer surgery. The study focused only on the hospitals where the operations were being done and did not mention the experience of the surgeons performing those operations. I suspect, though, that the surgeons operating at those high-volume hospitals were high-volume surgeons with years of experience. I expect that the best way to achieve a quality surgical outcome and minimize your risk of complications after surgery is to find an experienced surgeon who operates out of an experienced hospital. The next best way is to find a skilled, experienced surgeon.

Period. Since most community hospitals (based on size) have similar volume experience, with many of the common operations performed by surgeons of all specialties, all quality roads lead to finding that skilled, experienced surgeon. In a groundbreaking study published in the *New England Journal of Medicine* in October 2013, Dr. John Birkmeyer (director of the Center for Health Care Outcomes and Policy) and the Michigan Bariatric Collaborative scientifically revealed what most practicing surgeons already knew. Surgeons with greater skills inside the operating room have lower complication and death rates than those with lesser skills. Simply put, surgeons with better "hands" inside the operating room have better patient outcomes. The study had expert surgeons review videotapes of twenty anonymous surgeons performing surgery. All had similar operative experience. Based on certain criteria, the twenty surgeons were ranked on skills. Then, the authors reviewed the postoperative records of those twenty surgeons for complications and compared each with his individual ranking. What they found was important: Surgeons ranked (by previous skill level) in the bottom quartile had the highest patient complication rates and highest death rates, took longer to complete the operation, re-operated on their patients more frequently, and had the highest readmission rates. The study was the first to equate poor intraoperative skills to poor patient outcomes. According to Dr. Birkmeyer, "We now have a scientific way to evaluate a practicing surgeon's skill that is as reliable as about anything we measure in health care in terms of quality." What this study validated is that not all surgeons are created equal. The problem with this study is that if it were applied to all practicing surgeons, and the results made public, some of us would be out of a job. I am hopeful that this study will lead to legitimate surgical reviews that the public can use to evaluate a surgeon's skill set before entering the operating room.

———————

Mrs. Jamison was looking for an experienced surgeon when she stepped into my office. She was referred to me by her primary care physician because of a mass discovered in her pancreas on a workup for vague abdominal pain. She had not been feeling right for several months. She had no appetite and had lost about ten pounds. Otherwise, she was a healthy sixty-six-year-old woman with relatively few health problems.

I paused after reviewing her CT scan on a computer disc. "Mrs. Jamison, do you know what you have here?" I pointed to her pancreas on the image, cluing her in to the presence of the mass.

"Yes, I do, Dr. Ruggieri. I have a three-centimeter solid mass in my pancreas that needs to be removed." She definitely knew what was going on. "Can you perform this type of surgery and do you feel confident enough to perform it safely?" She paused without losing eye contact. "If not, can you find me a surgeon who does?"

Mrs. Jamison was not shy. Her opportunity for the best outcome was in the balance, and she wanted answers. She was educated and wanted to take as much control as possible of the choices she had for care.

"I admire your directness, Mrs. Jamison," I answered. "Can I perform this operation to remove part of your pancreas? Yes, I can. However, can I perform it safely enough to minimize your risk of complications and maximize your chance for a quality outcome? No, I cannot."

Nothing else needed to be said. Theoretically, I had the skill set to remove part of Mrs. Jamison's pancreas if I had decided I could (or should) perform the surgery. I was credentialed by the hospital to carry out the surgery, despite not having performed that particular operation in years. But practically speaking, I was not experienced enough with that procedure to morally act on those credentials. When I reapplied for operating credentials several years ago, no one questioned the number of pancreatic resections I had performed over the last two years. Someone should have. As a matter of fact, no one inquired about the numbers of any of the operations I was requesting privileges for. It is actually common for surgeons to check off operations they haven't performed in years when it comes time for recredentialing privileges. I sense many just do not want to give up the privilege out of ego or they don't want to miss out on business should the opportunity present itself. The problem is, hospitals are afraid to challenge surgeons on this lack of experience in certain operations, afraid to ask for clinical proof of competency.

No, I absolutely did not feel confident in performing the type of operation Mrs. Jamison needed. It had been more than ten years since I had removed part of a pancreas. And that operation resulted in a complication. Why would I start now? I was not a high-volume surgeon in this type of surgery. It was as simple as that. Mrs. Jamison's best chance for a quality outcome, her best chance to minimize her risk of dying after surgery from a complication, was for me to find a high-volume surgeon for her. And that is exactly what I did.

For a number of major operations, there is no denying the

direct relationship between quality outcomes and experienced surgeons. What is now being discovered is the relationship between cost and surgical volume. In a study published in the *Journal of Urology* in 2012, the authors looked at the influence of surgeons and hospital volume on costs related to performing a radical prostatectomy for cancer. Over a six-year period, more than eleven thousand patient outcomes were reviewed. The costs for surgery were lowest for high-volume surgeons, especially if they operated at high-volume hospitals. High-volume surgeons also had lower costs even if they operated at low-volume hospitals. High-volume hospitals had greater costs per patient, despite their experience, when low-volume surgeons did the operating. Again, in this study the surgeon was the deciding factor when it came to cost variations. If extrapolated nationwide, the cost savings from this study would have amounted to $29 million during the six-year period.

In a similar study published in the *Journal of the American College of Surgeons*, hospital volume and cost were reviewed in the elderly population undergoing three different types of operations: colon resection for cancer, coronary artery bypass surgery, and abdominal aortic aneurysm repair. For all three operations, low-volume hospitals had higher costs for each operation, in addition to higher thirty-day readmission rates.

The message is becoming clearer with each published study. High-volume surgeons, surgeons with experience, operating out of high-volume hospitals with experience give patients the best chance for quality outcomes. High-volume surgeons and high-volume hospitals also reduce cost by minimizing the risk of complications and readmission after discharge. Again, based on the data, the high-volume-surgeon part of the equation seems to be the most important factor. The spotlight now focuses on the number of operations needed to be a high-volume, competent surgeon. What is that number and who defines it? Is it five or ten specific operations a year, or maybe twenty? If you ask five different surgeons, you may get five different answers. Most national surgical societies offer guidelines, but even they have to be put in context. The big problem is that a patient has no way to know, or verify, the number of operations his or her surgeon has performed, regardless of the outcome.

If I had removed part of Mrs. Jamison's pancreas at my community hospital, I would have selfishly put her at risk for a bad outcome. I would have also burdened the system with unnecessary costs. The problem here lies in the fact that Mrs. Jamison—had she not asked—would have had no way of knowing I was a low-volume pancreatic surgeon who would increase her risk of a poor outcome. She had no single resource to help her find a high-volume surgeon who operated out of a high-volume hospital.

As the benchmarks for defining surgical quality become more defined, transparent, and linked to cost containment, there is another that affects millions of people. It's called Medicaid. More and more studies are examining the influence of a patient's insurance status on the quality of care received. Many of these studies are revealing that individuals covered by Medicaid (as well as the uninsured) have worse surgical outcomes than their privately insured cohorts.

In 2010, a study published in the journal *Cancer* showed the outcomes of more than 1,200 patients treated for throat cancer. The study found that Medicaid and uninsured patients were 50 percent more likely to die than those with private insurance.

This number held steady even after adjusting the data for other factors related to patient demographics. The study also revealed that Medicaid patients, when compared to those with private insurance, were 80 percent more likely to first seek treatment when the disease was more advanced.

Again in 2010, a study published in the *Annals of Surgery* reviewed more than 900,000 operations over a four-year period. The data showed that Medicaid patients had the longest length of stay in the hospital, higher hospital costs, and a higher risk of dying after their surgery when compared to the privately insured.

In 2011, the *Journal of the American College of Surgeons* reviewed 478,000 surgical patients over a four-year period who had undergone heart valve operations. The results supported the previously mentioned studies: Medicaid and uninsured status conveyed an increased risk of dying in the hospital when compared to private insurance.

In the November 2012 edition of *JAMA Surgery*, a study analyzing a national outcomes database of patients who underwent a craniotomy for a brain tumor discovered that those with no insurance doubled their risk of dying in the hospital when compared to the privately insured. In this study, Medicaid insurance also correlated to a higher risk for dying after brain surgery. When more analysis was completed, this risk was not as strong. But when other demographic factors were adjusted in the patient population, the risks remained present. All operations were performed at teaching hospitals with residents-in-training involved in the care. In the study, the authors write, "among patients with brain tumors with no other major medical condition, uninsured patients (but not necessarily Medicaid) have a higher in-hospital mortality than privately insured patients. This variation in postoperative outcomes remains unexplained." What stands out is the statement by the authors: "It is possible hospitals provide different care to uninsured patients, but our study does not prove this." Extrapolate this even further by asking the question, *Is it possible surgeons provide different care to the uninsured and Medicaid population?* The bottom line is that more studies are concluding that uninsured and Medicaid status increases the risk of a poor outcome after *many* different types of surgical procedures—for complex reasons scientifically unknown at this time. As more outcome evidence is gathered, can uninsured and Medicaid designations be considered benchmarks for poor-quality care? If so, the cost to society may greatly increase as states' Medicaid populations expand, supported by the financial subsidies mandated by the federal government in the Affordable Care Act. Until recently, the overall outcomes of Medicare patients have not been shown to differ from those of privately insured patients. In a 2013 study published in the journal *Health Affairs*, Medicare patients were observed to have a higher risk of dying after eight surgical procedures when compared to privately insured patients. It may be possible, as more studies are done, that having Medicare insurance will be a risk factor for a bad outcome after surgery.

Every hospital is responsible for monitoring its own benchmarks and defining quality surgical patient care. And, I believe, every surgeon is accountable for monitoring his or her own personal outcome benchmarks for quality care. Yet in this era of healthcare transparency, hospitals and surgeons have a long way to go before the public can accurately evaluate the quality of care they provide and the cost of that quality. Part of the problem: There is little transparency today in reporting quality surgical benchmarks such as surgical site infection rates. In addition, there is even less transparency in the financial cost to achieve those surgical benchmarks. If you do not link transparency of surgical cost to surgical quality, patients will have no idea whether a higher cost means better quality or a lower cost means poor quality. Patients and even surgeons today have no way of making that distinction because of the lack of transparency.

The price of true surgical quality may be difficult to define, given the financial pressures hospitals (and surgeons) are facing to attempt to keep costs down. If it does get legitimately defined, quality may not come cheap. As a colleague recently told me during a department of surgery meeting, discussing how quality may be taking a backseat to pure economics, "If I can't find out who the best surgeon in town is, I will surely find out who is the cheapest."

If a vascular surgeon cannot determine which surgeon in town has the best quality outcomes, how in the world can you?

6 STICKER SHOCK

Mr. Wilkes was in my office for a postsurgical follow-up visit. I had recently repaired his inguinal hernia; because I had used laparoscopic techniques, his incision had been small. He was healing well. He let me know right away that he was not concerned about his physical health but he was quite worked up about the bill he had received from the hospital. He held the paper out for me to see.

"From what I can make out, the hospital charged my insurance company seventeen thousand dollars. How could my surgery have cost that much? I was only in the hospital for three hours, maybe less."

Mr. Wilkes had Medicare as his primary health insurance and a secondary private plan. "My neighbor across the street had his hernia repaired three months ago, by you, at an outpatient surgery center. His bill was four thousand, six hundred dollars.

Why such a huge difference? You performed the same operation on him as you did on me, right?"

I smiled. "Yes, sir, it was the same. I'm not sure why your bill is so high." Like most surgeons, I had no idea what the hospital charged insurance companies for any operation I performed. I wasn't even sure what my office charged Mr. Wilkes for my fee. I was running my fingers over Mr. Wilkes's incisions. He had a little bruising in his scrotum but nothing out of the ordinary. "Was there a breakdown of charges?" I was curious but didn't want to expose my ignorance about what and how hospitals charge patients for surgery.

"No. Just the seventeen thousand. It's listed under 'Hospital Misc.' "

I finished the exam and took the piece of paper from him. The statement listed what the hospital had charged Medicare for his hernia repair, what Medicare had approved, and what it had paid. The numbers weren't even close. On a bill of $17,000, Medicare had approved just over $4,000, yet paid the hospital only $2,900, a mere 17 percent of what was charged. This figure did not include my fee or the anesthesiologist's fee, both of which tacked on another $2,900 combined.

"You can request a breakdown of the individual charges, Mr. Wilkes." Most hospitals never give patients a breakdown of charges until it's requested. They do this on purpose; hospitals don't want patients to scrutinize the charges. If everyone did ask, hospital billing departments would have a lot of questions to answer. The answers would defy logic.

"If you don't mind, Mr. Wilkes," I said, handing the bill back to him, "when you get that breakdown, send a copy to me, will you?"

A week later, the breakdown of Mr. Wilkes's bill arrived in my office mailbox. I looked it over and had no idea how the hospital had arrived at the numbers. There was an $8,000 charge under the heading "operating room services," with no further explanation. There was also a $3,300 charge for all devices and instruments used during the operation. There were charges for medications and the use of the recovery room. Some of the wording was so vague I couldn't tell what it meant. Buried several pages in was a separate bill for my fee. It showed I had charged Medicare $1,400 (the standard fee for a hernia repair) for my surgical services. Medicare approved a payment of $420 but wrote a check to me for $340. That, evidently, was what the federal government thought my twenty-one years of consistently good outcomes and expertise in laparoscopic hernia repair was worth. Still, I could not explain to Mr. Wilkes why his bill was so high. I also could not explain why the hospital cost of his hernia surgery was almost four times as much as his neighbor's surgery, performed at an outpatient surgery center, by me, several months earlier.

Deciphering the hieroglyphics of hospital bills, especially when it involves surgery, is not a job for the faint of heart. As Mr. Wilkes discovered when comparing notes with a friend, there's another puzzle: the huge variation in charges between hospitals and surgi-centers *for the same operation.* For surgeons, too, trying to figure out the logic behind insurance company reimbursement is a daunting task. Why is it that two surgeons operating out of the same hospital, *performing the same operation,* can receive two vastly different fees—regardless of the clinical outcomes? Making sense of it all is beyond human mental capabilities.

A study published in 2012 in the *Archives of Internal Medicine* analyzed the charges for an uncomplicated appendectomy after which the patient spent three days or less in the hospital. The results were fascinating. In a review of 289 California hospitals and twenty thousand patients, charges ranged from $1,529 to $183,000. You may have to read that sentence again. The average charge was $33,000. Where was the variation? All over the place: For-profit hospitals charged more for services than nonprofit community hospitals; charges increased with the age of the patient; and charges went up yet again for the uninsured and for Medicaid-covered patients.

Dr. Renee Hsia, the lead author of the study, noted, "There's no rhyme or reason for how patients are charged. Variations of two or three times is to be expected, but there is no industry where you see charges of more than 100 times for the same product." She concluded, "There is no method to the madness. No system at all to determine what is a national price for this condition or this procedure." While some of the price variation can be explained by surgical technique, a patient's underlying health conditions, and whether the appendix had ruptured, the study did not find specific, consistent reasons for the large differences in what patients and their health insurance carriers were billed. Other studies analyzing Medicare prices for operations among regions across the country have also found no rational reason why price variation exists.

No one is really sure of the origins of the discrepancies in healthcare billing today, but it is clear that the current mess evolved from a byzantine system that includes hospitals (for-profit and not-for-profit), insurance companies (private and federal), and physicians. And because few public resources are available to help you understand these fees, patients are left in the dark when it comes to understanding how a hospital arrived at the figures on its bill. What *does* "Hospital Misc." include? (I must confess, most surgeons are in the dark, too, unaware of the expenses the hospital incurs as a result of the decisions we make in the operating room.)

For decades, there has been no transparency whatsoever in hospital pricing, no accountability for what hospitals have been allowed to charge patients. And hospitals have been content to keep it this way. Behind the guise of "This is *medicine*—too complicated for a mere patient to understand," hospitals have been able to hide the price of services from the consumer. The entire pricing system exists in a cocoon, hidden not only from patients but also from market forces that could foster competition. This secrecy is so embedded in hospital billing and administrative bureaucracy that even those who manage operating rooms are clueless about cost and how final decisions are made.

Without transparency, prospective patients have no way of comparing prices, no way of gaining any bargaining leverage. In 2007, researchers at the University of Pittsburgh disguised themselves as patients, calling hospitals in advance of their fictitious upcoming operations, asking for pricing information. Only a third of the hospitals responded at all, and for those that did, much of the information provided was incomplete. Of the hospitals that did respond, the charges for a hysterectomy, for example, ranged from $3,500 to $65,000. The removal of a gallbladder cost from $2,700 to $36,000. The price of a routine colonoscopy ranged from $350 to $5,800. Despite this "transparency," the lack of details made the prices almost meaningless. In addition, unlike so many consumer purchases today, there was no way of knowing if the prices correlated to better clinical outcomes. There was no way of knowing if you got what you paid for.

Other studies have confirmed the difficulty a patient faces when trying to crack a hospital's pricing code. In 2013, a study published in *JAMA Internal Medicine* summarized efforts to obtain pricing for an elective hip replacement. The researchers repeatedly called 102 hospitals, posing as a sixty-two-year-old woman with no insurance who was willing to pay cash for her hip replacement. Each hospital was asked the same questions: What are the total hospital charges and total bundled charges (hospital charges plus surgeon's fees) for this operation? Of the 102 hospitals queried, 64 of them (63 percent) provided an estimate of hospital charges only. Only 10 hospitals (10 percent of the survey) could give a single, all-inclusive bundled price for an elective hip replacement. Of those, prices ranged from $11,000 to $125,000. Of the twenty top-ranked orthopedic hospitals queried, only nine (45 percent) provided an all-inclusive bundled price; these ranged from $12,500 to $105,000. Three hospitals were unable to provide the caller with *any* price. The mean price for the top twenty hospitals combined was $12,000 higher than the nonranked hospitals. The lead author of the study, a physician, concluded, "in aggregate, our results highlight the difficulty that consumers have in obtaining price estimates for common medical procedures." That might be the understatement of the year. Moreover, if it's that difficult for someone who *understands* the medical system, how in the world does the average American sort through all this?

What these studies reveal—the irrationality of hospital pricing, especially for surgical procedures—is not new. But while these studies were not breaking any new ground, they expose the subculture that hospitals and insurance companies have lived in for years. It is a subculture shrouded in secrecy that has taken full advantage of the current fee-for-service reimbursement system. It is a subculture where hospitals, insurance companies, and physicians negotiate reimbursement deals far from public scrutiny. Protected from the competition of market forces, it is a subculture where I can perform the same hernia repair, using the same instruments, on four patients with four different insurance plans (Medicare, Medicaid, private insurance, and uninsured) at the same hospital and generate four different prices for each case—regardless of the clinical outcome.

The truth is, hospitals can and do charge whatever their hearts desire for any operation because there has not been an entity holding them accountable for proving (with clinical outcomes data) that the service they provide is worth the cost. Sure, any hospital administrator will tell you they have a (secret) scientific formula for creating sticker charges for any service offered or device used in the operating room. Good luck trying to uncover it or, if you do, trying to decipher it. What is the science behind a hospital pricing formula that charges Medicare $1,300 for a six-inch by six-inch single piece of hernia mesh that was purchased for $300 and made by a medical device company for far less than that?

According to one bold hospital administrator at a Long Island, New York, facility, his hospital calculates the price charged for an MRI scan "based on such factors as the cost of buying or leasing the machinery, the wear and tear on that machine, staff salaries, the climate control and electric bill, cleaning costs, local competitive pricing, and other costs related to the hospital's overhead, like malpractice insurance." Now, that is a lot to digest.

Even though hospitals work in an environment where they can charge whatever they want, it is up to the insurance companies and the federal government (Medicare, Medicaid) to decide how much any hospital gets paid. On the other hand, individual hospitals or multifacility systems can negotiate with private insurers for reimbursement rates. In the past, many of these negotiations were based on quantity, market share, lobbying efforts, and other factors unrelated to clinical outcome data. Hospital systems with brand name recognition often could charge more for the same operation (and receive more) than a community hospital, despite outcomes. Hospital name recognition has always carried clout when negotiating reimbursement contracts with health insurance companies. It has traditionally been a numbers game for hospitals and insurance companies, all about patient volume. The game is changing, however, as insurance companies begin to use clinical outcomes data (infection rates, readmission rates, and so on) as leverage during these negotiations, demanding to see documented quality data that's better than the competition before completing reimbursement deals.

Once reimbursement contracts are signed, the money paid to a hospital for that hip replacement, heart bypass procedure, hysterectomy, or colon removal doesn't even remotely resemble the initial eye-popping charges. To the public and professional eye, the discrepancies are unexplainable. To hospital administrators, it is business as usual. Even with markups on every charge and markdowns on actual reimbursement, most hospitals still have a 20 to 30 percent profit cushion to sit back on.

"Dr. Ruggieri, Mr. Wilkes is on the phone."

"Put him through to my office, Terri." I wasn't surprised he was calling me. He was probably curious about what I thought about the copy of the bill he had mailed to me.

"Mr. Wilkes. How are you feeling?"

"Fine, fine. Great job with the hernia, Dr. Ruggieri. Definitely got my money's worth," he said. "What did you think of my bill? Are all the charges legitimate?"

I wasn't quite sure how to answer that since I had no idea how the hospital arrived at the charges.

He continued. "I had no idea they charged my insurance company for all that stuff. Not that it matters." He laughed. "What the hell, I pay enough for health insurance! I'm just thinking about my neighbor. I hope you didn't skimp on his hernia!"

I would have loved to enlighten Mr. Wilkes about the relationship between cost and quality surgical care—and it would have been a short conversation—but the truth was, he didn't care. Much of the literature suggests there is no direct correlation between the amount of money spent on a surgery and its outcome. Mr. Wilkes is not alone in his naïveté or in his lack of interest in understanding hospital charges, true costs, and the quality of care. A study published in 2013 in *Health Affairs* discussed the topic of cost and healthcare with two focus groups. The findings confirmed Mr. Wilkes's attitude as the norm. Not surprisingly, most people believe the more money you spend, the better care you get. The focus group participants were not interested in what insurers have to pay to cover their hospital care, as long as they perceived that their care was the best. This price-desensitization attitude will change as patients are forced by their insurance carriers to take more financial responsibility for their care.

Hospitals have been the beneficiary of this disinterest and misperception for years. In general, patients have been shielded from knowing what their operations cost and what is paid for their care. I believe that if people found themselves having to contribute more to their healthcare expenses, they would eventually show more interest in cost comparison, especially when it came to paying for an operation. The 2013 *Health Affairs* study supported this conjecture. Over a four-year time period, enrollees in the California Public Employees' Retirement System (CalPERS) were given incentives to select designated low-price hospitals over high-priced hospitals when having knee or hip replacement surgery; quality was rated the same for all the hospitals available under the initiative. The incentive: CalPERS enrollees would pay more out of pocket if they chose one of the higher-priced hospitals for their surgery. When the enrollees understood that the quality ratings were the same, and that they would pay more to have surgery at a hospital that did not demonstrate better outcomes, the result was encouraging. Surgical volumes increased by 21 percent at the lower-price hospitals and decreased by 34 percent at the higher-price hospitals. Over the four years, in response to consumer choice, prices for hip and knee replacement surgery declined in *both* groups; the low-price hospitals dropped rates by 5 percent, and high-price hospitals dropped rates by 34 percent, resulting in $2.8 million in savings.

In 2013, as accountability became a buzzword in healthcare, studies showed that hospitals were responding with greater transparency in billing as well as outcomes data. As they did, and consumers were encouraged to become actively engaged in their healthcare choices, costs actually decreased.

When it comes to your hernia repair, cesarian section, joint replacement—you name it—as soon as you enter the hospital on the day of your operation, the charges begin to accrue. Nurses will prepare you in the preoperative area. Here, charges will be incurred for everything needed to get you ready for the surgery—intravenous lines, catheters, tubing, and so on—as well as all medications you'll be given (perhaps morphine or antibiotics) before you enter the operating room.

Once you are wheeled into the operating room, the number and value of the charges increases dramatically. The hospital will charge for everything used inside the operating room, and there will be separate charges for medical devices and equipment as well as charges for medications. There will be separate charges for supplies and drugs used by the anesthesiologist, which will be in addition to another separate charge for the actual services provided by the anesthesiologist. Nothing is free once you are placed on the thin steel operating table. Even the small amount of oxygen Mr. Wilkes was asked to breathe through a mask before being put to sleep for his hernia operation was listed as a charge on his bill. I could not even begin to figure out how the hospital came up with the charge of $53 for one minute of sweet-smelling "perioperative" oxygen used.

Once you are under anesthesia, you will also be billed for the amount of time you spend in the operating room. Some hospitals will go so far as to charge you separately for the fifteen to twenty minutes it takes to organize the instruments in the OR before you enter. It reminds me of the automatic $2.30 charge I see on the meter when getting into a taxi, before it even moves one foot. I have always wondered how taxi drivers calculate this charge. The operating room "initial setup" charge may be listed as a separate charge. Most often, it's buried under some vague heading. There is no standard for what hospitals can charge for operating room time. Some hospitals charge by the minute (the most common method), others by set minute intervals; some will not divulge their criteria. Some hospitals also charge a patient by the "level" of service provided in the operating room. Each level is based on the equipment used, the number of staff in the room, the number of instrument sets opened, the case level classification (minor, major, or major extensive), and any other category a hospital's charge expert can legitimize.

A hospital can have up to fourteen levels of charge categorization based on its unique charge formula. Some levels include charges for operating room time usage and some do not. Level charging is a vehicle for hospitals to secretly include the costs of supplies and equipment normally not readily billable. For instance, hospitals cannot charge separately for the use of capital equipment, such as the use of a heart monitor during anesthesia. They are, however, allowed to charge (at inflated prices) for the disposable sticky sensors that are placed on your skin and hooked up to the monitor.

To further complicate the unregulated world of operating room billing, some hospitals use a system called "specialty-based" charges. Specialty groupings include orthopedics, general surgery, gynecology, ENT (ear, nose, and throat), and all the other surgical subspecialties. With this system, charges are based, in part, on the number of minutes the patient is in the operating room. Each specialty has its own required instruments and devices, technical staff, and monitoring equipment so hospitals can come to a total unique charge for each operation in each specialty incorporating all these factors, including minutes. Blurring the lines further, some hospitals include the charge of an implant (such as an artificial hip or hernia mesh) in the total specialty charge, while others bill separately for it.

In addition to time spent in the operating room, a hospital's second biggest charge category during any surgery involves the implants, devices, and instruments the surgeon uses. For instance, compared to "open" surgery (when the surgeon makes a large incision and opens that part of the body to readily expose the area being worked on), the charges generated for laparoscopic procedures are higher. That's because the cost of disposable laparoscopic instruments is higher. Disposable instruments are used once during any operation, either open or laparoscopic. Once used, they are then discarded. Usually. In an effort to save money, however, hospitals have been legally sterilizing disposable instruments in order to get more than a onetime use out of them. Hospitals love this because they save money by not buying new disposables for every operation, while they can charge for that single disposable item's use more than once. The medical device companies who produce these so-called disposable instruments are not happy because resterilization reduces the number of disposables they sell. If you ask company reps, they will argue that sterilization of disposables may not be completely safe in eradicating all bacteria. If you ask the Food and Drug Administration (FDA), the process meets its standards and *is* safe. Regardless of whom you ask, you will never know if you are getting charged for resterilized disposable instruments used during your laparoscopic procedure.

Disposable devices, such as surgical staplers, clip appliers, or fixating devices to tack hernia mesh can be marked up considerably by hospitals and end up costing insurance companies and patients thousands of dollars. Many of the implantable devices, such as artificial knees or hips or hernia mesh, can also generate a large charge number (including markup) on any operating room bill. Robotic surgery can raise these costs and markups even higher, a topic discussed in Chapter 8. As for Mr. Wilkes, the disposable supplies unique to laparoscopic hernia surgery that I used in his case came to a total charge of more than $3,300 to Medicare. Normally, to purchase this equipment hospitals pay less than half of what they charge patients for its use. One charge really jumped off the page when compared to its actual purchase price. As I reviewed Mr. Wilkes's bill, I saw that the disposable device I used to create a space underneath the muscle to access the hernia was marked up 900 percent. It was clearly the winner in the charge markup race. In addition to that, the implantable mesh I used to repair his hernia and the device I used to fix it in place added another charge of $2,800 to his bill, a more than 300 percent markup over cost.

As for Mr. Wilkes's surgery, it went well and took about thirty minutes to perform. He woke from the anesthesia without any problems and was placed on a gurney headed for the recovery room. As he left the operating room, the hospital was preparing a bill for just over $15,000. One would think, based on that number, the charges for his hernia operation would have stopped there. But for Mr. Wilkes, and in fact for every patient leaving an operating room, the hospital charges continue; there is PACU (the post-anesthesia care unit), also called the recovery room, where you are monitored and cared for as the anesthesia wears off. Recovery room charges are an entirely separate bunch of expenses a patient accumulates. Similar to operating room charges, recovery room charges are usually by the minute. Depending on the type of surgery you had, the staff needed to give care, drugs administered, and supplies used, more charges accrue during recovery. This second fee can be one number encompassing all the factors previously listed, but it is a number open to manipulation based on its arbitrariness. As for Mr. Wilkes, he spent sixty minutes in the recovery room at a going rate of $10/minute for a total cost of $600. This charge did not include anything but a physical stop in the recovery room. His second charge generated in the recovery room (listed under the heading of "major procedure") totaled $1,700. How this number was arrived at and what the charges included were as much of a mystery to me as da Vinci's model for the *Mona Lisa.*

When it was all over, the hospital billed Medicare $17,000 for Mr. Wilkes's laparoscopic hernia repair. Again, this charge did not include the anesthesiologist's fee or mine. As I mentioned earlier, Medicare approved payments of $4,000 but ended up paying only $2,900 while his secondary insurance contributed $350. Unfortunately for Mr. Wilkes, the hospital went after him for the $750 difference.

With such diverse methods of determining patient bills, who actually decides how much a hospital can charge? The Centers for Medicare & Medicaid Services (CMS) *does* provide hospitals with general guidelines on what to charge (and what not to charge). CMS does not, however, offer up lists of specific chargeable items. For instance, supplies used routinely during surgery by operating room staff (gloves, gowns) cannot be charged to a patient. Other supplies commonly used for all patients are also generally not chargeable. For instance, the sterile sheets used to drape out a patient's body part during surgery cannot be charged for separately. And capital equipment (such as a heart monitor) used in the operating room cannot be listed as a separate charge in an operating room bill. Yet even with these constraints, there is no uniformity in the way charges are generated from hospital to hospital. There are no constant standards that can be used for comparison. No way of knowing what goes into every hospital's unique secret charge formula. All a patient will ever see is the final product this formula spits out. Even with total transparency, hospitals would still have a lot of explaining to do to justify what they charge for and why it costs what it does.

Hospitals and insurance companies are not the only culpable ones in this scenario; doctors themselves contribute to a culture that ignores the importance of cost control. A study published in *JAMA* in 2013 surveyed 2,500 physicians regarding their thoughts on controlling costs in medicine. Sixty percent pointed to trial lawyers as the biggest contributor to spiraling healthcare costs. Lawyers were followed by insurance companies, hospitals, pharmaceutical and medical device companies, and, finally, patients themselves. At the very bottom of the list, identified as the least significant factor, a small number of those surveyed stated that *physicians* bear a responsibility to control costs. More than 50 percent of those surveyed agreed that reducing the compensation of highly paid specialists would help control costs. Sounds to me like a primary care physician point of view. . . .

I suspect that not many in that group were surgeons.

As a surgeon, I have never had any serious interest in controlling costs in the operating room. Historically, surgeons have gotten whatever their hearts desired. Our mantra has been, "I don't care what it costs. If you can't buy that new device for me, I will be forced to take my business across town." For years, many surgeons used their status to get what they wanted. We expected, and got, carte blanche treatment because of our place in the physician hierarchical chain. We also believed that controlling costs was not our problem and that a mere administrator should not be able to question a surgeon's choice of tools. For a long time, it did not matter how much new devices cost because hospitals would simply pass along the expense to your insurance company and, ultimately, to you, the consumer.

Traditionally, surgeons have not concerned themselves with cost because no one held them accountable for it. Even today, with the growing emphasis on controlling expenses, surgeons are largely shielded from concentrating on the ledger sheet for the operations they perform. We just don't have to think about it, and I am as guilty of this as the next surgeon. Why should we? There are no positive or negative consequences if the total cost for me to remove an appendix is consistently 25 percent less than the expenses generated by the surgeon in the next room. There are no personal financial rewards if my lower complication rates translate into lower hospital costs, even though the surgeon with higher complication rates will burden the hospital (and patient) with higher hospital costs. As a matter of fact, under the fee-for-service model, surgical complications *pay off* for hospitals by generating more charges.

Another etiology of cost generation in the operating room has to do with the surgeon's skill set. Many of my colleagues may not agree with me on this point, but I believe experienced surgeons improve not only clinical outcomes but also operating room costs. How can this be? As I mentioned, many hospitals charge patients by the number of minutes spent in the operating room. The more time a patient spends on the operating room table, the higher the charge. The patients of surgeons who are more skilled and, therefore, perhaps faster at a particular procedure will spend less time in the operating room and see a smaller bill for that part of the costs.

Now, it's only fair to point out that any patient can present factors that will mean the case will take longer than average, no matter what the skill or experience of the surgeon. In addition, I need to emphasize there is *no* data to support a direct relationship between speed in the operating room and skill, or better outcomes. A fast surgeon can get into trouble in the operating room by not paying attention to detail. Although patients may perceive a surgeon's speed inside the operating room as a marker of a higher skill level, it isn't consistently true. What *is* true is this: If your surgeon spends an hour longer to take out your gallbladder than your coworker's surgeon spent on his surgery, the operating room charges on your bill will invariably be higher.

Anesthesia will also influence what your hospital will charge for your surgery. If your surgery took thirty minutes but it took an abnormally long time, say forty-five minutes, to "wake" you from anesthesia, your charges will reflect the prolonged time in PACU. If you are having general anesthesia versus intravenous sedation, your time inside the operating room will also be longer because it will take longer for general anesthesia to leave your system. Later, you will spend more time in the recovery room waking up from a general anesthetic than from other types of anesthesia.

In addition to influencing operating room time charges, surgeons have a direct influence on the medical device charges attached to your bill. Your surgeon decides which devices he or she needs to complete your operation successfully. All hospitals have an operating room "preference card" for every surgeon. This preference card lists every instrument and device that surgeon normally uses during every specific operation. It is created when a new surgeon arrives on staff and is modified over the years as a surgeon's preferences change with time, experience, and new technology. Operating rooms use the preference card to determine which device packages to open and which instruments to set up before the patient is brought into the operating room. Often, this preference card needs updating and the information on it is not accurate. In such instances, when instruments listed on an old preference card are opened but never used, they are still added as charges to the patient's bill. Sometimes a surgeon will change his or her mind in the middle of an operation and not use some of the already opened devices; the patient will still be charged for them. Sometimes a nurse will open the wrong instrument by accident, increasing operating room charges. Sometimes surgeons deviate from their norm, asking for instruments not on the preference card. Sometimes a surgeon will ask for one device but actually mean another, only realizing the mistake after the package is opened. Sometimes a surgeon will encounter a defective medical device during surgery and need to use a second one. No matter the reason, once these expensive devices are hatched from their sterile packages (and whether or not the surgeon uses them), they become added charges to the patient's bill.

Here's a common example. A $1,200 surgical stapler misfires in the middle of my attempt to connect two ends of colon; I need to ask for a new stapler. Sometimes surgical stapling devices are accidentally dropped on the operating room floor; when that happens, a new one is required. Sometimes the stapler is opened but not used because the surgeon decides to hand-sew instead. (Hand-sewing instead of stapling drastically reduces the expense; the cost of simple sutures is roughly $4 apiece.) The patient's bill will still reflect the cost of the stapler.

I'm not recommending we eliminate surgical staplers and go back to the days of only using sutures. Every week, thousands of surgical staplers are successfully used by surgeons in operating rooms across the country—for removing sections of organs and reconnecting anatomical parts. They are efficient, faster than sewing, and a major component of all laparoscopic surgery performed today. They do not, however, come cheap. If multiple staplers are used during an operation for whatever reason, charges for that operation will dramatically increase.

The bottom line is that surgeons have a direct influence on what patients are charged. We have to be more aware of how we affect cost and use that awareness to minimize waste. We have to get away from the old attitude of "You need to get this hernia mesh because it is the latest and greatest" or "I have always used this device and I don't care what it costs." A study published in *Health Affairs* in 2014 surveyed orthopedic surgeons at seven academic teaching hospitals, asking them to estimate the cost of thirteen medical devices they often use in the operating room. Twenty-one percent of 503 surgeons correctly estimated the cost of each device. A third stated they had "poor" knowledge of the entire pricing process. Surgeons must be more open to using alternative, equally effective, less costly devices in the operating room. I was once approached by a medical device company rep, eager to show me the newest model of a laparoscopic hand port for colon surgery I already used in the operating room. It was a device I have loved using since it came on the market. But the upgraded model was priced much higher than the older version, out of proportion to its clinical value. Even though I don't pay for it, the "sticker shock" forced me to give the competition a second chance. I ended up trying the competition's less expensive model and liking it. I still use it today.

In today's world, with an expectation of transparency and "affordable care," surgeons have to become more active in accepting accountability for the costs we generate. The handwriting is on the wall: If we don't discipline ourselves to control costs inside the operating room, hospitals and insurance companies will do it for us. I'd rather make those choices myself.

Anyone can see that the relationship between surgical charges (inflated or not) and payments to hospitals and surgeons resembles an absurd negotiation between a seller and buyer at a prehistoric bazaar. Is there any agency in a position to decide what those charges and payments should be? For Medicare-covered care, there is. The Medicare Payment Advisory Commission (MedPAC) is charged with determining how much surgeons are paid for procedures. The organization, made up of seventeen individuals, is an independent arm of Congress. All seventeen members are appointed by the comptroller general of the United States, who is appointed by the president. MedPAC was established in 1997 by the Balanced Budget Act to advise Congress about the Medicare program; it has no legislative ability to make policy. MedPAC's role is to make recommendations that Congress will evaluate and approve or disapprove on matters related to the Medicare payment system.

What I find interesting about the makeup of the current board is that only four individuals have M.D. after their names, and only three have experience in the actual practice of medicine. The rest have Ph.D., J.D., or M.B.A. as credentials and are policy geeks. All three practicing M.D.s are medical specialists. In addition, of these three, only one board member currently practices medicine in a community setting. Unfortunately for surgeons, none are found within 100 miles of the MedPAC board. Surgeons do not have any representation on the decisions that affect what Medicare will pay them. Consequently, I have the MedPAC board to thank for reimbursing $340 for Mr. Wilkes's successful hernia repair.

As for private insurance companies, payments to hospitals and surgeons are negotiated through contracts, behind the scenes, on a variety of economic and political fronts. In the past, these contract negotiations to set fees for hospitals and surgeons have had nothing to do with the quality of care being offered but everything to do with political influence. Larger academic hospitals can use the value of their branded name as clout to obtain higher fees, particularly when it comes to reimbursement for surgery. Private insurance companies have paid higher fees just so they can attach a brand name to their products. Higher fees to larger institutions are often paid regardless of outcomes or cost. For the smaller, private practice surgical groups without name recognition, private insurance companies are in a position to negotiate lower reimbursement fees. That is why two surgeons—one affiliated with a larger hospital system and one in group private practice—can perform the same operation with the same outcome at the same hospital and get reimbursed differently.

As I finished my phone conversation with Mr. Wilkes, he seemed happy with his outcome but a little unsettled about the fact that his neighbor (who had the same surgery, by my hands, and the same good outcome) had one-upped him on cost by having his procedure at the outpatient surgery center across town. What was dawning on Mr. Wilkes is actually a dirty little secret that surgeons and private insurance companies have known for years (and that hospitals don't want you to know): It is much less costly to have an outpatient operation at a free-standing, independent surgery center than at a hospital.

Independent free-standing surgery centers have their roots in the 1970s. At that time, surgeons were becoming frustrated with the inefficiencies of hospital operating rooms and the costs of operations to patients. They were looking for an alternative, so many started to set up their own surgery centers. They were usually owned by groups of surgeons and had to be licensed by the state. It quickly became apparent that surgi-centers offered a more efficient, less costly place for surgeons to take their business. Once hospitals realized they had real competition for surgical revenue, they tried to put them out of business. Hospitals used their political muscle to squash the growth and economic viability of surgi-centers, sending a message loud and clear to the owner-surgeons. The lobbying influence that hospitals had with private insurance companies was put to use to attempt to stop reimbursement to surgery centers. Yet despite enormous pressure, surgery centers continued to grow in popularity with both surgeons and patients. Today it is accepted that surgicenters can offer the same high-quality surgical service as a hospital across the street, but at a much lower price.

Independent surgery centers do not receive the same reimbursement as hospitals do. Surgery centers charge Medicare or a patient's private insurance a flat facility fee for the use of the building. As with hospitals, this fee was determined by negotiations with private insurance companies. A different facility fee is predetermined for every operation performed at the facility. This fee does not include the surgeon's or anesthesiologist's fee, but other than that it is all-inclusive, covering all charges from the time you enter the surgi-center to the time you leave. The facility fee also includes any implantable devices (such as hernia mesh) used. Unlike free-standing outpatient surgery centers, hospitals can charge for implantable devices separately, in addition to their other operating room fees.

Traditionally, outpatient free-standing surgery centers have been paid lower facility fees than hospitals by private insurance companies for each operation. Hospitals can point to higher facility expenses and therefore have lobbied and received higher fees for the same operation.

Surgeons are motivated to work at surgery centers, despite the lower fee structure, because the environment allows them to provide more efficient, cost-effective care for most outpatient procedures. They don't have to deal with the bloated middle layers of administration costs inherent to most hospital bureaucracies. Most outpatient free-standing surgery centers are owned by the surgeons who work there. They are competing for the same patients hospitals want to attract, and their cost efficiency has become a threat to the surgical business of many community hospitals.

As for Mr. Wilkes's neighbor, Medicare was charged $4,625 for his outpatient surgery center hernia repair, compared to the $17,000 charged by the hospital for the same operation. Medicare paid $1,660 to the outpatient free-standing surgery center for the repair of Mr. Wilkes's neighbor's hernia versus $2,900 to the hospital for his own. A savings of $1,240 was achieved for Medicare (which is funded by all of us who pay taxes). With over 700,000 hernias repaired in this country every year, Medicare (and private insurance companies, too) could achieve enormous savings if more of them were performed at free-standing outpatient surgery centers. In light of this potential savings, Medicare is now thinking of reimbursing hospitals the same lower fees for uncomplicated outpatient procedures as it currently reimburses surgery centers.

Now that everyone acknowledges there is virtually no transparency, or logic for that matter, in the methods hospitals use to charge patients for surgery, the question becomes, *Is there anyone to blame?* Answer: Oh, yes, there are many.

The blame can be shared by *all* parties involved. Hospitals, for the way they mark up and charge for every item inside the operating room, knowing they will not receive close to what is on the bill. ("It's the way business has always been done," was a phrase I continually heard from operating room managers whenever I questioned costs.) Hospitals are also at fault for their extreme reluctance to reveal pricing to the public.

Health insurance companies are to blame for fostering a culture where hospitals are not held accountable for outcomes and are reimbursed *regardless* of the quality of surgical care. Health insurance companies *could* link reimbursement contracts to clinical outcomes data. The information exists. They could also pressure hospitals to allow patients to have their surgeries at less expensive outpatient surgery centers.

Surgeons need to step up and take some of the blame for the charge culture that exists in operating rooms today. Most are either not interested in or unaware of the costs they produce in the operating room.

Lastly, patients must also share in a portion of the blame for not taking an active role in trying to uncover pricing before being wheeled into the operating room. I realize hospitals make it difficult to find out what things cost, but if more and more prospective patients would ask, would shop around and dig into surgical prices, hospitals would have to become more transparent about pricing and costs. As a prospective patient, every one of us has to lose the outdated "My insurance covers it—why should I care what it costs?" attitude.

You should care and you can get educated about healthcare costs pretty easily. Several websites offer hospital pricing for different types of operations. FAIR Health (fairhealthconsumer .org), pricing healthcare (pricinghealthcare.com), and the Healthcare Bluebook (healthcarebluebook.com) offer information on the costs of specific operations. The state of Massachusetts recently passed a law setting up a toll-free phone number and website with information on the costs of various operations by hospitals and surgeons. Other states are following the Massachusetts model.

The federal government is beginning to help, too. In 2013, for the first time, the Centers for Medicare & Medicaid Services published the prices at more than three thousand hospitals for the 100 most common inpatient stays and procedures during 2011. Prices covered both medical and surgical charges for a variety of diseases. As you would expect, the prices charged to Medicare by different hospitals for the same operation were all over the map. According to the former secretary of health and human services Kathleen Sebelius, "average inpatient charges for services a hospital provides in connection with a joint replacement range from the low of $5,300 at a hospital in Ada, Oklahoma, to a high of $223,000 at a hospital in Monterey Park, California." She went on to state that "even within the same geographic area, hospital charges for similar services can vary significantly." In accordance with these astounding findings, the Affordable Care Act mandates that all hospitals publish prices for common surgical services beginning in 2014. A new era is dawning.

You can contact your hospital or insurance company directly requesting the total cost of an upcoming surgery. Ask for details of the total, too. After surgery, when you are recovering at home, request a breakdown of your hospital bill. Take a close look at what your hospital charged for and what your insurance company actually paid. A precaution: You'll need to hire a consultant to interpret the breakdown.

7 | MONEY, MARKETING, AND MEDICAL DEVICES

There was blood everywhere. I was sucking it out as fast as I could, but I was losing ground. The clock was ticking. If I did not cut open Mr. Bowmore's belly within the next sixty seconds to get a clamp on the bleeding artery, his blood loss would be substantial. I would also have some explaining to do to his family.

"Damn it. Artery tore right off." The jet pulse of blood hitting my camera lens and obscuring my line of sight was coming from Mr. Bowmore's inferior epigastric artery; it had somehow ripped from his abdominal wall muscle.

A nicked or torn artery, bleeding uncontrollably, is a serious complication that can occur during surgery. Your arteries carry oxygenated, clean, nutrient-rich blood from your heart to every part of your body; the veins return the blood to your heart. It's a process that never stops. Even at rest, your heart is pumping more than five liters of blood throughout your body every minute.

Consequently, uncontrolled arterial bleeding can quickly cause a severe loss of blood. At the very least, this complication can lead to serious negative effects on all your organs including your brain; at the worst, it leads to death.

"I can't see a thing in here." Blood continued to pool in Mr. Bowmore's abdomen, the space where I was working, trying to perform a simple hernia repair. I struggled to place a laparoscopic clamp on the bleeding artery.

One of the benefits of laparoscopic surgery and the use of high-definition camera monitors is the magnification of anatomic detail that can be seen on the screen. Colors are also more distinct and intense—a tremendous help to the surgeon. When the bright red of arterial blood fills the screen, however, it induces pure terror.

"Son of a bitch." This was supposed to be a routine operation. I had barely started the laparoscopic repair of Mr. Bowmore's left inguinal hernia—an operation I have done a thousand times—when something went horribly wrong. The device I was using (called a dissecting hernia balloon) to create a space underneath the muscle during the operation had torn off a branch of a main artery.

"Dr. Ruggieri"—the anesthesiologist's voice started to crack—"his blood pressure is dropping. You need to open him up now and stop the bleeding or we are going to be in trouble." Suddenly, the head of the operating room table tilted downward, almost standing Mr. Bowmore on his head, a maneuver used to keep blood flow to the brain in times of low blood pressure caused by profuse bleeding.

"I know, I know." My scrub top was drenched with sweat. For a second, I glanced over at the two medical device company representatives (referred to in the OR as "reps") standing in a corner of the operating room. They worked for the company that promoted and sold the dissecting hernia balloon device. It was a device I had used for many years to perform laparoscopic hernia repairs. Now that very same device had ripped the hole in the main abdominal muscle artery I was trying to close.

One of the reps was someone I had known for months because my hospital was one of his accounts. Initially, he had made a serious effort to target me, knowing I was an avid user of his product. He would visit my office on the days he knew I would be there. He would show up in the operating room to make sure things were going well for me. He knew I had been using his company's device for years and wanted to keep me (and the other surgeons who also used it) as a satisfied client. He was a salesman, plain and simple, selling the hospital a product that I relied on to perform laparoscopic hernia surgery. I expected him to be in the operating room, monitoring the effectiveness of his products and the satisfaction level of the surgeons using them.

The other rep was not a rep at all, but a regional manager. A company boss. He'd introduced himself while I was scrubbing in before the case began. Now, it's common knowledge that medical device company bosses rarely show up "in the field," at hospital operating rooms. His presence meant something was up. Maybe the field rep was in line for a review and promotion. Or, he could have been there if sales numbers were down, or if a new product line was about to be released. Most of these bosses have worked as medical device sales reps themselves; they've paid their dues. After years of catering to surgeons' desires, egos, and appetites, the successful ones move up the corporate ladder and out of the operating room. I had never met this particular boss before; unfortunately, as it turned out, he had picked the wrong day to make a field visit. He would be disappointed in the effectiveness of his "new and improved" product, and in my level of satisfaction with it. As I glanced at them, I could see their ashen faces and wide-eyed stares above their surgical masks. Both were fixed on the sea of red filling the monitor, horrified at what was transpiring. I was livid.

"You guys need to get the hell out of here. *Now*." Enough said. They were all too happy to oblige. Both exited without a word. I would deal with them later. At the moment, I had more important things to do.

"Can't stop this damn bleeding." I was blindly jabbing my laparoscopic grasper into the red hole of blood, hoping to get lucky. "I wish I could just get my hands in there." After a few more unsuccessful jabs, I capitulated. "Hand me a knife, please." I stuck my hand out, trying not to take my eyes off the monitor. Swiftly, with two quick strokes of the blade, I parted his skin, fascia, and muscle. A volcano of blood erupted all over his skin as soon as my knife pierced the last layer of tissue holding everything together. I had no choice but to convert a routine outpatient laparoscopic hernia repair (which should have resulted in minimal blood loss) into an open operation that had already experienced major blood loss. Conversion to almost any "open," traditional surgery often necessitates a longer stay in the hospital and, of course, a higher hospital bill. Fortunately for Mr. Bowmore, he recovered well and left the hospital two days later without any further problems. Before he left, however, I had some explaining to do, to both him and his family, as to why he had to be transfused two units of blood. I also had to explain why he was left with a painful six-inch cut in his left groin, not the standard three tiny incisions.

This scenario—medical device company reps in the operating room, monitoring the use of their products—is common. Every day of the week, company reps are scrubbed, masked, and gowned, standing in a corner of operating rooms across America, watching as surgeons use their medical device products. *Is the surgeon happy? Is the device working as promised? Will I be getting a year-end bonus?* Or, *Is the device malfunctioning? Is the surgeon getting frustrated? Is the competition trying to move in on my surgeon?* I imagine these are the questions that occupy their thoughts. Most of the time, I don't pay much attention to them.

The day of Mr. Bowmore's hernia repair had started out like most routine days in the operating room. By the end of it, though, I realized I had been ambushed. Unbeknownst to me, the medical device company rep had approached the hospital's manager of operating room materials several weeks earlier. He was hawking the "new, improved" version of the hernia dissecting balloon I had been using for ten-plus years to the person in charge of purchasing. Meanwhile, I had no complaints about the device and no idea it needed improving. As a rule, most new, improved versions of existing medical devices normally don't add much "improvement." In my view, it's an excuse for the company to raise the price of the device and make more money. Hospitals already pay a hefty markup for medical devices. In 2012 the *Wall Street Journal* quoted a Government Accountability Office (GAO) survey of thirty-one hospitals and found that "some hospitals pay thousands of dollars more than others for big-ticket medical devices." The designation of "new and improved" usually adds to cost. What often accompanies the release of an upgraded device is "discontinued production" of the existing version. I suspect companies purposely do this to force hospitals to buy the new upgrade.

In any case, the medical device company rep had persuaded someone at the hospital to purchase the new version and get rid of the older version, all without much if any input from the surgeons who actually use them. The problem: I was not aware the hospital had decided to replace the hernia dissecting balloon device I was accustomed to using. I learned about it as I was making the incisions in Mr. Bowmore's skin.

"Dr. Ruggieri?" The rep wanted my attention. "We just stocked the shelves with a new, improved version of the hernia dissecting balloon. I think you'll like the upgrade." I listened as I drew blood. He reassured me of its similarity to the older version, certain I would "love" the minor improvements. My eyes met his for a few seconds. He was also confident he could help me "walk through" the use of it if I had any questions or got into difficulty. Most surgeons cringe when these words are spoken inside the operating room. Fortunately, patients never hear these words because they are asleep. We hate surprises when a live patient is on the table. We hate the risk that the unfamiliarity of new instruments brings to the operating room. (I am also positive that the words *walk you through* would not instill confidence in anyone about to undergo an operation.)

Most of the "walking" done by surgeons is supposed to be carried out well in advance of entering the operating room. The reality of today's rapidly changing operating room technology, however, means that on rare occasions surgeons do need help mastering the finer points of a new device during an operation.

One of the rep's jobs is to be available to answer any questions regarding the use of a new surgical device. I now suspected why the two company reps were present. Maybe the entire scenario was carefully orchestrated in order to get the improved version on the shelves before surgeons could evaluate it. He had access to the right people, knew about my affinity for his device. Maybe he had even stretched the truth to get the hospital to agree to buy it. Whatever he had done or said, I was now in the uncompromising position of having to try it.

I had been ambushed. I had no recourse but to use the new version; the old version had been removed from our shelves. I had to make a decision: Should I proceed with the new device, a device with which I was not familiar, or should I open up Mr. Bowmore and repair his hernia the old-fashioned way (not what I had described to him when he consulted with me for the operation). I chose to proceed using the new version of the device, thinking I could figure it out. In retrospect, it was one of the worst decisions I have ever made. It was a decision I blame myself for making since I—not a company rep—am responsible for what happens to my patients in the operating room. I struggled with placing the device in what I thought was the proper position. As I inflated the balloon underneath the abdominal wall muscle, its incorrectly placed position damaged a major muscle artery. The rest was history. As enraged as I was by the rep's ploy, Mr. Bowmore would be the one to pay the price for this ambush.

Within weeks of my operation on Mr. Bowmore, I was informed by the operating room manager that the old version of the hernia dissecting balloon was being resurrected. It would be on the shelves within days. So much for its being "discontinued."

I also learned that surgeons around the country had been critical of the new device, encountering the same positioning problem I had struggled with. Eventually, it was revealed that the new version had a design flaw that prevented accurate placement.

In the United States today, the medical/surgical device business is a $150-billion-a-year industry. Globally, the industry approaches $400 billion. The money spent on medical/surgical devices accounts for roughly 6 percent of the $2.7 trillion spent each year on healthcare in this country. The hernia market alone approaches $1.5 billion with its use of medical devices and mesh implants. Surgical staplers, frequently used during both open and minimally invasive surgery, amount to a $1.5 billion market. The joint replacement market continues to grow, with close to three million procedures done worldwide yearly and implant sales totaling over $13.8 billion. When a general surgeon sutures in a piece of synthetic mesh to repair a hernia, or when an orthopedic surgeon replaces an osteoarthritic knee with an artificial joint, many entities benefit financially. The manufacturing company producing the devices, the company reps selling them, the hospitals purchasing them, and the surgeons using them—all have a stake in the money generated from their use.

The Food and Drug Administration (FDA) offers medical device companies two pathways to approval. The first is called the premarket approval (PMA) process, used most often for what the FDA considers uniquely new devices. It is a process that costs more (for both the FDA and the company seeking FDA approval), has stricter requirements, and requires a human clinical trial in support of safety and efficacy. The second approval pathway is called the 510(k) process. This pathway is less expensive, has fewer regulations, and does not require any supportive human clinical trial proving its superiority over what is already on the market. All the FDA requires in the 510(k) pathway is for the manufacturer to prove the medical device is "substantially equivalent" to an existing device already on the market. Along with no human clinical trial data, the device is not subject to premarket inspection or postmarket studies to determine safety and efficacy once physicians begin using it. Not surprisingly, companies use the fast-track 510(k) process whenever they can because it is cheaper and allows approval of a new device without the time and expense of extensive human testing before and after its production.

The problem is that when a device has inherent flaws, the expedited process may not reveal them, as was the case with the hernia dissecting balloon I used in Mr. Bowmore's surgery. As a matter of fact, medical device defects often manifest themselves *after* the item is FDA-cleared and in use. A study published in 2011 in the *Archives of Internal Medicine* looking at 115 medical devices recalled by the FDA between 2005 and 2009 for causing undue harm found that 88 (78 percent) had been cleared by the expedited 510(k) process. In 2011, the Institute of Medicine concluded that the 510(k) approval process needed to be significantly revised or abolished because it was allowing flawed devices to come onto the market.

You don't have to read medical journals to be aware of this phenomenon; all you have to do is watch television. Note the number of commercials for lawyers searching for clients who have been injured by defective medical devices. Or pay attention to the news. There have been some high-profile recalls in the past. C. R. Bard's parent company, Davol, had to recall hernia mesh in 2005 because of harm it was causing. Turns out, even when properly placed by the most expert of surgeons, the mesh was coming loose, puncturing holes in intestine and causing the individual to require multiple operations to repair the damage. To this day, some nine years since its recall, I still get patients asking me whether I use this type of mesh when I repair hernias. The answer is no, but occasionally I do have to perform an emergency surgery to remove it; when it erodes into a segment of intestine, fixing it can't wait. Lawsuits are still evolving as a result of this defective product.

Another high-profile medical device recall happened in 2010 when Johnson & Johnson's European joint manufacturer unit, DePuy, recalled a hip implant. The primary reason for the recall was the implant's high failure rate (more than 30 percent at five years, compared to the standard hip failure rate of 5 percent at five years). In addition, there were reports of pieces of implant metal breaking off and accumulating in a patient's bloodstream. As a result of the recall, thousands of lawsuits made their way through the courts, with accusations centered on what company officials knew and when they knew it. In November 2013, Johnson & Johnson announced a $2.5 billion settlement to all the defective hip lawsuits, with patients receiving $160,000 each for pain and suffering while the lawyers received a third ($800 million).

In the world of minimally invasive surgery, disposable and nondisposable surgical devices are used every day in operating rooms across the country. Surgeons rely heavily on these devices to perform most operations today. Over the course of a week, I must use tens of thousands of dollars' worth of surgical devices during the minimally invasive operations I perform. Surgical device companies know this. They know who their target audience is. The colorectal surgeon performing minimally invasive abdominal surgery, the general surgeon performing hernia surgery, the orthopedic surgeon performing joint replacements, the neurosurgeon performing spinal surgery, the urologic surgeon performing robotic prostatectomies—for all of us, these surgical devices are essential to our work. That's why no surgeon who enters an operating room is spared from the marketing influences of surgical device companies and their sales representatives.

Surgical device company reps have been hanging around operating rooms, like bookies in a bar, since my internship days. Back then, there were no rules restricting reps' presence in the operating room. To my mind, they often mimicked the three wise men of the Bible, bearing gifts (usually edible) for the surgeon-child, trying to ingratiate themselves early on in our careers; the bigger gifts were for the practicing surgeons. During those years of surgical training, we young surgeons were useless to them. As surgical trainees, we had no control over our own lives, never mind the decisions a hospital made regarding the purchase of surgical devices. We had no impact on a rep's ability to make money. Only later in our careers as practicing surgeons would we have the power to impact the earning potential of surgical device reps.

During the last several years, access to the operating room by reps has become more restricted by hospitals. Reps are no longer free to roam in and out of a surgeon's operating room, no longer free to show up with a new product for surgeons to look at. In spite of the restrictions, many still have access to the inside of an operating room. Every day, reps diligently watch their surgeons use their products, doing whatever they can to make sure their use goes smoothly.

Most patients undergoing surgery have no idea that a company rep may be in the corner of the operating room, answering questions your surgeon might have about the medical devices being used on you. Contrary to what you may have heard, medical device company reps do not scrub in and physically help surgeons perform surgery. Most often, they are present for technical (or moral) support. Yet there is a surgical procedure (robotic partial knee or hip replacement) where a competent company rep has to be in the room, assisting the surgeon. In this case, the rep is indispensable to the operation, and the surgeon cannot proceed without his or her presence. Some surgical specialties attract more reps to the OR than others. Artificial joint company reps are regularly spotted in operating rooms, watching as orthopedic surgeons perform joint replacement surgery. The artificial joint industry is a highly competitive and lucrative business. Most of these reps are trying to protect their turf. They keep an eye out for the competition while making sure their orthopedic surgeon clients remain satisfied.

Device companies devote significant resources to develop finely tuned sales plans to persuade surgeons to use *their* product. The plan of attack is multifaceted. At the center of the campaign is a rep's ability to sell himself or herself. (In the old days, it was mainly the ability to sell *herself* to the male-dominated profession of surgery; yes, looks counted.) The rep needs you to like him or her. If, on top of that, the surgical device being promoted is adequate and useful, the rest is usually easy. I can attest to this scenario. For years, I was loyal to a device that allowed me to perform minimally invasive colon surgery. This device was more expensive than that of the competition, but I *had to have it*. One day the competition's new rep stopped by to introduce himself and his competing device. He wasn't overbearing, wasn't trying to massage my ego. He respected my decision not to use his product. He was the perfect gentleman and a restrained salesman. Over time, I got to know him better, got to know about his family, his hobbies. My wife and I even had dinner with him and his wife several times. Eventually, I took a liking to him, enough to try his surgical product during one of my operations. Since that time, I have been using his device rather than the one I had been devoted to for years. It also helped that his device was cheaper than the one I had been using.

In the old days, reps had unrestricted expense accounts to spend on surgeons (those days are essentially gone now, thanks to federal laws that largely prohibit device companies from giving "gifts" of any kind to surgeons). Once a rep penetrated a surgeon's office, he or she had an array of weapons to use to get a surgeon "on board," to be an advocate for the product. These weapons were aimed at specific parts of our anatomy, usually the stomach or the brain. Napoleon Bonaparte's observation more than two hundred years ago—"an army marches on its stomach"—applies to the marketing of devices to surgeons. Surgeons (and all physicians for that matter) march on their stomachs. Reps had unlimited funds to bring lunches to surgeons' offices and to take them out to fine restaurants. Once the gastric relationship was fully developed, it could open the door to the operating room. Believe me, these expenditures helped reps develop relationships with surgeons, relationships that allowed them access to the operating room and the opportunity to get their devices used.

Surgical device reps are deftly trained to diagnose what I call the Triple E Syndrome in surgeons: ego, economics, and expertise. I cannot tell you how many times I have heard the words, "I hear you are the best and the busiest thyroid [or colon, spine, joint, or whatever] surgeon in town." This is often followed with, "When you use our device, my company has resources to help market your skills and generate new business." Finally, if you are a special case, you might hear, "Why don't you become an expert consultant for our company? We can train you. You can educate your colleagues on our device. Speak at conferences. Benefit financially." Paying physicians to educate their colleagues and promote products was the norm in the industry for decades. It is only recently, in 2013, that some in the industry are stopping this practice altogether.

Upon the release of a new product, reps dedicate themselves to finding the surgeon equivalent of Moby Dick, the fabled white whale. All reps need is one big "whale" surgeon advocate and *wham!* their product is on operating room shelves. They need the support of that one influential (i.e., busy) surgeon to influence the hospital purchasing geeks. They need that surgeon, a true believer, to infuse the veins of hospital administrators with the "fear and greed" infection that often supplies the motive for purchasing new technology. The fear of losing surgical business to the hospital across town, coupled with the greed of getting into new and greater revenue markets, drives many purchasing decisions.

Medical device companies (along with the pharmaceutical industry) are adept at offering proof of the benefits of their products over lunch. These companies can present their own internal data promoting efficacy, the so-called white papers. These articles, however, are written by surgeons who happen to be paid consultants for the company. These papers look professional on the surface. They present themselves with all the legitimacy of published scientific articles, yet many are never scrutinized or published in peer-reviewed journals. Many are flawed studies and not scientifically conducted to truly analyze the effectiveness of their product when compared to the competition. In addition, companies splatter these articles on their websites to convince the unsuspecting public that their device or technology has legitimacy. Despite these marketing tactics, most surgeons are astute enough not to fall, at least not for all of it. I rarely have the time to scrutinize a scientific article handed to me by a company rep in support of a new device.

Other weapons that reps were able to use in the past included the ability to pay in full for whatever trip, course, or conference remotely connected to an educational need you might have. Those were the good old days when all expenses would be paid—bring your spouse!—no questions asked, and the expensive wine flowed. Today, medical device companies can legally pay for educational trips but within a much stricter set of guidelines.

Unfortunately (or fortunately, depending on whom you ask), the days of surgeons benefiting from the unlimited generosity of the surgical device industry are over. For the last five years, the states and the federal government have passed regulations limiting what company reps can spend on physicians without getting anything in return. For instance, in 2008 the state of Massachusetts passed a law prohibiting pharmaceutical and medical device companies from paying for dinners attended by physicians, regardless of whether an educational component was present. The state also banned all other gifts to physicians as well. For decades, companies sponsored educational dinners for physicians where expert speakers would talk about new treatments or medical devices. I looked forward to attending these talks to learn about the potential of new surgical techniques and to socialize with colleagues. The fact that they were held at a nice restaurant did not dampen my enthusiasm. Did these educational dinners influence my decision to use a specific product inside the operating room? Not at all. They did, however, give me the opportunity to try new restaurants. I miss that.

Apparently, Massachusetts state representatives concluded that my decision to use a specific surgical stapler when resecting a segment of colon or a specific type of hernia mesh had the potential to be influenced by a free filet mignon and a glass of cabernet. As a result, these dinners were banned by new laws. The loss of business to the hotel and restaurant industry in Boston was significant enough for both industries to lobby state representatives hard to overturn the law. In July 2012 the state legislature surprisingly reversed course and voted to do just that. The new law stated that pharmaceutical and medical device companies can pay for "modest meals and refreshments." The word *modest* was to be defined at a later date. In the end, Massachusetts state representatives (after attending a few lobbying dinners, I suspect) came to the startling revelation that physician decision making might not be influenced by a free baked stuffed lobster or tiramisu after all.

In addition to changing the rules about access, over the last few years several states (including my state of Massachusetts) have made it mandatory for pharmaceutical and medical device companies to report annually the amount of money paid to physicians for any reason. This information is then publicly reported on each state's medical board website.

Supporting states' desire for more transparency on monies or gifts physicians receive from private industry, the passage of the Affordable Care Act in 2010 mandated public reporting of payments to physicians. Deep within the pages of the Affordable Care Act is a law requiring all pharmaceutical and medical device companies and group purchasing organizations (GPOs, which act as distributors of medical devices) to publicly report to the government any single payment (or equivalent gift value) of $10 or more made to healthcare providers, primarily physicians. Companies are also required to report payments under $10 if the yearly total value exceeds $100. As mandated by the Physician Payment Sunshine Act, payment information will be posted on the Centers for Medicare & Medicaid Services (CMS) website for public scrutiny. The collection of data started August 1, 2013. Starting in September 2014, you, the public, will be able to see if the general surgeon about to repair your hernia with a new mesh is receiving any money from the manufacturing company. You will be able to find out if the orthopedic surgeon about to replace your left knee owns stock options in the company that manufactures that knee. You will be able to research whether the urologist who has scheduled your robotic prostatectomy is receiving any speaking honoraria from the company that created the robot assisting in removing your prostate gland.

The CMS website will post payments under the physician's name, license number, address, and specialty. The website will also break down the payments into a dozen categories, such as payments for meals, travel, research, speaking honoraria, stock options, dividends received, and consulting services. Before the payments are posted, each physician will have forty-five days to review the accuracy of the data and fifteen more to correct any misinformation. Still, many physicians worry that the posted data will be inaccurate, leaving the public with misconceptions about the nature of their relationships. Many physicians worry also how they might be perceived if a six-figure payment is listed next to their name. Along with payments to physicians, the CMS website will also post payments to teaching institutions from private industry.

The goal of the Physician's Payment Sunshine Act is to make clearer to the public the financial relationships that exist between physicians and private industry. The hope is that potential conflicts of interest will be reduced by increasing transparency. The CMS website's purpose is only to reveal the financial payments received by physicians and other healthcare providers. It is up to the public who view this data to decide its significance. You will have to decide for yourself if there is a potential conflict of interest between your physician and the company writing him a check.

If a person needing surgery is unaware of his or her surgeon's financial relationships with the medical device industry, does that surgeon have an obligation to inform the individual before the operation? Do I have an obligation to disclose my financial relationship with a company that manufactures the mesh I will insert in your abdomen or the robot I might use to remove your gallbladder? If I am an orthopedic surgeon, should I be required to tell you about my financial relationship with the company that manufactures the implant I will use in your knee or hip? The question is controversial in physician circles, and the answer will vary depending on which surgeon you ask. As of today, there are no laws that require doctors (or hospitals, for that matter) to disclose to patients their financial relationship with the pharmaceutical industry before prescribing a drug, or the financial relationship with a medical device company before entering the operating room.

The relationship between surgeons and medical device companies throughout the years has always been one of a symbiotic nature. Surgeons rely on private corporations to develop new instruments, new technologies that allow them to operate in places where no one has gone before. On the other hand, private corporations rely on practicing surgeons to use their devices during surgery so they can turn a profit. The entire field of minimally invasive surgery has its roots in the private practice sector and has flourished as a result of the innovative device inventions born out of the for-profit corporate world. Despite this, some question whether the relationship between surgeons and private industry has become too close, too codependent. The main concern of health policy wonks is the potential for money and gifts to affect clinical decision making in and out of the operating room. Is there an inherent conflict of interest when there is a financial relationship between a medical device company and a surgeon who uses the very devices made by that company? In 2008, the federal government (MedPAC—the Medicare Payments Advisory Commission) looked at this relationship and, as a result, called for a national reporting system listing physicians and industry payments received. In 2009, the Institute of Medicine also looked at the potential for a conflict of interest between physicians and the medical industry and recommended more public transparency regarding gifts and financial relationships. Most recently, in 2012 the Affordable Care Act brought us the Sunshine Act.

How common are financial relationships between physicians/ surgeons and private industry? A *New England Journal of Medicine* study published in 2007 surveyed more than three thousand physicians in six specialties: general surgery, anesthesia, family practice, pediatrics, internal medicine, and cardiology. Ninety-four percent of the physicians reported "relationships" with private industry, while 83 percent reported receiving gifts. Of those surveyed, 35 percent had received reimbursement for educational meetings and trips, while 28 percent reported receiving money for "consulting" services. Of all the specialties, cardiologists benefited the most from these relationships, while specialists (including surgeons) bettered their primary care colleagues.

Another *New England Journal of Medicine* article published in 2013 looked at the distribution of payments to physicians in Massachusetts from 2009 to 2011. Massachusetts is one of a handful of states with laws requiring pharmaceutical and medical device companies to report payments to physicians. During this two-year time frame, $77 million was distributed to physicians around the state, with an average payment of close to $5,000. Within the surgical specialties listed, 61 percent of the urologists surveyed had received payments, compared to 22 percent of general surgeons. Orthopedic surgeons received the highest amount of money per surgeon over the length of the study, with each receiving approximately $18,500. Most of these payments were reported for "services provided" and not actual gifts.

Cardiologists received the most money (just under $8 million during that two-year period), closely followed by orthopedic surgeons, coming in at $7.6 million. General surgeons, like me, came in at number seventeen on the list, receiving just under $1 million. Primary care physicians came in at the very bottom. The most common payment was in the form of food, which is not surprising. The study concluded that medical specialists and surgeons received more payments than primary care physicians, with most of these being listed as nonspecific "compensation for bona fide services." Even the lead author of the study, however, was not able to state exactly what that phrase meant.

Such studies demonstrate that surgeons, because of the nature of the work they do and the revenue they generate for the hospital and the device company, are aggressively targeted by private industry. Consider this: The cost to manufacture an artificial knee joint (over 700,000 of which are used by orthopedic surgeons in this country every year) is $500, yet it is sold to a hospital for over $4,000. Why *wouldn't* orthopedic surgeons be a primary marketing target for joint manufacturing companies? The same can be said for a six-inch by six-inch piece of mesh with a tenfold markup produced by a medical device company, being used hundreds of thousands of times by general surgeons across the country. Medical device companies would not be performing their fiduciary duty to stockholders if they did not market their product to surgeons or financially reward those surgeons for championing their product.

In a 2013 *Wall Street Journal* article titled "Medical Conflicts of Interest Are Dangerous," Dr. Robert Pearl, executive director and CEO of the Permanente Medical Group/Kaiser Permanente, was quoted as making the following (telling) statement:

"For years, pharmaceutical and medical device companies have engaged in a marketing and promotion strategy in which they develop 'consultative' relationships with a large number of doctors, recruiting them to work on behalf of the companies by paying them to use their products—and more important, to promote the products to colleagues. For other doctors who are high users of their products, these companies invite them to attend extravagant dinners and participate as 'faculty' at conferences being held at resort destinations with all expenses paid by the pharmaceutical or medical device manufacturer."

Given the extent of the financial relationship between physicians and private industry, how do physicians themselves view the nature of this relationship? In a study published in *Archives of Surgery* in 2010, an anonymous survey was taken of all specialties regarding attitudes on gifts from private industry. The survey was completed by 590 physicians and medical students, 131 of whom were from surgical specialties. The study revealed that 72 percent found free lunches appropriate, and 25 percent found large gifts appropriate. The study also indicated that surgeons and surgical trainees exhibited more positive attitudes than other specialties toward gifts, reimbursement for travel expenses, and payments for attending lectures. The conclusion was that surgeons, despite the potential for a conflict of interest, continue to exhibit a favorable view toward the marketing tactics (including financial "gifts") of the medical device industry. How do patients feel about a surgeon's financial relationship with a medical device company? A study published in the *Journal of Bone and Joint Surgery* surveyed 252 patients who had knee or hip surgery. Most patients were not worried about a potential conflict of interest between their surgeon and a medical device company, although 63 percent said it was "inappropriate" to receive outright gifts for no reason at all.

That said, other prominent voices in my profession strongly believe that an inherent conflict of interest exists when physicians or surgeons receive payments from companies who manufacture the products they use to treat patients. Many believe that the amount of money being distributed by companies makes it impossible for a physician's clinical treatment decisions to remain sterile, uncontaminated.

Over the last few years, several high-profile cases have shed light on the complicated and potentially dangerous relationship between surgeons and private industry when enormous amounts of money are involved. In 2007, four of the five manufacturers of artificial knees and hips settled a federal lawsuit in which the government alleged they violated anti-kickback laws. According to Christopher J. Christie, the then U.S. attorney in Newark prosecuting the case, "this industry routinely violated anti-kickback statutes by paying physicians for the purpose of exclusively using their products. Prior to our investigation, many orthopedic surgeons in this country made decisions predicated on how much money they could make—choosing which device to implant by going to the highest bidder."

The four joint-making companies paid a total of $310 million to settle the lawsuit without admitting any guilt. What came out in the settlement was the fact that in 2007 the four companies paid close to $200 million to 939 orthopedic surgeons. In 2008, the manufacturers paid $228 million to 526 orthopedic surgeons. No surgeons were charged in the lawsuit.

One of the prominent voices speaking out about the detrimental influence of monies paid to surgeons by private industry is Dr. Steven Nissen, cardiologist and chairman of the department of cardiovascular medicine at the prestigious Cleveland Clinic. Dr. Nissen, in an article in *Medical Economics* in March 2013, stated:

"Physicians acting ethically should have nothing to fear [in regard to the Sunshine Act]. But anybody who says physicians are not influenced is simply not being realistic. Studies have shown over and over again that physicians are influenced."

Dr. Robert Pearl, too, expressed his concern about the effect of private industry payments on a physician's ability to remain unbiased when making treatment decisions. In the *Wall Street Journal* article mentioned earlier in this chapter, Dr. Pearl was quoted as saying:

"Physicians want to believe that their clinical judgment cannot be influenced by these types of partnerships, but medical literature is full of examples of the pernicious impact that gifts and financial arrangements have on treatment decisions, ranging from excess prescribing of more expensive medications to increased use of specific medical devices. Ultimately, these payments inappropriately influence the decisions physicians make, driving up health-care costs."

There may be some truth to what Dr. Pearl and others espouse, certainly the part about driving up healthcare costs. Over ten years ago, I was approached by a major medical device company and offered an opportunity to be a paid consultant for them. At the time, I was using a specific minimally invasive operative technique during colon surgery. It was a technique that other general surgeons who were not adept at minimally invasive colon surgery were becoming interested in because it was easier to learn than older techniques. Also, patients benefited greatly in their recovery. During the operation, I relied on a device that allowed me to place my hand inside the abdomen without making a large incision. I had been using this device for several years, under the radar, because I believed in it. I never received any money for using it, promoting it, or teaching my colleagues how to use it. At the time, I had no financial motives to use it whatsoever. My interest was purely clinical. I was the only surgeon in the region with extensive experience using the device, and I had been gathering patient data on my outcomes.

Several months after I had changed jobs and moved to a different state, the medical device company rep approached me with an offer. His company wanted to give me a contract to work as a consultant. I would be paid for giving lectures and presenting my outcome data. I would also be obligated to go to hospitals in the region, teaching surgeons the new technique using the medical device. I would also be responsible for promoting their product at major medical meetings with all my expenses paid. It was all perfectly legal and commonplace.

How did I feel about being offered a financial contract by a medical device company to educate and promote their product to my colleagues? In the beginning, I was fine with it. I had no conflict of interest in being paid as a consultant because I was already using the product by choice. The device worked well and the technique helped my patients recover faster. Frankly, it felt good to reap some financial reward from an expertise I had labored to perfect and now found in demand. Deep down, I felt I deserved the compensation. My ego felt good because my colleagues now would look to me as *the* expert in the technique. It was also an opportunity get my name out there, and I'd be paid for it. Nothing was going to change my clinical decision making even though I would be reimbursed by the company for the time

I devoted to teaching my colleagues. I was not getting paid to *use* their device. I was also not receiving anything for the *number* of patients I used it on. Plus, I was never told to lie about the benefits of the company's product or the faults of the competition. It felt like a professional, ethical arrangement.

Over the next two years, I continued to be a consultant, proctoring surgical colleagues on minimally invasive techniques using the company's medical device. At the beginning of my third year, the company decided not to renew my contract. No reason was given. I wasn't upset about it and didn't pursue the company for an answer. I suspected I had filled a need the company had at the time to "promote" their product. I also suspected I had outlived my marketing usefulness after two years since I was not a well-known academic surgeon with lengthy biographical credentials. I did not publish papers or have the power to influence great numbers of people; at the time I was proctoring one surgeon. My professional coattails were short. It was time for the company to move on to a more influential surgeon consultant. Time for the company to find someone with a broader ability to influence others. It was also time for me to go back to anonymity.

Looking back on that experience, I have asked myself if getting paid as a consultant by a medical device company influenced my clinical judgment or decision making inside the operating room. The answer is, no, it didn't. What it did do, however, was indirectly make me a promotional agent for their device. As the "expert" giving educational lectures to my colleagues, I was in effect telling them to use the company's product. As the proctoring surgical expert, I was a vehicle muting the competition's cheaper version of the same device. Yet, I justified the money I received because of the work I did to earn it.

I have no doubt the medical device company justified the money they paid me for services rendered because I know how much their sales increased in the region during the two years I was a consultant.

How would you know if your surgeon's motives for using a specific medical device or implant on you are influenced by factors outside pure clinical judgment? You wouldn't. Do you think a surgeon who receives millions of dollars in royalties from a company for helping design a medical device can be totally unbiased in deciding which device to use on his or her patients? I don't. Hospitals also need to do a better job at policing the financial relationships their "busy" surgeons have with medical device companies, and not let their enthusiasm for surgical volume partially blind them. I am a firm believer in getting full public disclosure of all financial ties surgeons may have with the medical device industry before taking a trip to the operating room. At least the Sunshine Act is a step in the right direction, opening the "transparency" window into the operating room a crack. I encourage you to take a look.

8 THE ROBOT WILL SEE YOU NOW

had just finished my last case of the day, removing a colon cancer using a minimally invasive technique, and had made my way to the surgeons' locker room to change. Dr. Jonathan Rye, a gynecologic surgeon who had practiced in the community for the last twenty years, was there changing into street clothes, ready to call it a day, too. Rye had a thriving practice; his reputation as an excellent surgeon had made him well respected among his peers.

"Hey, Jon, you have experience using the robot, don't you?" I asked.

He nodded. "Just finished a case, as a matter of fact. A robotic hysterectomy. My twentieth, I believe."

"What do you think of it? Are there tangible benefits to the patient's recovery compared to what we are already doing?" I really did want to know. *How could a robot's "hands" remove a uterus better than those of a skilled, experienced surgeon? I* opened my locker. "How does it feel to be sitting at a television console in the corner of the operating room, manipulating robotic arms in a patient's abdomen?"

I had not ventured into robotic surgery and wasn't particularly attracted to it. The growing public interest, however, was forcing me to take a serious look at it.

He looked at me, a half smile on his face. "Paul, let me be frank. When I tell a patient I can remove her fibroid uterus using robotic arms and small incisions, she's pretty taken with it. Sounds fabulously state of the art."

And it is. The technology itself is like something out of a *Star Trek* episode.

He continued, "I find that patients are mesmerized when they hear the word *robot*. From an operative standpoint, it is a surgical tour de force. The robotic hand movements are more precise; they have more rotational flexibility. No doubt about it. And the three-dimensional depth perception is better. You can operate with more confidence in small spaces." He was struggling to get his right leg inside his pants. "Plus, I have to tell you, sitting at a console is much easier on my back."

"I bet. So, when it comes to hysterectomy, must be a lot of benefits to using that robot."

"Yes and no." He paused. "Despite the benefits to the surgeon—and I should say 'potential benefits'—to date there is no legitimate data proving patient benefit compared to other minimally invasive techniques. But, you know, it gives me another option. Right now, I have the ability to remove a uterus four different ways." He had finally gotten his other leg inside the pants. "If I open someone up the old-fashioned way," he continued, "she may be in the hospital an extra day. Recovery may take longer. If I use traditional laparoscopic techniques, most of my patients only stay in the hospital overnight, and they do recover faster." He was looking for socks in his locker. "The only real difference between using a robot and the other laparoscopic techniques is the cost." The socks emerged, fuchsia cashmere.

"You thinking about testing the waters, Paul?" He looked up from his sock-tugging. "Surgical robots do not come cheap and are not stress-free."

Several studies have supported Jon's assessment. One study published in *JAMA* in 2013 covered a three-year period and looked at more than 260,000 women undergoing hysterectomy for benign disease. The data revealed the median cost of a robotic-assisted hysterectomy to be $2,000 more than a conventional laparoscopic hysterectomy—*without any difference in patient outcomes* (complication rates, length of hospital stay). The report prompted James T. Breeden, M.D., president of the American Congress of Obstetricians and Gynecologists (the governing organization of gynecologic surgeons in this country), to publish the following statement: "Robotic surgery is not the only or the best minimally invasive approach for hysterectomy. Nor is it the most cost-efficient. It is important to separate the marketing hype from the reality when considering the best surgical approach. . . . There is no good data proving that robotic hysterectomy is even as good as—let alone better—than existing, and far less costly, minimally invasive alternatives."

Hysterectomy is one of the most commonly performed operations in America today, and if the last five years represent a trend, it is going to become increasingly common. Three years ago, fewer than 1 percent of all hysterectomies were performed robotically. Today, that number is close to 10 percent and climbing.

I had to ask. "So why are you doing robotic surgery if there haven't been any legitimate scientific trials proving patient benefits? How can an insurance company justify the added cost?" I could see by the expression on his face that he was eager to confess.

"Let me tell you a story." He sat down in front of his open locker. "Before conventional laparoscopic surgery took off in the nineties, I was removing a uterus one of two ways: through the vagina or an open abdominal cut. As more gynecologic surgeons gained experience with laparoscopic techniques, I learned them to stay competitive." He checked his watch. "But I discovered that laparoscopic meant the patient spent more time under anesthesia. There was a learning curve, greater potential for mistakes. It increased the hospital's costs. And it increased physical stress. On me." He smiled. "Ultimately, laparoscopic technique was not a lot better than what I was already doing. But I decided to add it to my offerings based on the needs of my practice." He pulled on his shirt. "At the time, actually, I wanted to wait. So did a lot of my colleagues."

"What happened? What convinced you?" I wanted to know. He had almost finished dressing, so I knew our conversation was coming to an end.

"Competition. Once a few gyn docs here starting doing laparoscopic hysterectomies . . . I'm sure you remember the ads. You couldn't miss them. Billboards, city buses." He was running a comb through his hair now. "'Surgery without a scar!' A thin, attractive, middle-aged woman pointing to three small Band-Aids on her flat abs." He fiddled with his watch. "I started to lose business, pretty quickly actually. Patients who needed a hysterectomy wanted three tiny incisions. No supportive scientific evidence? Did not matter. Higher cost? Insurance would pay it."

He slammed the locker door shut. "The handwriting was on the wall back then, as it is now. Hey, do you think I wanted to go back and learn robotic surgery at my age? Who needs the stress and the potential for mistakes? I had to, to maintain a viable practice."

A message came over his pager. "Listen, Paul, nice talking with you. I know I'm not telling you anything you don't know. Sometimes, to survive in this business, you have to be flexible." With that, he shook my hand, saying, "Best of luck," as he left.

The da Vinci surgical robotic system was approved for use in general laparoscopic procedures by the Medical Devices Advisory Committee of the Food and Drug Administration (FDA) on June 16, 1999. It was the first of its kind—a robotic device to facilitate minimally invasive general surgery—ever approved by the FDA. Today, the da Vinci Surgical System is the only robotic game in town. It is used for all robotic surgical procedures, except joint replacements, in hospitals across the country. Further approval for gynecologic procedures came in 2005. The manufacturer is a company called Intuitive Surgical. All the company had to do was convince the FDA that its device was safe and as effective as similar technology already being used in the practice of surgery. At the time of approval, the FDA did not require the company to have comprehensive training programs in place for surgeons. It also did not require the company to have a centralized data system to monitor clinical outcomes and complications. Such programs are often designed by the company after approval. In the case of Intuitive Surgical, two years after approval the company shortened its surgeon training requirements in order to hasten the device's use by surgeons. This kind of leeway is very different from the FDA's approval requirements for new pharmaceuticals.

The FDA's Medical Devices Advisory Committee based its approval of the da Vinci robotic system on one study comparing 113 patients who had undergone robotic procedures for gallbladder removal and reflux disease to 132 patients who had undergone traditional minimally invasive surgery. The clinical study took place in Mexico and was not designed to see which approach was better. I suspect the reason the company turned to Mexico was to hasten the study's completion by taking advantage of a less restrictive regulatory environment for human clinical trials. It also cost less to do it outside the United States. The study itself was designed to show only comparable safety and effectiveness to traditional minimally invasive techniques already being used by surgeons. It was not designed to prove superiority over existing surgical approaches because that was not required for approval. Today, based on one small study carried out in another country, the maker of the da Vinci robot surgical system has grown into a two-billion-dollar-revenue-producing giant.

The da Vinci robot is a computerized system of robotic arms and a camera. These are placed inside a body cavity through three or four small surgical incisions or one larger incision, depending on the application. The system's primary use is to assist surgeons performing minimally invasive surgery inside the abdominal cavity. The surgeon performing the surgery sits at a television monitor, manipulating the robotic arms from levers and foot pedals on a console directly in front of him. The robot was invented to be used as an accessory tool for the surgeon to use in the operating room. It does not take the place of a surgeon's skill or make up for a lack of it. It will not make your surgeon a better minimally invasive surgeon just by its presence alone. The robot does not perform surgery on its own. Despite what you may imagine, the robot does not turn a mediocre minimally invasive surgeon into a good one. Without a competent surgeon manipulating the robotic arms, it is nothing more than a dangerous multimillion-dollar piece of equipment.

The benefits to a surgeon of computerized remotely controlled arms with fine fingerlike instruments attached to the ends appear to be many. With traditional minimally invasive surgery, the ability of the human wrist to move in all directions is limited by the technique itself and the rigid instruments used. The human wrist has seven degrees of motion. Traditional minimally invasive surgery instruments have only four degrees. With robotic surgery, the "wrist" at the end of the robotic arm has six degrees of movement, greatly enhancing the surgeon's dexterity. There is also greater flexibility in the robotic hands, significantly more than the fixed movements of conventional laparoscopic instruments. The robotic system gives improved visualization of the operative field compared to traditional laparoscopic surgery. Three-dimensional visualization provides a picture on the monitor that is more "real time" than a traditional laparoscopic television monitor. Depth perception is also improved, which helps a surgeon's hand-eye coordination. Other benefits afforded by the robotic operating system include minimizing a surgeon's natural hand tremor. Another plus: Sitting at a console while operating is better ergonomically for the surgeon than standing, hunching, or leaning over the patient on the operating table for hours.

There is no denying the benefits that robotic arms add to a surgeon's technique. The issue that has yet to be decided is whether these benefits translate into better patient outcomes and justify the cost.

The system has some technical disadvantages. Despite the improved visualization, the actual visual field a surgeon sees is smaller than the view on the larger monitors used during traditional laparoscopic surgery. It takes some time to get used to this reduced visual field. Another disadvantage is the loss of haptic feedback (force and tactile) during robotic surgery. With traditional laparoscopic instruments, a surgeon has the ability to feel surrounding structures, including nearby blood vessels, because he or she has a hand on one end of the instrument. By its nature, robotic surgery does not allow this feedback. A surgeon's hands are on levers at a console and not on the end of the robotic arm. Without the ability to tactilely sense nearby organs, a surgeon loses an important tool that's necessary to avoid getting into trouble.

In the beginning, robotic surgery takes longer than traditional laparoscopic surgery. There is also a surgeon learning curve. Throughout the learning curve, there is an increased risk for complications and poor outcomes. As surgeons progress through this curve, their operating times shorten, their confidence increases, and mistakes become less frequent. Most patients will never know where their surgeon is on this learning curve unless they specifically ask. Proponents of robotic surgery emphasize the shortness of this learning curve as an advantage to the surgeon, but there is no scientific evidence to back that up.

Another growing disadvantage of robotic surgery is the cost. The da Vinci robotic system costs a hospital between $1.5 and $2.2 million to purchase, depending on the model. In addition to that, there is a yearly service contract that ranges from $100,000 to $200,000. The robotic instrument arms themselves have a finite life and have to be replaced periodically, adding thousands of dollars to every operation. Indirect added costs result from longer operating room time and anesthesia services.

No one, proponent or critic, will deny the fact that performing robotic minimally invasive surgery costs more than traditional laparoscopic surgery or open surgery, regardless of the operation. Study after study has shown that using robotics can add approximately 20 percent (anywhere from $2,000 to $4,000) more to an operation. Whether it is removal of a uterus, prostate gland, segment of colon, gallbladder, or urinary bladder, costs increase when a robot is involved. In addition to the study that revealed the higher costs of robotic hysterectomies, a 2008 Swiss study published in *Annals of Surgery* showed the cost of a robotic gallbladder removal to be approximately $2,000 higher than a traditional laparoscopic removal. Johns Hopkins published a study in 2013 in the journal *JAMA Surgery* comparing robotic-assisted, traditional laparoscopic, and open colon operations. The study looked at close to a quarter of a million operations. Its authors concluded there was no difference in outcomes between robotic and traditional laparoscopic, the robot added $3,000 more per operation, and, if universally adopted, robotic-assisted surgery would add billions of dollars to our national healthcare tab.

According to Intuitive Surgical, more than 1.5 million da Vinci robotic procedures have been performed worldwide as of 2014; most (80 percent) were operations to remove diseased prostate glands and uteruses. In 2004, only 15 percent of the ninety thousand prostatectomies (removal of the prostate) performed in this country were carried out with robotic techniques. Today, that number exceeds 80 percent. The number of hysterectomies performed using the robot has increased dramatically over the last three years. As robotic surgery is used to treat more surgical diseases, two definitive statements can be made about its clinical benefits. The first centers on safety. The FDA, prior to approval of robotic surgery in 1999, deemed the robot safe to use on humans. Since then, the consensus within the surgical profession is that robotic surgery *in competent surgical hands* is as safe as traditional laparoscopic surgery.

The second definitive statement that can be made, based on the published data, is that robotic surgery has some patient benefits over traditional open surgery. In the first national analysis of robotic surgery outcomes, published in the *Journal of the American College of Surgeons* in 2012, the authors retrospectively looked at 368,000 patients who underwent different types of surgery over a fourteen-month period and concluded that robotic surgery patients had a shorter hospital stay and had less chance of dying than open surgery patients. The final conclusion of the study also showed a higher median cost of each robotic operation when compared to an open procedure. Other studies since then have also supported the benefits of robotic surgery over open surgery. One study published in the *Annals of Thoracic Surgery* in October 2013 revealed robotic-assisted lung surgery to have lower complications, death rates, and shorter hospital stays when compared to open lung surgery.

The surgical community was not surprised by these findings, given the fact that robotic surgery is minimally invasive by nature. Minimally invasive surgery, using conventional laparoscopic instruments, has been around since the late 1980s. It offers well-documented clinical benefits to patients when compared with traditional open surgery. Regardless of whether there is a robot or human manipulating the surgical instruments, the benefits of a decreased hospital stay and quicker recovery (not to mention smaller incisions and less postoperative pain) are common to both. This point is also supported by a study published in the journal *Urology* in 2013. Here, the authors compared the outcomes of more than 4,000 minimally invasive (robotic and traditional laparoscopic) prostate operations to 1,280 open procedures over a five-year time period. They concluded that the minimally invasive approach (combined robotic and laparoscopic) was associated with a decreased length of stay, fewer complications, and a decreased risk of dying. The authors, unfortunately, did not separate the data produced by the robotic operations from the traditional laparoscopic operations in the study. In order to know which technique had the greater influence on patient outcomes, that information is needed.

In light of this data, the question has to be raised: Are the added patient benefits afforded by robotic surgery over open surgery due to the "minimally invasive" component (which has been around for over two decades) and not the actual robot component? The answer depends on whom you ask.

Thousands of studies have been published on robotic surgery,

but to date there have been no large-scale, prospective, randomized trials comparing traditional laparoscopic operations head-
to-head with robotic operations. In the eyes of the scientific
world, the two words that legitimize a study's results are *prospective* and *randomized*, meaning that patient variables that
might prejudice results are removed. Without these two words, a
study's claims about which technique is better must be digested
with a grain of salt. Add the terms *large scale* and *double-
blinded* to the study and the results take on further credibility.
Anyone can design a study, and make it look official, to fit their
needs. Like two opposing lawyers arguing a case, the medical
literature is full of studies supporting differing points of view.
When it comes to truly determining the benefits of robotic surgery over what most traditional laparoscopic surgeons are
already doing, what's needed is a properly run large-scale, randomized, prospective study. Only then can surgeons, insurance
companies, and society decide whether the increased costs of
robotic surgery are justified. This kind of data is also what is
needed for the company that manufactures the da Vinci robotic
surgical system to silence its critics.

Unfortunately, such a study may never be done. The FDA felt
it wasn't necessary and gave the company its stamp of approval
on the use of its robot. In the minutes of the June 1999 FDA
panel meeting that approved the da Vinci robot, "some panel
concern was expressed over the advisability of approving costly
new technologies without measurable benefit, but it was noted
that by regulation, the basis for device approval rests upon safety
and equivalence, not cost considerations."

A large study comparing robotic to traditional laparoscopic
surgery would also be very costly to carry out and would take

years to complete. (It might also be impossible to find patients to participate.) But why would the company that manufactures the da Vinci robot want to participate? Why would it want to kill the cash cow?

At the moment, there is no financial incentive for Intuitive Surgical to carry out such a study because hospitals are buying their robots and surgeons are using them. In addition, there is no competition on the horizon. A growing number of traditional laparoscopic surgeons are now beginning to dip their surgical toes in the robotic waters. Whatever their motivations may be, they are doing so despite the lack of legitimate clinical data showing its cost-effectiveness over what they already know how to do. Interestingly, this phenomenon of the technology getting ahead of the scientific data occurred at the beginning of the laparoscopic era in the early 1990s. Back then, the outcome benefits of laparoscopic surgery over traditional open surgery were obvious to the naked eye. Although visually a tour de force, robotic-assisted surgery has not passed the outcome eye test.

One of the few prospective, randomized studies that compared robotic to traditional laparoscopic hysterectomy was published in May 2013 in the *American Journal of Obstetrics and Gynecology*. It looked at complication rates, length of stay, postoperative pain, and operative times for both techniques. After the analysis, the authors found no difference in outcomes. The only observed difference was that a robotic-assisted hysterectomy took longer to perform than a conventional laparoscopic procedure. The study did not analyze costs.

While there is scientific criticism regarding Intuitive Surgical's inability to justify the costs a robotic system adds to an operation, it seems to be falling on deaf ears. More than 1,500 hospitals in this country have at least one da Vinci robot. The number of robotic procedures has risen approximately 25 percent a year for the last several years. The manufacturer is eyeing new markets, trying to persuade more surgeons to use their robot. As I write this, the company is looking to expand use of the robot to heart and spine procedures. The lack of legitimate large-scale clinical trials proving cost-efficient superiority does not seem to be dampening robotic fever.

Since its initial public offering on the NASDAQ stock exchange in 2000 at $9 per share, Intuitive Surgical's stock had passed the $500-per-share price and now has retreated because of slowing future growth. Along the way, this Silicon Valley–based company has solidified its monopolistic position in the surgical robot space by purchasing competing companies. One of those companies was in the process of suing Intuitive Surgical for patent infringement when it mysteriously decided to be bought out. From 2008 to 2013, Intuitive Surgical experienced incredible growth. Its revenue from sales and maintenance fees from the da Vinci robot increased from $600 million to over $2 billion. However, the company experienced some strong financial headwinds in 2014 with its seeing decreasing sales to hospitals, facing continued criticisms about cost, feeling the full effects of the Affordable Care Act, having to recall faulty equipment causing harm to patients, getting investigated by the FDA, having to answer to the increasing rate of robotic injuries to patients, and subsequently addressing lawsuits from those injuries.

Yes, robotic surgery appears to be as safe as traditional laparoscopic surgery. But it costs more without adding any proven benefits yet. Why, then, is your gynecologist, urologist, or general surgeon so eager to say, "You are a candidate for robotic surgery." *Marketing.* Dr. John Mulhall, a urologist performing prostate cancer surgery at Memorial Sloan Kettering Cancer Center in New York, was recently quoted in a Bloomberg News business article on robotic surgery, saying, ". . . if there was a Nobel Prize for marketing, it would go to Intuitive Surgical."

When the corporate heads at Intuitive Surgical developed a plan to crack the minimally invasive surgery market, they were brilliant to recognize the two operations where the da Vinci robot would have the most impact with surgeons. The first, and probably the most significant in terms of the company's early financial growth, is the radical prostatectomy (removal of the prostate gland). Prior to the explosion in minimally invasive surgery in the 1990s, urologists had been removing prostate glands the old-fashioned way. It involved a large incision and several days in the hospital. In capable hands, complications were minimized and outcomes good. When minimally invasive surgery became commonplace, many urologists attempted to apply these techniques to their most common operation, the prostatectomy. They saw the benefits of minimally invasive surgery on other patients and hoped to see it translate to their own.

Traditional minimally invasive removal of the prostate gland never become popular with urologists. For those persistent urologists who eventually perfected the technique, their patients did benefit from smaller incisions and less time in the hospital. Most, however, found it a difficult operation to learn. Part of the reason was that the minimally invasive instruments available did not enhance their skills. In addition, urologists found that they required hundreds of operations in experience to get to a point where their confidence level was acceptable. Many just did not have the time for it because the operation markedly increased their operative times, not to mention that complications were common during the learning curve and outcomes compromised.

Prolonged operating times, complications, poor outcomes, and learning curves do not sit well with surgeons, especially those in private practice. These things bring on more stress, whispers of incompetence, and less income. Not a good combination. The bottom line: Most urologists who tried performing traditional laparoscopic prostatectomies soon realized the operation was not worth the effort.

As one of my urology colleagues put it, "Why should I spend three hours struggling to take out a prostate gland through four small incisions, increasing the risk of complications, when I can do it in less than an hour with a bigger incision and much more confidence? I get paid the same amount and my patients do just as well, if not better, in the end." As soon as most practicing urologists began to abandon the minimally invasive approach, the marketing pressures to compete for patients miraculously dissipated.

Intuitive Surgical knew it would have a difficult time justifying the cost of the da Vinci robot if it pushed for a broader application, encroaching on operations where traditional laparoscopic surgery had been making a difference for years. Their approach was to take one piece of the surgical pie at a time. Early on, most other surgeons saw no obvious difference between the patient benefits that robotic and traditional laparoscopic surgery brought. For urologists, the market was ripe. Urologists were primed for a new technique to come along and assist them in performing prostatectomies. Never, though, did they think it would arrive in the form of a robot. The da Vinci robotic system allowed urologists to overcome the previous difficulties they had removing a prostate with minimally invasive technique.

Now that the company had found its target, it had to figure out a way to maximize its marketing potential. Since most prostatectomies were still being done by traditional open surgery, the company focused its marketing efforts on the comparison of robotic prostate surgery to traditional open surgery. Private practice surgeons were listening, excited about adding a new surgical weapon to the arsenal. Hospitals were eager for a competitive edge with new technology, too. The company was smart to avoid direct comparison with traditional laparoscopic surgery, a battle it could not win. With the unsuspecting help of urologists, Intuitive Surgical was able to get a big robotic foot in the operating room door of hospitals. Once inside, the company would have the opportunity to speak forcefully into a hospital CEO's bad ear about the robot's marketing benefits over open prostate surgery. It would also have the opportunity to whisper into the same CEO's good ear about the potential for financial gain if other surgeons got on board.

What came next was the opportunity to convince urologists that it was worth their while to start performing robotic prostatectomies. The company had to show data supporting the procedure's benefits over open surgery while minimizing the added costs. With all the studies published on the use of robotic prostate surgery, the consensus is that there *are* potential patient benefits when compared to traditional open surgery. Robotic prostatectomy does appear to be associated with less blood loss or a decreased transfusion rate, less postoperative pain, and maybe a shorter stay in the hospital when compared to open prostatectomy. But much of this consensus was arrived at from studies that were not ideally scientifically designed. And there is *no* data supporting any differences in outcomes for the second and third most important considerations for men (the first being cancer-free): urinary incontinence and erectile dysfunction.

As its marketing machine began to churn, Intuitive Surgical developed a three-pronged approach to selling the da Vinci robotic system. The first and most important target was the surgeon, followed by the hospital, and then the public. Intuitive was one of the first companies ever to market directly to consumers of surgical care, as well as to the providers of it. As company reps began to call on urologists, they accentuated the benefits a robot could bring to men undergoing prostate surgery. They also argued that learning robotic surgery was easy and could be mastered in a short period of time. There were also whispers the robot would make it easier for surgeons who lacked the confidence or skill to finally learn minimally invasive techniques. Could the cold steel of the robotic arms take a surgeon "to the next level"? The company reassured surgeons that it would train them adequately once they were on board, regardless of their baseline surgical skills. All of this is now being challenged by the existence of ongoing multiple lawsuits brought by harmed patients currently making their way through the legal system.

For the surgeons willing to listen, the company reps appealed to their desires to increase business while simultaneously leaving the competition in the dust. These were the surgeons who, once converted, needed to persuade their hospital administrators to write a check for a da Vinci robot. While the new robotic champions were persuading hospital administrators, the company reps were offering to assist the hospitals in their marketing campaigns.

While all this persuasion was going on, the company was directly marketing its robot to the public with billboards depicting beautiful people embracing a futuristic surgical robot. This all put more pressure on surgeons to join the vanguard. It was smart for Intuitive to blanket traditional and social media with marketing extolling the technological wonders of robotic surgery. As consumers were convinced of the surgical healing powers of the robot, more people were walking into surgeons' offices wanting their organs removed by "virtually scarless" techniques. Surgeons were forced to choose between what their scientific hearts told them and what their business minds worried about.

The true believers had no problem supporting the company line, with assistance from glossy company brochures telling a story that sounds almost too good to be true. The benefits of robotic surgery listed in the company's free brochures sound incredibly familiar to surgeons who have been performing less costly, traditional laparoscopic surgery for years. One study, published in *Archives of Surgery* in 2011, referenced in the slick marketing literature (in fine print at the bottom), done at a Veterans Administration hospital, was led by two paid consultants for Intuitive Surgical. The study looked at clinical data from robotic cholecystectomy (removal of the gallbladder) performed on nine VA patients. It compared it to data obtained from ten traditional laparoscopic operations. This very small study concluded, *based on only nine operations*, that robotic cholecystectomy was "feasible and comparable with standard laparoscopic cholecystectomy." That was all. No other information regarding patient benefits came out of that study. Nevertheless, Intuitive Surgical was not shy about claiming numerous patient benefits in large print.

The company's marketing plan was devised to pressure all the parties involved to jump in or get left behind. An American Hospital Association marketing survey concluded that hospitals in regions where other hospitals had a robot were more likely to purchase one as well. Not surprisingly, once a robot was purchased, the number of prostatectomies performed at that hospital increased 30 percent.

Urologists have given the robot their seal of approval, as evidenced by the rapid rise in robotic prostatectomies in this country. As a result, more hospitals have invested in the da Vinci robotic surgical system. Almost 25 percent of American hospitals have one sitting in one of their operating rooms. Some are being put to work by surgeons, while others are collecting dust. Along with the large up-front and ongoing costs, every hospital has to train its own special team to assist in robotic surgery, adding a human resource cost to offering robotic surgery.

Once a robot arrives in an operating room, a hospital is pressured by its elephant-size footprint to find ways to pay for its added costs. Many are unable to do so. Some never have an actual business plan in place. They hope that, with the help of the company, more surgeons will be enamored with the technology, pulled in by the gravitational forces of its marketing or pressured by public demand. But hospitals today lose thousands of dollars every time a robotic arm enters a person's abdomen. Some understand the unfavorable economics up front. It doesn't, however, stop them from writing out the $1.5 million check.

To date, insurance companies and Medicare reimburse a hospital the same amount of money for a traditional laparoscopic procedure as for a robotic procedure. Surgeons performing robotic surgery get reimbursed roughly the same amount of

money whether an organ is removed using traditional laparoscopic techniques or the robot. Hospitals can inflate the charges
for a robotic operation, akin to what they can do for a traditional
laparoscopic hernia repair or a piece of hernia mesh. Third-
party reimbursements, however, will not increase.

Once a hospital has a surgical robot crouched in an operating room corner, it cannot be allowed to collect dust. Hospitals
feel a financial pressure to keep their robots employed. Surgeons
under hospital employment may also feel pressure to perform
robotic surgery or risk being replaced by someone who can.
Intuitive Surgical knows how to take full advantage of the
change in operating room dynamics when their robot has landed.

Soon, hospitals have to find more work for their robots,
broaden its applications to balance the cost. The manufacturer
of the da Vinci robot was all too eager to encourage hospitals to
recruit robotic surgeons, increase their robotic caseload, and
market their new technology to surrounding communities. Consequently, the next group of surgeons lured by the advantages of
robotic surgery were the gynecologists. Gynecologic surgeons,
like urologists, were not satisfied with the limitations of traditional laparoscopic techniques when performing certain operations. In particular, when it came to removing a woman's uterus,
traditional minimally invasive laparoscopic surgery hadn't become
the norm as with other surgical procedures. Laparoscopic hysterectomy was difficult to learn, was physically demanding on
the surgeon, and took longer, and many patients were simply not
candidates for it. Shortcomings notwithstanding, laparoscopic
hysterectomy did become more popular with surgeons as time
went on. Most gynecologists I know, if they had their druthers,
would have continued to remove a uterus using traditional open

techniques. So a gap existed in this surgical market, and the makers of the da Vinci robot were happy to fill it. It was a perfect storm. Hospitals could increase their robotic operations beyond the prostatectomy. Gynecologists would be able to offer robotic surgery to women and become more marketable, while the company expanded its market share. As Dr. Myriam Curet, surgeon and chief medical advisor for Intuitive Surgical, stated in an interview published in the *Wall Street Journal* in 2013, "We did not develop the robot to compete with laparoscopic surgery. We developed the robot to bring the benefits of minimally invasive surgery to more women." Unfortunately, any clarity this statement might bring only gets lost when translated by the marketing department.

Up until Intuitive Surgical's marketing blitz, most hysterectomies (70 percent) were performed by traditional open methods. Over the last several years, despite the increased cost and lack of superiority when compared to traditional laparoscopic surgery, the number of robotic hysterectomies has continued to climb. In a randomized trial published in the journal *Obstetrics and Gynecology* in 2013, the authors compared traditional laparoscopic to robotic hysterectomy in sixty-two cases. Both techniques were safe. No difference in clinical outcomes was observed. Robotic hysterectomy did require a significantly longer time to complete. According to the lead author, Dr. Marie Paraiso of the Cleveland Clinic, "Robotic surgery does help me when I have to go really deep in the pelvis or use a lot of sutures. But we haven't really defined which patients it helps most and it's never been shown to be cost-effective."

Still, the number of robotic hysterectomies increased by 26 percent in 2012 while the number of robotic prostatectomies decreased by 15 percent. It appears the use of the surgical robot by urologists may have plateaued. The robotic baton seems to have been passed to the gynecologic surgeon, with the general surgeon next in line.

What is fascinating regarding the evolution in use of the da Vinci robot for intra-abdominal surgery is the circle it has traveled. It was initially approved by the FDA based on a study evaluating its effectiveness and safety for removing gallbladders and treating gastroesophageal reflux. Once approved, I believe the manufacturer intended to introduce it to traditional laparoscopic general surgeons who perform surgery inside the abdominal cavity. Early on, however, the technology did not appeal to general surgeons. About eleven years ago, I was briefly employed by a large academic teaching institution in Boston. It had purchased a da Vinci robot that was gathering dust from lack of use. I was offered the opportunity to "play" with the robot in my spare time. I politely declined. I had no interest; traditional laparoscopic surgery satisfied all my professional needs. I soon learned that many of my colleagues felt the same way.

How times have changed. Today, more and more general surgeons are looking at what robotic surgery can do for their practice (first), hospital (second), and patients (third). They have witnessed the marketing effects on patient volume for urologists and gynecologists. Not surprisingly, more and more hospitals are encouraging general surgeons as well as cardiac and spine surgeons to take another look at robotic surgery. As you would expect, the manufacturer of the da Vinci robot continues to encourage hospitals to expand their robotic markets and will make available to them specific "surgical rep" teams to assist any way they can.

Since the birth of the da Vinci robotic system, the manufacturer has been in what I call a "honeymoon" period of clinical and financial growth. There are reasons for this. On the clinical side, studies supporting the safety and effectiveness of robotic surgery are growing in number. The studies behind the claims of its benefits over traditional open surgery are gaining some credence within the surgical community. The studies comparing robotic surgery to traditional laparoscopic surgery are also beginning to trickle out. So far the general consensus is: no outcome or cost advantage to robotic surgery. However, a recent (2014) study published in the *Journal of Minimally Invasive Gynecology* did show an outcome advantage to robotic-assisted surgery when compared to a traditional laparoscopic procedure after analyzing 2,500 hysterectomy operations. Despite this preliminary study, and the fact that the author is a paid consultant for the company that makes the da Vinci robot, many questions remain unanswered.

In light of this data, it *is* difficult to justify its routine use based on cost. Nevertheless, the number of robotic operations increases every year in this country. Within the next five years, the worldwide market for robotic surgery is projected at more than $20 billion.

The numbers will continue to increase because surgeons will continue to be enamored with technology, not only in this country but throughout the world. They will also recognize the publicity a surgical robot can bring to their practice. Hospitals, once they invest in the da Vinci robot, will continue to encourage their surgeons to learn the technology. The manufacturer will continue to encourage the broadening of its applications. The company will continue to pay its "consultant" surgeons $2,000 to $3,000 per case to go to hospitals and proctor surgeons interested in learning robotic surgery. It will also continue to write a check to consultant surgeons every time another surgeon watches them do a robotic operation. It will continue to offer hospitals financial incentives to generate more robotic business, despite the money lost on each case. All of it will continue despite the lack of large-scale clinical trials designed to see if the claimed benefits of robotic surgery are true and justify its long-term cost. Throughout it all, factors outside the operating room will continue to drive the popularity of robotic surgery.

With no real competition on the horizon, Intuitive Surgical is free to market itself to surgeons, hospitals, and the public as it wishes. With no large-scale, scientifically designed clinical studies refuting its marketing claims, the company is in a position to control its message and to define the applications of its product to surgeons, hospitals, and the public. During these halcyon days, the company continues to educate hospitals on how to maximize their returns with the robot. It continues to promote its robotic surgeons in the communities where they practice without revealing much about their individual operative experience. (The company leaves that discretion up to each individual surgeon.) Finally, it continues to influence the public via the Internet. Its visually stunning, futuristic website is an impressive marketing vehicle. As you browse through it, you are left with the impression that maybe only their robot is necessary to perform your surgery. If you happen to have a problem finding a robotic surgeon, the company's website will direct you to one in your community, without conveniently mentioning that surgeon's robotic experience or clinical outcomes.

This halo effect is working, too, for hospitals that purchase the da Vinci robot. A study published in 2012 in the *American*

Journal of Obstetrics and Gynecology looked at the websites of 432 hospitals in Florida. Forty-four percent (192) contained marketing information on the use of the robot in gynecologic surgery. More than 75 percent of those with robotic marketing information on their websites made favorable statements supporting its use, without citing any scientific studies. Many also stated it was "the best surgical approach" without offering any evidence. Fewer than 4 percent of the hospital websites mentioned complication rates, increased costs, or increased operating times associated with robotic surgery. The authors concluded that "much of the content is not based on high-quality data and can be misleading."

The manufacturer of the da Vinci robot is enjoying a financial heyday because it is in a position to charge hospitals whatever it wants for its goods and services. With the dearth of competition, Intuitive Surgical can pressure hospitals into becoming more reliant on their products and future upgrades. The company has the time to convince surgeons and hospitals that they need to purchase the newest attachment in order to stay competitive in the robotic surgery market. If a cheaper competitor does materialize, hospitals will be too deeply invested in the da Vinci product line to even think about changing. Once hospitals and surgeons become absorbed in the Intuitive Surgical culture, it can be difficult to escape its cult influence. I call this the "Apple phenomenon," the iPhone being the surgical equivalent of the da Vinci robot—you *have* to have it or your credibility is questioned. Once you purchase and incorporate the iPhone into your everyday life, it is hard to live without it. The technology becomes addictive. Its applications define you. When it all falls in line, the technology holds you hostage. It has you waiting in line to purchase the next generation da Vinci/iPhone because you must have it. Intuitive Surgical knows this and obliged in 2014 by introducing its first major upgrade to the original robot. It is called the da Vinci Xi, and it costs close to $2 million. The only problem for hospitals who spent close to $2 million on the original robot is that the old one is not compatible with the upgrade. If hospitals want the new, improved robot, they have to pay up another $2 million.

As more robotic operations are performed over the next five years, the surgical profession will continue to fine-tune the robot's clinical benefits and applications. Some inexperienced surgeons, wanting to increase the number of robotic operations they perform, will lower their diagnostic threshold for removing gallbladders. This could lead to unnecessary operations and unnecessary complications. The same trend was seen when traditional laparoscopic surgery became popular. In a study published in *BMC Surgery* (an online journal) in 2013, in which the authors looked at over 800 patients who underwent a traditional laparoscopic gallbladder removal from 1999 to 2008, it was found that 21 percent (160 patients) had their gallbladder removed for no apparent reason.

As with any new surgical technology, as more patients become exposed to it, poor outcomes increase and inherent defects become unearthed. Surgeons saw this phenomenon when traditional laparoscopic surgery first became popular in the 1990s. As more surgeons learned the new techniques, there was a rise in unique complications and deaths. Surgeons were cutting common bile ducts or accidentally creating holes in patients' intestines during routine laparoscopic gallbladder surgery at alarming rates. Most of these mishaps were the fault of inexperienced surgeons and not the fault of the new technology. In May 2013 the manufacturer of the da Vinci robot issued an "Urgent Medical Device Warning" on potential problems with its robotic arms during surgery that could cause injury. The crux of the problem: cracks in the insulation surrounding the ends of the robotic arms. When scissor electric cautery was used to coagulate blood vessels, an arc of electric current would escape and burn nearby organs. Much of this was out of the sight of the surgeon. Unfortunately, the damage would only manifest several days after surgery in the form of a perforated bowel. Many patients had to be taken back to the operating room. Some even died.

According to the FDA in the warning letter sent to the company in July 2013, the company had known about the increase in adverse event reports or AERs (patient burns from robot malfunction) for almost two years before it acknowledged the problem. From 2011 to 2012, the number of reported AERs including patient deaths associated with the da Vinci robotic system increased 34 percent, while the number of operations increased 26 percent. In November 2013, the company sent out an "urgent medical recall letter" to its customer hospitals warning that the robotic arms could malfunction in the middle of an operation. The FDA recently cleared the company of any failure to report violations listed in their 2013 warning letter. The number of lawsuits against the company by patients claiming their product is unsafe and that surgeons are inadequately trained has also increased. Some, such as Johns Hopkins surgeon researcher Dr. Marty Makary, have suggested the real percentage may be even higher but has been underreported. I suspect that is the case. It is a survival instinct for surgeons and hospitals to underreport complications, especially those that may slow the momentum of a new technology.

One of those reported adverse events occurred with a patient of mine I shall call Mr. Ardmore. He was a sixty-one-year-old father of three who had undergone a robotic prostatectomy for newly diagnosed prostate cancer. The operation seemed to have gone well until three days into his recovery, when he became very ill. I was called to see him. After laying my hands on his exquisitely tender abdomen, I knew immediately he needed to go back to the operating room. Mr. Ardmore had a perforated intestine, and the damage had occurred during his robotic prostatectomy. I was forced to open his abdomen, wash out his infection, and remove a foot-long segment of small intestine. After several more operations, abscess drainages, and months in the hospital, he was finally able to return home. Was the perforation caused by a burn from electricity escaping the robotic arm, or was it surgeon error? It was impossible to determine, but the final pathology on the segment of intestine I removed suggested the former.

Invariably, as surgeons learn new techniques there must be a learning curve; that's how we gain experience. It is during this learning curve that most surgeon mishaps and complications occur. Learning how to operate with the da Vinci robot is no exception. There is no good, scientific data to indicate the number of robotic operations necessary to become an expert. One of my urology colleagues who performs robotic surgery put it this way: "It takes at least fifty robotic prostatectomies to feel safe performing the procedure. It may take another two hundred to become proficient at doing it. Beyond that, it is anybody's guess how many robotic operations a surgeon needs to do to be called an expert. Some say it may even be in the thousands."

There is no nationwide professional standardization for credentialing surgeons to perform robotic surgery. Hospitals today are granting privileges for robotic surgery to surgeons who have attended a weekend course taught by the robot's manufacturer. It includes operating on a pig and some online training. Once the course is complete, surgeons have to be proctored by an experienced robotic surgeon for a small number of cases, generally from five to ten operations. After that, they are on their own, regardless of how confident they feel.

It will take many years before definitive scientific data can prove that robotic surgery results in better patient outcomes and can therefore justify its cost. In the meantime, more and more hospitals are investing in robotic systems, giving more and more surgeons the opportunity to use them and leaving me with more questions. Should all surgeons be allowed to use the da Vinci robot—given the learning curve, the potential for complications, and the reality that most surgeons will never do enough robotic operations in their professional lifetimes to become experts? The fact is, many robotic operations are being done by "low-volume surgeons." As I mentioned earlier, low-volume surgeons tend to have worse outcomes and generate higher costs than high-volume surgeons. Hospitals today need to develop strict clinical criteria for using the robot on patients, and the surgical profession needs to develop a vigilant oversight program to follow outcome and complication trends. Surgeons like Dr. Marty Makary, author of *Unaccountable: What Hospitals Won't*

Tell You and How Transparency Can Revolutionize Health Care, have called for a national database registry to monitor robotic surgeons' experience, clinical outcomes, complications, and costs.

Young surgeons in training are being exposed to the technologic uniqueness of robotic surgery. Many are embracing it like they embrace most new technologies. I wonder this: If the enthusiasm over robotic surgery continues, will the next generation of surgeons gain enough experience during their training to perform traditional open surgery? Some of the data coming out now says no. Will they even know what a scalpel handle or a live organ feels like in their hands? Will they feel competent enough to get their hands dirty with blood or stool when forced to leave the comforts of the robotic console chair and emergently open an abdomen?

I worry that too much reliance on new surgical technology in the operating room has the potential to lull surgeons into a false sense of complacency and make them feel even more detached from their patients. Between a surgeon sitting at a television console, manipulating levers inside the operating room without actually laying a hand on you, and "physician extenders" caring for you outside the operating room, does the bond between patient and surgeon get diluted even further? Old-fashioned clinical judgment, the fading art of medicine shaped by the blood, sweat, and tears of experience, may be supplanted by robotic fever. As more surgeons transfer their skills to a robot, what will they have left? Will the steady reliance on robotic technology ultimately transform the human surgeon behind the controls into a robot as well? In the future, will the robot surgeon be training the human surgeon to operate? Will robots take over and, in a *Terminator*-like scenario, eliminate the need for a human surgeon in the operating room?

Robot technology does make it easier for some surgeons to perform some complex minimally invasive operations, and robotic-assisted surgery has advantages over traditional, open surgery. There is no denying the higher costs robotic surgery brings into the operating room. There is also no denying the unique marketing fervor the manufacturer brings to the job of promoting its technology. Which leaves me wondering, *Is robotic surgery just having its fifteen expensive minutes of fame, or is it a technological black swan that will revolutionize the way all surgery is done in the future?* Time will tell.

In the meantime, my assistant will continue to step into the waiting room at my practice and say to my next appointment, "The doctor, not the robot, will see you now."

9 OBAMACARE, MEDICARE, AND THE FUTURE OF YOUR HEALTHCARE

How do my incisions look?" Mrs. Jansson was in my office for a follow-up visit. I had removed her acutely inflamed gallbladder two weeks earlier, shortly after she had arrived at the emergency room, very sick, with a serious infection from gallstones. At the time of her operation, her gallbladder was partly gangrenous. Luckily, she did well after her surgery despite having several comorbidities such as atrial fibrillation, high blood pressure, and coronary artery disease, all of which put her at risk for problems after any operation.

"They're healing nicely," I answered. The four small laparoscopic incisions still had some bruising around them, but nothing out of the ordinary. I was thankful to have dodged a bullet with her; I'd gotten her out of the hospital without any serious complications.

Six months prior to showing up in the emergency room with a gangrenous gallbladder, Mrs. Jansson had lost her health insurance when her employer decided to drop its coverage. She had no choice but to go to her state's health exchange marketplace, set up as a result of the Affordable Care Act, to obtain a health insurance plan. On the exchange, she was able to find an insurance plan that fit her budget, but the coverage benefits were less comprehensive than her previous plan. In addition, she had to drop her primary care physician (PCP) because he was not in her new network plan. Once she located a primary care physician in her coverage's network, it took another several months to get an appointment. All this time, she continued to have intermittent abdominal pain from her gallstones. When she finally got in to see the primary care physician to tell him about her pain, he was reluctant to send her to see a surgeon. He thought it could have been her stomach and wanted to "just watch things for now, see if we can avoid surgery." Why did he wait so long? If she had been referred to a surgeon for a consultation earlier, an ER visit and emergency surgery could have been avoided. Both are expensive, inefficient ways to use healthcare, not to mention dangerous to the patient.

Finally, her new PCP referred her to a surgeon. But Mrs. Jansson didn't like him. He spent about five minutes talking with her, looking at his tablet computer screen the whole time, typing in her health information. He barely examined her and at the end of the visit decided to "just keep watching things." He told her she was too high risk and that he wanted to wait.

The next week, Mrs. Jansson asked her primary care physician to refer her to the surgical group across town for a second opinion. She had heard good things about their work from a friend who worked at the hospital. The problem was, this was an independent surgical group and not in her insurance's network. If she went to see one of these surgeons, she would have to pay a higher co-pay and more money out of pocket if surgery was needed. There was another surgical group in her network in the next town over, but she would have to get on the highway and travel twenty minutes for an office visit. It was not an ideal situation.

Mrs. Jansson's primary care physician and the surgeon to whom he'd referred her were both employed by the local hospital. The physician group, along with their hospital affiliation, were members of an accountable care organization (ACO). All three worked together to deliver healthcare to their patient members and all were financially linked. An accountable care organization is an integrated system of physicians (primary care and specialists) and hospitals working together to care for their patients. In regard to the Medicare population, the federal government's plan is to reimburse each ACO a lump sum of money, based on its patient population, at the beginning of the year. The ACO will be responsible for using that reimbursement money to care for its Medicare population. It will have total control over how that money is spent in the delivery of healthcare. The federal government will financially encourage the ACO to practice quality medicine. If the ACO runs out of money, it (and its physician members) may be at a financial risk. If, on the other hand, quality medicine is practiced and there is money left over, the surplus can be shared among the ACO's physician members as bonuses.

As a key component of the Affordable Care Act, the formation of ACOs is being "urged" by the federal government with the goal of delivering cost-efficient, quality medical care. In particular, ACOs are intended to rein in Medicare spending by holding hospital systems and physicians accountable for the care they deliver to that population. So far, the ACO experiment has received mixed reviews. A 2014 study published in *JAMA Surgery* looked at Medicare data over a two-year period to see if pilot integrated delivery systems (the generic term for accountable care organizations) decreased costs and improved surgical quality when compared to nonintegrated delivery systems. The study found no differences in surgical quality and cost savings between the two entities.

With the birth of the ACO when the Affordable Care Act was signed into law, some in the medical profession thought they had traveled back in time to the 1990s and the days of managed care and health maintenance organizations (HMOs). It was as if the HMO had risen from the dead, reincarnated as an ACO, ready to relive the horrors of the era of managed care. These horrors included rationing or withholding care in the name of cost, diminished physician choice, and poor-quality care overall. Does the word *capitation* bring back any memories? Many a surgeon's income decreased during those times because primary care physicians were reluctant to send their patients for elective surgery because of the cost. Remember the "gatekeeper" approach? The gatekeeper was your primary care physician, the person who exerted total control over testing and specialist referrals. To propagate this concept, many hospitals were buying up primary care practices with the hope of managing their care costs effectively. Frankly, it was a scenario not too different from what is happening today. The gatekeeper was created in an attempt to control healthcare costs but ended up limiting patients' choices. This concept failed miserably back in the 1990s for several reasons, not the least because patients rebelled against its negative impact on their ability to choose a physician and have access to quality care.

An ACO is considered a different animal than the HMO dinosaur, mainly because the federal government is feeding it and not just the insurance companies. ACOs emphasize efficient delivery of quality care while trying to contain costs. And today there are financial incentives to practice quality medicine and keep costs down that did not exist in the 1990s. Built into the definition of an ACO for the treatment of Medicare patients is the accountability of cost and the potential for monetary bonuses to physicians if money is saved. Will this organizational drive to save money and potential conflict result in the delivery of quality care? Will physicians' medical decision-making behavior change as a result of the emphasis on cost control and bonuses at the end of the year? One way for ACOs to save money is to have their patients avoid the operating room if at all possible. Operations cost organizations money—money that could otherwise be distributed to the ACO members at the end of the year. Operations cost even more if high-risk patients experience complications and have a prolonged hospital stay. Did the surgeon Mrs. Jansson initially consulted seem hesitant to operate on her because of her risk for a bad outcome, a prolonged hospital stay, and a potential cost to his ACO? This is a difficult question to ask and an even more difficult one to answer.

The birth of ACOs and payment of physicians as members is just one aspect of the Affordable Care Act's goal to reform the way healthcare is delivered in this country and how it is going to be paid for. Payment reform is an important goal because it is hoped it will improve the quality of the care delivered *and* lower the costs. As a surgeon, I get paid for every operation I perform, regardless of the patient outcome, good or bad. The fee-for-service system has been around forever and the authors of the ACA want to change or virtually eliminate it. The new mantra for the way many physicians will be paid in the future, especially for Medicare patients, is called pay-for-performance or P4P. Pay-for-performance is fee-for-service with a twist. Under this method, physicians will still be paid a fee for their service but at a negotiated, reduced rate. The twist: A physician receives a bonus if specific quality and cost measures are reached, individually or by the physician organization as a whole. Under this system, the payers (now the federal government, later private health insurance companies) typically set the quality and cost standards. As a surgeon belonging to (or being contracted out by) an organization under the P4P model, I potentially would have received a lower fee for Mrs. Jansson's Medicare surgery, lower than the fee paid out by private insurers. As the year progressed, if I continued to have good clinical and cost-reduced outcomes, I would receive a monetary bonus for my "performance." If some of my outcomes were unexpected or bad and cost the organization more money than anticipated, there would be no bonus. Under the P4P roof, I not only have to think about making the correct clinical decisions concerning Mrs. Jansson, I will be pressured to think about how those decisions will affect the bottom line. Interestingly enough, the Centers for Medicare and Medicaid Services (CMS) has developed an app physicians can use ahead of time to see if they will get penalized by not meeting certain quality measures or receive a bonus if they have exceeded them. Will this new clinical-financial link affect the overall quality of care I provide and who I provide it to? Will I eventually view Mrs. Jansson as an outcome number indicating the quality or a cost I need to reach in order to get a bonus? Or will I view her as a real person with a diseased gallbladder who needs surgery?

In a commentary piece published in *JAMA* in June 2012, Dr. Christine K. Cassel (past president of the American Board of Internal Medicine) and Dr. Sachin H. Jain (Harvard Medical School) asked this about pay-for-performance: "Does Measurement Suppress Motivation?" Both authors expressed concern that pay-for-performance may harm the physician-patient relationship. According to the authors' commentary, "Close attention must be given to whether and how these initiatives motivate physicians and not turn them into pawns working only toward specific measurable outcomes, losing the complex problem-solving and diagnostic capabilities essential to their role in quality of patient care, and diminish their sense of professional responsibility by making it a market commodity."

The question that has to be answered is, will the pay-for-performance model improve the quality of care delivered in the country? It is too early to tell, but a study published in the *New England Journal of Medicine* in April 2012 may provide some insight. The study compared 252 hospitals involved in a pay-for-performance program to a control group of hospitals (not involved in a pay-for-performance program). The study looked at thirty-day mortality rates for six million patients who had undergone a coronary artery bypass graft (CABG) or had had a heart attack, congestive heart failure, or pneumonia. The authors found no evidence that pay-for-performance led to a decrease in the thirty-day death rates for these patients.

Several other payment models for hospitals and physicians

are being evaluated in the name of improving quality and saving money. With all these payment models being tested, it looks a lot like the government (Medicare administrators) and insurance companies are throwing darts at a board to see which ones hit their mark. There are the so-called bundled payments, where hospitals receive one lump sum of money for the cost of services provided by all physicians involved for a single episode of care. As a surgeon, if I am not employed by the hospital organization that receives the lump-sum payment, I would need to negotiate up front with the hospital what my fees would be. The risk for physicians in this model is that if the lump sum provided for the episode of care is not enough because of a patient's complications after surgery or a prolonged hospital course of treatment, the difference may have to be absorbed by the physicians. Under this payment structure, I might think twice about operating on a Medicare patient with multiple medical problems who is at risk for a costly, bad outcome.

Once the Patient Protection and Affordable Care Act (aka ACA or Obamacare) was signed into law in March 2010, payment to the organizations that deliver healthcare and are accountable for its quality was changed forever. (Fortunately, the physicians and the way they are trained are still the same.) The goal of the ACA is admirable: to make access to healthcare available to the roughly fifty million uninsured people in this country who go without health insurance every day. It has a number of good qualities, such as making sure people with pre-existing conditions have access to affordable healthcare and allowing young adults to stay on their parents' health insurance plan until age twenty-six. The law itself is a massive restructuring of our healthcare system, which accounts for almost one-fifth of our economy. Within its two thousand pages are mandates and rules that create more than 160 new "boards, agencies, and commissions" to oversee and monitor the quantity and quality of healthcare delivered in this country. Many of the regulations inside the law were purposely left open-ended, to be shaped and defined at a later date. What Congresswoman Nancy Pelosi from California said on the eve of the passage of the ACA has come to be prophetic given the fluidity of its contents: "We have to pass the bill so that we can find out what is in it."

The bill rests on two major pillars that will make health insurance available and affordable. The first is state-based health exchanges, an option for individuals to purchase a healthcare plan that fits their budget and medical needs. The second is an expansion of state Medicaid coverage to the very poor, with family incomes defined as less than 138 percent of the poverty line (133 percent per adult). According to the Congressional Budget Office, this could add an additional twelve to eighteen million people to the Medicaid rolls, on top of the sixty-plus million current enrollees (nearly one-fifth of the population).

Some argue that the health exchanges offer health plans that sacrifice quality and choice for affordability. It's true; many of the plans on the state exchanges are affordable but offer limited choices. In order for insurance companies to keep monthly premiums within people's budgets, they had to solicit price concessions from hospitals and physicians on services rendered. In return, the insurance companies promised to direct more business to them to increase their volume. Once the insurance companies agreed to lower premiums and hospitals to lower service prices, the latter would be considered "in network" and patients would pay the negotiated reduced rates. The problem with this system lies in the fact that many of the major medical centers in this country were not too keen on offering discounted rates on their services and hence are not involved in many of the exchanges. As a result, some of the best medical expertise and technology is simply not readily available under many of the exchange plans because they are considered "out of network." A patient choosing an out-of-network hospital or physician (ostensibly for better care) would be required to pay much more out of pocket. Many cannot afford these fees, so their choices are limited and their access to quality care impeded because of cost.

In addition to some of the best hospitals, some of the biggest insurance companies are not involved in many of these exchanges because of the health risk classification of those looking for affordable exchange insurance. Many of those going to exchanges for affordable healthcare have underlying preexisting conditions that put them at a higher risk for costly healthcare later in life. Preexisting conditions were probably the reason they did not have insurance in the first place. I suspect many were uninsured or on Medicaid with very little coverage. As you can understand, insurance companies are not jumping over one another to insure the fifty-year-old man with a history of COPD from smoking, diabetes, and high cholesterol, and who is eighty pounds overweight. They are not jumping onto the exchanges for these patients because insuring them would take too much away from the profit margin. Can you blame them? As a surgeon, I know the logic behind any major insurance company not offering healthcare plans on the Affordable Care Act's health exchanges. When I take an obese fifty-year-old diabetic male with COPD and heart disease to the operating room for abdominal surgery, he is at a very real risk for complications (as he would be after *any* major surgery), complications that would prolong his hospital stay and cost his insurance company money. These are the type of patients many insurance companies are trying to avoid, despite the momentum of the Affordable Care Act. Frankly, these are the type of patients I would like to avoid myself, knowing the work involved in caring for them afterward and the potential for a bad outcome—costly both personally and financially. Maybe cost crossed the mind of Mrs. Jansson's first surgeon when he evaluated her for elective gallbladder surgery. Maybe he was also evaluating her cost risk to his ACO's bottom line, in addition to evaluating her physical risk for an operation.

The other pillar of the Affordable Care Act intended to broaden health insurance coverage to the poor, previously uninsured population is the expansion of state-run Medicaid programs. Under the ACA, the federal government has agreed to foot the bill for the first three years for all states and pay 90 percent of the cost of Medicaid coverage thereafter. Initially, the ACA mandated that all states expand Medicaid health coverage to those who could not afford health insurance. In 2012, however, the Supreme Court of the United States ruled that states could opt out of this Medicaid mandate and participate voluntarily. Roughly twenty-five states have opted out, while many others have agreed to expand their Medicaid coverage to more of the poor. Consequently, more previously uninsured poor will finally have healthcare coverage under Medicaid. Overall, this is a good thing for hospitals and surgeons because it will lessen the weight of uncompensated care (estimated at $75 billion) both are currently providing in acute settings. Currently, according to a 2008 Health Tracking Physician Survey, 74 percent of surgeons provide care they never get reimbursed for. On average, surgeons use more than eleven hours per month of their time to care for patients without insurance. The problem lies in the coverage itself and the complexity of the patients. Medicaid reimburses physicians poorly for their services when compared to private insurance— to the point where many physicians cannot afford to accept new Medicaid patients. Practices lose money every time they see a new Medicaid patient. Today, some 33 percent of primary care physicians do not accept new Medicaid patients. This number is even higher for surgeons, approaching 40 or 50 percent.

The other reason many physicians and surgeons limit their Medicaid population is that many in that population are sicker overall than the general population. For complex reasons, many Medicaid patients have underlying medical problems that have been neglected. Care for Medicaid patients involves more work and costs more for practices. Numerous studies show that Medicaid patients have a higher risk of complications and death overall after elective surgery. Many surgeons simply do not want to get involved operating on Medicaid patients electively because of the risk of a poor outcome and the reality of extremely poor reimbursements. Yes, the Affordable Care Act will bring health insurance coverage to many of the poor in this country through its expansion of Medicaid. Yet many of those covered will have limited choice of quality care because many physicians' practice doors will be closed to them.

The ACA's mandate to insure most people in this country does not mean this health coverage is free. It comes at a cost. The price tag on the ACA's mandate to insure the uninsured is estimated by the Congressional Budget Office as just under $1.5 trillion over the next ten years. Critics of that estimate believe, based on the Massachusetts experience in universal healthcare (the so-called Romneycare), that $1.5 trillion could well be much higher. According to a *Boston Globe* article published in June 2011, when universal care was implemented in 2006, the state of Massachusetts contributed $33 million of the $656 million total spent within the state on healthcare reform. The rest came from the federal government, hospitals, and insurers. By 2011, that $33 million state contribution had ballooned to $406 million and the total spent was $2.1 billion. Today, spending by the state of Massachusetts on healthcare comprises more than 40 percent of the state budget (it was 29 percent the year before universal coverage was implemented in 2005). This is projected to reach 50 percent by 2020. According to the official website of Massachusetts (mass.gov), "historically healthcare spending has crowded out key public investments. . . . These spending growth trends are unsustainable." With all the money spent and the Boston area having the most physicians per capita, it still ranks at the top of the list for longest waiting times to get in to see a physician.

The $1.5 trillion cost of the ACA to the American people is being paid for on several budget-cut and added tax and penalty fronts. The taxes that pay for the universal health coverage mandated by the ACA do not discriminate. They are levied on average Americans, hospitals, physicians, and medical device companies in a variety of ways. It all starts with a tax on the average American, who will pay a yearly tax if he or she does not have health insurance by 2014 ($95 per adult, increasing to $695 per adult by 2016, or a percent of household income). There is a Medicare payroll tax on high-income earners, along with extra taxes on unearned income such as stock dividends or rental income. There is a 40 percent tax on people who have the best healthcare plans, the so-called Cadillac plans. There are taxes on businesses that employ over fifty people if they do not offer health insurance that meets the ACA's requirements. There is even a 10 percent tax on tanning salons, which, I am sure, will just pass it along to their customers. The medical device sales tax (just over 2 percent) is a federal tax on all implantable devices such as artificial joints, pacemakers, defibrillators, cardiac stents, and hernia mesh. As with most taxes, I have no doubt the medical device companies will pass this added cost along to hospitals, which, in turn, will pass it along in patients' hospital charges after they receive that new artificial knee, pacemaker, or hernia mesh.

In 2013, most lawmakers woke up and realized what they had voted for when all of the medical device companies in certain states (especially Massachusetts) complained bitterly that the new tax was not business friendly and would affect local jobs. Politicians on both sides of the aisle tried to repeal the medical device tax based on their constituents' lobbying during the negotiations to reopen the government in 2013. The efforts were unsuccessful. Now the federal government takes a small financial piece of that new hip or knee you just had replaced.

On top of the taxes in the ACA, financial penalties (many consider them a tax) will also contribute to paying for its implementation in addition to helping to decrease the rate of growth of Medicare spending. Hospitals are currently penalized for excess readmission rates for a variety of diseases. According to the Medicare Payment Advisory Commission (MedPAC), two-thirds of U.S. hospitals will be penalized for unwarranted readmission rates, with the average being $125,000 per hospital. Another interesting penalty mandated by the ACA will be assessed to physicians. The Medicare Physician Quality Reporting System (PQRS) was born before the ACA was signed into law. When it was created, the PQRS mandated physicians to report their work on specific healthcare quality measures. The reporting was voluntary, and each specialty had its own quality measures to meet and report. For instance, surgeons had to meet specific quality measures for administering intravenous antibiotics one hour before surgery or for ordering medicine to prevent blood clots after surgery (called DVT prophylaxis). According to a *New England Journal of Medicine* commentary published in November 2013, many of the quality measures listed by the PQRS may have nothing to do with the clinical quality of your physician. As a surgeon, the "quality measures" I have to meet reveal nothing about my intraoperative skills, my complication rates, my experience, or my outcomes. All they indicate is that I am diligent about following and writing orders. I can be the surgeon with the worst outcomes in a community yet, in the eyes of the PQRS, have a quality rating! To me, meeting requirements for this specific system reminds me of a surgeon I had to expose because of his danger to the community. He looked absolutely fantastic on paper, with all the correct board certifications, published papers, and recommendations. The problem: He had poor judgment along with dangerously below-average operative skills, both of which have no bearing on his quality rating in the eyes of the PQRS.

Before the ACA, most physicians blew off reporting to the PQRS. Now, starting in 2015, the PQRS will penalize a physician's Medicare total yearly reimbursement (between 1 and 2 percent) if he or she does not voluntarily report on specific quality measures. I suspect that in 2015 most surgeons will look at reporting a little differently since failure to comply will hit them in the pocketbook.

If providing affordable health insurance to every American is the number one priority of the Affordable Care Act, then the next priority is to reduce the rate of growth of Medicare spending. The ACA does this by cutting more than $500 billion from the Medicare coffers over the next ten years. In addition, the bill calls for cutting close to $200 billion from the Medicare Advantage budget, primarily covering eleven million senior citizens in this country. The Medicare Advantage program is very popular with those over sixty-five. It is administered by private health insurance companies in conjunction with the U.S. government to add medical benefits beyond the normal Medicare benefits. The private payers are given blocks of money and administer the Medicare Advantage plans to senior citizens for an added monthly premium. So, where will these cuts come from? The bulk of these Medicare/Medicare Advantage cuts are coming right out of reimbursements to hospitals and physicians (mainly specialists and surgeons). Senior citizens should not have to pay any more into the Medicare system than what they already have. Your primary care physician may not feel the pinch over the next ten years, but your gastroenterologist who is about to perform your colonoscopy or your surgeon about to remove your diseased segment of colon will, in the form of decreased reimbursements. Will these Medicare cuts to surgeons affect the access and quality of care delivered to senior citizens or their outcomes after an operation? I can see a point when surgeons will severely limit the number of Medicare patients they decide to electively operate on in their practice. They will do this for several reasons, reasons that involve the risk of bad outcomes coupled with declining reimbursements. As people enter the Medicare program, they are at the age when their physical health starts to decline. As the Affordable Care Act starts to place more emphasis on my surgical outcomes, linking them to reimbursements, I may start to reconsider the risk of operating on that eighty-two-year-old woman with colon cancer who recently had a stroke, is on blood thinners, and has a long history of smoking. In addition to surgical risk, I may also be forced to factor into my decision making the financial risk to the system if a bad outcome occurs, resulting in a prolonged hospitalization and added costs. As Medicare reimbursements keep trending downward, the cost of operating on a patient at risk for complications and a poor outcome may just be too high.

An interesting study in the journal *Health Affairs*, published in October 2013, asked the question, "How will hospitals respond to the decreased Medicare reimbursements mandated by the Affordable Care Act?" The study examined data from hospitals in ten states from 1995 to 2009, looking at their care of elderly patients in the face of the Medicare cuts during that time period. The study concluded that the hospitals reduced their volume of Medicare patients in response to Medicare cuts in reimbursements. They achieved this by reducing the number of "staffed beds" available to senior citizens, and thus potentially available services. The study concluded that "it appears that Medicare price cuts affect the volume of care that the elderly receive." The study went on to ask whether a decrease in hospital Medicare inpatient reimbursement will have any negative effect on the quality of care delivered or outcomes. The jury is still out, and more scientific studies will have to be done.

One of the more controversial and powerful components of the Affordable Care Act is the Independent Payment Advisory Board (IPAB). It is made up of fifteen presidentially appointed, full-time members (not necessarily physicians), who will have a six-year term and earn $165,000 each. The sole purpose of this board is to set policy to keep the growth of Medicare spending in line with the targets mandated by the ACA guidelines. This board will do the dirty work if Congress cannot when it comes to making decisions that lower Medicare payments to hospitals and physicians for the services they provide. It can set Medicare payment policy without the approval of Congress. The IPAB is essentially the existing MedPAC (Medicare Payment Advisory Commission) on steroids. The controversy surrounding the existence of this board began when it was politicized on the eve of the law being signed and again during the 2012 presidential campaign. It was this very board that politicians and media talking heads were referring to when they talked about the "death panels" created by the ACA, death panels with the potential to withhold care from the elderly and decide who gets treated and who dies. What added to the firestorm was the fact that the IPAB was initially going to reimburse physicians for "discussing end of life issues with patients." Imagine, physicians able to bill for spending forty-five minutes with a patient in a well office visit discussing potential scenarios of dying, in addition to doing screening tests to increase their longevity. Talk about a contradiction, regardless of the financial incentives involved. Obviously, this IPAB proposal did not go over well with physicians, patients, and some politicians. As with many controversial topics, this one was politicized during the run-up to the ACA enactment and, ultimately, dropped before the law was signed.

Despite this, there is still a major concern within the medical profession as to whether the IPAB's policies and the Affordable Care Act's cuts to Medicare will lead to the rationing of medical care within the elderly population. Dr. Donald Berwick (administrator to the Centers for Medicare & Medicaid Services from July 2010 to December 2011), a prime supporter of the Affordable Care Act, added fuel to the debate when he stated in a 2009 interview, "The decision is not whether or not we will ration care. The decision will be whether we ration care with our eyes open." In the beginning, the rationing of care to keep costs down within the Medicare population may just be a very subtle raising of the age requirement for procedures. It may start with an eighty-year-old grandmother with severe sciatic-type nerve pain having to wait at least six weeks before an MRI of her lower back will be approved, despite the fact that an orthopedic back specialist will not even look at her without one. It could continue with a seventy-eight-year-old mother of seven who suddenly finds out Medicare has stopped paying for her yearly Pap smear testing. Yes, she can still get one, but at an out-of-pocket price of three hundred dollars. The rationing of care may end with Medicare refusing to pay for a colonoscopy in a retired eighty-five-year-old Coast Guard enlisted man who happened to be a hero in one of the greatest maritime rescue operations in the history of this country.

While policy states that the IPAB is "forbidden from rationing care," its goals of keeping Medicare spending in check may clash with the costly reality of delivering healthcare to the Medicare population today and in the future. Consider this: Up to 30 percent (over $200 billion) of the total Medicare budget each year is spent on the last year of life. Medicare patients who die spend six times as much in the last year of life as compared to any other year when they were living. In regard to surgery, a third of Medicare patients undergo a costly operation in the last year of their lives.

No matter how one massages the statistics, a fair amount of Medicare money can be saved by somehow cutting back on emergent or nonemergent care to the elderly in the last year of life. This is really the big elephant in the room, the hot topic that no public official with thoughts of reelection dares address.

So the government, as it often does, will either vote to revisit the issue at a later date or transfer the responsibility to some other entity, in this case the IPAB. The IPAB knows it must reduce spending on the Medicare population in the last year of life in order to realistically make a dent in the growth of spending. They know this because they tried to gently approach the topic in their original policy by reimbursing physicians extra money for discussing quality-of-life issues during a routine well-check office visit. I believe it was a valiant effort to begin the battle of reducing Medicare spending in the last year of life. I also believe the IPAB's Trojan horse attempt at persuading primary care physicians (by paying them) as "first responders" to the Medicare cost-cutting war was deliberate. Political pressure quickly wiped out the policy.

Nonetheless, the seeds have been planted that will cause physicians and surgeons to factor cost into their medical decision making for Medicare patients. As more studies are published on the science of predicting longevity or risk factors for bad outcomes in the Medicare population before surgery, I believe the brains that make up the IPAB will gradually become more comfortable establishing policies (augmented by financial incentives) that may amount to the rationing of healthcare. For now, the IPAB is in a hibernating state. I suspect it will stay this way for a while, given the partisan emotions it generates. If the political winds change in Washington, it may never even come out of its cave.

The University of San Francisco published a study in *JAMA* in March 2013 assessing the health risks of older people. The authors of the study looked at data from a national health survey taken by more than twenty thousand older Americans. From this survey, they developed a "mortality index" based on twelve factors that may help determine the ten-year survival rates of the Medicare population. Will there come a day when the IPAB uses the science of predicting longevity to justify policies of not reimbursing physicians for certain screening procedures or even needed surgery in the high-risk elderly population?

Mrs. Tucker was a pleasant ninety-six-year-old woman I had been asked to see after a newly diagnosed colon cancer. She was admitted to the hospital because of abdominal pain and anemia. I had operated on her ten years earlier for the same problem, when she was a very young eighty-six-year-old. Mrs. Tucker had expressed a desire to live to 102, the same age as her grandmother. Her overall health was actually pretty good outside a little dementia setting in.

A colonoscopy in the hospital discovered an ugly tumor in the midportion of her colon that was partially obstructing her bowels. The family asked me whether she could tolerate major surgery. They trusted me and would accept my assessment and advice. Every physician who had come in contact with Mrs. Tucker said surgery was necessary, but none of them were surgeons. None of them had to accept responsibility if her outcome was bad. I said I would. As her surgeon, I would be the one to get her through a difficult postoperative course, not the other physicians, and I knew she undoubtedly would have a difficult time recovering from major surgery given her age. If it came to it, I would be the one to coax the family into changing direction; cases like this can mean pneumonia and ventilators. As I evaluated Mrs. Tucker for surgery, I went over the survival statistics in the back of my mind. I was aware that if I did nothing, she would probably live to see only ninety-seven. I was also keenly aware of the fact that an operation could easily end this woman's life if her postoperative course did not go perfectly. Along the way to a final decision, nothing outside clinical factors biased my thought process in any way. The clinical choices were not great. Will the day arrive when the IPAB's policies of reducing spending in the Medicare population based on longevity pressure my medical decision-making process when evaluating another Mrs. Tucker? I believe it will.

As each day passes and the mandates in the Affordable Care Act continue to bloom, every hospital, patient, and insurance company will continue to feel its effects on the way healthcare is delivered, by whom it is provided, and how it is paid for. Hospitals will try to make up for the decrease in reimbursements under Medicare by finding creative ways to decrease your length of stay and expedite discharge planning. They will also be trying to gain additional Medicare revenue by "upcoding" their diagnosis for every patient discharged in an attempt to enhance their reimbursement. Hospital coders will be combing every patient's chart at the time of discharge more than ever, searching for new diagnoses and services to bill for. They will be looking for diagnoses related to complications after surgery (since complications pay) or any new diagnoses that patients may have at the time of discharge. Hospitals will all be vigorously educating their employed physicians and hospitalists in the art of coding now that electronic health records makes this process much more efficient.

As I mentioned earlier in this book, hospitals are all too eager to classify a patient's admission as "inpatient" versus "observation." This classification distinction can require a complex process, but the result is more money for inpatient admissions. After I remove a diseased appendix on a patient and he is admitted overnight, I often receive a call from the hospital's case manager wanting to change the status of that patient from observation to inpatient. This change cannot be done without a physician's order. In the past, it did not matter to me because clinically all I wanted was the patient to stay one night. I never understood why the hospital cared, until I started paying more attention to the financial ramifications of it. Inpatient versus observation status can also have profound financial implications on patients, depending on the coverage details of each plan. Some insurance plans may not offer complete coverage for an observation status, and require more money out of pocket. Billing Medicare for inpatient versus observation can be gray enough that hospitals can get a little overzealous in an attempt to maximize revenue. One Boston hospital found this out the hard way when it was fined more than $5 million in 2013 for overbilling Medicare for services it billed as inpatient but that were ultimately deemed to be observation. In order to bring clarification to this type of billing, Medicare passed a "two-midnight" minimum rule, requiring patients classified as inpatient to be in the hospital two consecutive midnights.

In addition to trying to maximize revenue, hospitals also want to minimize the financial sting from penalties that Medicare has handed down for specific requirements. Readmitting patients within thirty days of discharge will cost hospitals. Hospitals, therefore, are finding creative ways to do whatever they can to prevent patients from getting readmitted within thirty days from a recent admission, including classifying as observation patients who are treated in the ER and go on to spend the night (and subsequent nights) in the hospital.

Insurance companies, too, are being impacted by the broad mandates of the Affordable Care Act. For instance, the high-deductible plans offered today mean a patient pays more out of pocket for healthcare than at any other time in history. These high-deductible plans were around before the signing of the ACA, but insurance companies have accelerated their use in order to save money. Health insurance companies on the ACA's health exchange markets are keeping premiums down for the exchange population at the expense of the deductible. Health insurance companies (along with the hospitals they contract with) are also categorizing physicians into "tiers." Where I practice, there are three tiers (1, 2, and 3). The insurance companies and the hospitals they contract with want you to believe tiering is based on meeting both quality and cost benchmarks. The reality of physician tiering is all about cost and alliances. In my community, as an independent practitioner I am considered a tier 3 surgeon in the eyes of one of the local hospitals because I am not employed by them. If I were hospital-employed, I would be a tier 1. It is that simple. I have always felt tiering places a scarlet letter on my white coat for all to see and for patients to make assumptions about—erroneous assumptions, since quality is not a factor in tiering.

Patients referred to me by hospital-employed physicians have to pay a higher co-pay and more out of pocket (higher deductibles) if they choose to be operated on at the competing hospital across town simply because of my tier 3 classification. If I were a tier 1 hospital-employed surgeon, patients would pay a smaller co-pay and very little out of pocket for an operation by my hands. Physician tiering is a way for hospitals and insurance companies to apply financial pressure that directs patient and physician behavior. In my case, regardless of the quality of surgery I practice, I will lose referrals by default because most patients will follow the path of least financial resistance. As a result, I may feel compelled to reevaluate my independent status based solely on the current financial pressures of the marketplace.

Tiering is a way for hospitals and the insurance companies they contract with to maximize cost control on the physicians they employ. It is an effective method of directing their patient base to these same physicians, who will, in turn, direct them to the hospitals they work for. Hospitals want their tier 1 employed primary care physicians to refer their patients to their own tier 1 surgeons. In turn, tier 1 employed surgeons will take these patients to their operating rooms and not to the competition across town. Tiering physicians is a way to limit a patient's choice of physician by making cost a factor. In theory, you have a choice when it comes time to choose the surgeon to operate on you. You also, in theory, have a choice in picking the hospital to have your operation at. The problem with this is that your surgeon may not have a choice. Despite all the *potential* for choice, when it comes time to pay, reality may leave you with very little choice.

As Mrs. Jansson left my office, I peered into the waiting room. Patients waiting to see me were overflowing into the hallway. I looked at my watch and shook my head. I was already an hour behind schedule.

I turned to my secretary, who was checking in patients. "Janice, where are all these new patients coming from?"

"I'm not really sure." She sounded flustered and didn't even look up from her computer.

"I just don't know how long I can keep up this pace," I said, even though I knew she wasn't listening. I had been up until two in the morning, operating on a young man with a perforated stomach ulcer, and I was exhausted.

I could hear the television in the waiting room. A reporter was commenting on the huge number of previously uninsured people, many with preexisting conditions, who were now able to obtain health insurance under the Affordable Care Act. A middle-aged woman was being interviewed and expressing her relief at finally being able to have the surgery she needed, now that she had health insurance to pay for it. The only problem: She would have to wait several months to get in to see a surgeon.

So this is where we're headed, I thought as I picked up the folder Janice had placed on the counter for my next consultation. My shoes felt like they were lined with lead. More people than ever—and sicker than ever—finally able to get in to see a doctor, and fewer and fewer doctors willing or able to see them. By 2025, the demand for surgical specialists is estimated to increase by 18 to 31 percent, depending on the specialty. Then, to top it all off, reimbursements are declining so drastically that no one wants to be a doctor anymore, let alone a surgeon. It was all very discouraging.

I headed back to an exam room to introduce myself to a sixty-five-year-old diabetic man with a newly diagnosed colon cancer. His medical history indicated multiple abdominal operations and a recent diagnosis of blocked coronary arteries. As I shook his hand I could see he was clearly scared, still shaken by the news that he had cancer. He wanted me to know he had a lot to live for. "I'm not ready to die," he said, pulling out his wallet and opening it to an accordion sleeve of photos. I could feel my energy pick up as I began reviewing strategies in my mind. I could help him.

"Would you excuse me a moment, Mr. Benigni? I need to get something from my assistant," I said as stepped out of the room.

"Janice, put on a new pot of coffee, will you? Thanks." I walked a quick loop through the staff-only space behind the receptionist's desk and back to the hallway.

I returned to Mr. Benigni. His surgery and postsurgical course would be challenging. I began explaining the details to him, including the risks. He listened closely and the more we talked, the more hopeful he became.

He had questions, mostly about what he could expect after surgery, but he also wanted to know if he should have any concerns about cost. "I have Medicare," he told me.

Oh, there will be costs, I thought to myself. I took out my mental notepad and did some quick calculations: hospital charges, anesthesiologist's fee, my fee, post-op visiting nurse home care. The real question was how many pennies on the dollar Medicare would pay toward any of those bills.

There *was* one item I hadn't included in the calculation. It was the net result of a series of numbers: long summers of manual labor as a steelworker to pay for medical school, thirteen years of study and training, and thousands of hours standing in an operating room, bent over a patient, working with my hands. The culmination—helping another human being—remains an honor and thrill that never gets old. It's a sum beyond measure.

10 PERFECTING THE ART OF MAKING MONEY

Money had nothing to do with it." I was working on an inflamed appendix with a new laparoscopic stapling device. The patient was a young girl and her intestinal appendage was on the precipice of bursting. A few more hours and it would have exploded, spewing pus and infection in all directions. If it had ruptured before I opened her up, her risk for infection would have increased dramatically. Her parents would have been angry, and her hospital stay would have been prolonged. *Glad I didn't wait,* I thought as I assessed the situation.

Maria, my first assistant, asked me again, "Are you sure you didn't go into surgery for the money?" She was goading me. She had seen my new car in the parking lot that morning.

Truth be told, money was a long-term factor in my decision to become a surgeon, but it wasn't the driving force. It was a practical consideration—I could see $100,000 of education debt looming on my horizon like an albatross. But I was drawn to it as a craft, as a way to make a person well with my hands and the tools of surgery. The sad fact today is that many medical students are focused on money first, forgoing careers in primary care medicine for careers in surgery or other better-paying specialties because of the potential earnings.

For the moment, I ignored Maria's questions. As I fired the stapling device to amputate the diseased appendix, pus oozed out the sides.

When I was applying to surgical residency programs, it was obvious that established surgeons were at the top of the medical earnings food chain. All I had to do was look at my general surgery mentors' cars in the doctors-only parking lot. The cars owned by cardiologists and radiologists indicated they also did quite well. I never considered this a bad thing. When I was a surgical resident, it seemed everyone wanted to be a heart surgeon. Cardiac surgery fellowships were extremely competitive. Heart surgeons were considered the big men on the surgical campus, well above the lowly general surgeon in stature and pay grade. By directly repairing maladies of the heart, heart surgeons were considered to be a special class. Besides the gravitas, they also earned the money to back it up; in those days many made well north of $5,000 for every operation.

Times have changed. Now cardiac surgery fellowships have trouble filling their yearly slots with qualified individuals. The seven to ten years of sacrifice it takes to become a heart surgeon, coupled with declining reimbursements (it's 50 percent less now) and a dwindling patient base, have taken the professional and financial shine off it. The growth of the cardiac stent industry has also threatened the livelihoods of cardiac surgeons. Many of the patients who, twenty years ago, would have undergone heart surgery for blocked coronary arteries are now getting stents—placed by interventional cardiologists, not cardiac surgeons. The cardiac stent business is a billion-dollar industry for interventional cardiologists and the hospitals who employ them. Like surgeons, they perform high-end procedures that generate substantial income for themselves and the hospitals where they work. Like surgeons, they are reimbursed for the *quantity* of their work, not the quality. The more stents a cardiologist puts in, the more money he or she makes. Interventional cardiologists are under the same workplace pressures as surgeons to produce and earn their salary in the face of declining reimbursements and cost cutting. They are also under the same personal ethical pressures as surgeons to insulate their medical decision making from the influences of personal financial gain.

Most surgeons I know have worked hard to get where they are in life. Why shouldn't they enjoy the financial fruits of their long and arduous labors? In today's medical reimbursement system, surgery pays. It certainly pays better than seeing patients in the office all day. In the world of private practice, the more operations you do, the more money you make. It's that simple. At the time of my decision to become a surgeon, what wasn't obvious to me was how hard I would have to work to get there. It also wasn't obvious how hard I would need to work to stay there.

I grabbed the freed appendix with a laparoscopic instrument and stuffed it into a clear bag. It was ready for extraction from the abdominal cavity. I looked at the clock; I got lucky this time. "Not bad . . . a little over four hundred dollars for fifteen minutes of work," I whispered. I knew this would get a reaction from Maria if she heard it.

"This should make up for the last appendectomy I did in the

middle of the night, on a patient with no insurance," I said more loudly. That appendix had been an angry blob of gangrenous tissue and had taken almost three painful hours to remove. "I almost put a hole in his colon in the process of trying to get the thing out. That one cost me many sleepless nights of worry." I had been exceedingly happy to see him leave without a complication. "Never saw the patient again after he was discharged." I paused, checking the view on the monitor. "I suspect it all evens out in the end."

Out of the corner of my eye I could see Maria shaking her head. As soon as I removed the bag from the abdomen, she grabbed it deftly and placed it on her back table, not a drop of its purulent contents spilled.

"Hey, I knew I'd make a good living eventually—draining pus, repairing hernias, and taking out diseased organs." I could tell Maria had stopped listening, but I kept going. "Once I finished four years of college, four years of medical school, five years of surgical training, and three years of a military obligation—I knew the money would be there at the end if I worked hard enough."

By now, I was clearly talking only to myself. Everyone in the room had tuned me out. I started to close my incisions. "After sacrificing thirteen prime years of my life, I was ready to capitalize on the personal investment I had made." Maria was humming, her back to me.

The current payment system that reimburses surgeons more for their services than other medical specialties dates back more than thirty years. In the late 1970s, studies done out of the Harvard University School of Public Health by William Hsiao were used by the federal government's Medicare program as a basis to create relative value units (RVUs) for physician services. The Centers for Medicare & Medicaid Services places a specific RVU number on every service (including every operation) carried out by a physician or surgeon. Once the Medicare and Medicaid programs adopted the RVU system to reimburse physicians, many private insurance companies soon followed.

The creation of a specific RVU for a surgical procedure is about as complex a process as a hospital's formula for calculating the total charges on a laparoscopic hernia repair. The task of defining this process is well beyond the scope of this book and I would not even begin to do it justice. What I can say is that once an RVU is established, conversion factors are used to determine the specific dollar amount Medicare reimburses for each service provided by a physician.

One component (there are three) making up the definition of an RVU incorporates what is called physician-specific work. Physician-specific work, according to the federal government, is measured by stress, skill, time, and the effort that goes into performing whatever service is defined. This is interesting because the American Medical Association's Relative Value Scale Update Committee (RUC) has the most influence in defining this physician-specific work component to the federal government. Medicare uses recommendations made by the RUC to factor in their reimbursement RVU formula for Medicare. The committee uses information from physician surveys in each medical or surgical specialty, inquiring about the time, effort, and stress level involved for a procedure or service to develop value numbers for the physician-specific work component of the RVU. The survey feedback from surgeons of all specialties regarding time, effort, and stress level has a major impact on the RVU value for any operation. Critics state that the times used in the reimbursement formula are inflated, leading to higher reimbursements for specialists who perform procedures and surgeons who operate.

The RUC is made up of thirty-one physician members, each representing a specific medical or surgical specialty. Of the thirty-one members, twenty-one represent specialty societies whose physicians perform procedures or surgery. It appears that primary care specialists have been outnumbered by their surgical brethren on this committee for a long time. The irony of the entire RVU reimbursement formula is that many surgeons, including me, do not belong to the American Medical Association, the very group that has had a significant influence with Medicare and private payers on paying surgeons to be at the top of the medical food chain. As a matter of fact, roughly 20 percent of physicians (most are primary care) in this country belong to the American Medical Association. As for surgeon membership, the percentage number is probably in the single digits. Most surgeons would rather belong to their specific specialty societies (such as the American College of Surgeons) and have long believed the AMA has always put the interests of primary care medicine ahead of the surgical specialties.

A recent study published in *JAMA* in August 2013 examined the time allotments used by the Centers for Medicare & Medicaid Services to calibrate payment for three common medical services: a screening colonoscopy, cataract removal, and a primary care office visit. The authors calculated the physician work per hour for the two specialist/surgeon procedures and compared them to a primary care office visit. In terms of time spent, the authors concluded that "Medicare spends almost 4 times as much for a screening colonoscopy and almost 5 times as much for cataract extraction as it does for a complicated office visit" carried out by a primary care physician. The authors continued, "We believe the strong financial incentives described compromise access to primary care. The gap between what Medicare pays for procedures verses what it pays for office visit services encourages specialists to favor more procedures . . . and discourages physicians from choosing a career in primary care."

Many surgeons, including me, have problems with this study: how it was done and the sample procedures used to arrive at its conclusions. First of all, surgeons are reimbursed by Medicare and private insurers a onetime, all-inclusive dollar amount for whatever operation they perform. Unlike my plastic surgeon colleagues (who deal in an all-cash-and-debit-card world), I do not have the luxury of receiving money up front, although at an earlier point in my career, I did have the luxury of receiving tangible goods for my services when there was no money to be paid. The Amish father of a child I had operated on to remove a gangrenous appendix could not afford to pay me the traditional way for helping his son. He was eternally grateful and showed it by building (and surprising me with) a beautiful oak desk and bookshelf, both of which I still have today. In retrospect, it was one of the best reimbursements I have ever received.

I receive a fee after all the work is done, nothing before, and it often takes four to six weeks to get it—*if* there are no mistakes in the paperwork filed for its claim. During this wait, Medicare is looking aggressively for reasons to reject any surgeon's reimbursement claims. If rejected, the claim must be refiled, adding months more to the wait for payment. The fee I receive for any operation covers the time and care invested in the patient before I operate, the operation itself, care of the patient while in the hospital and/or while recovering at home (taking phone calls, faxing prescription changes to a pharmacy, etc.). As a general surgeon, I often perform complex intra-abdominal surgery on complex patients, surgeries that can take hours to perform. The care afterward can also occupy a significant number of hours each day and night, depending on the operation. The two examples in the previously quoted study (colonoscopy and cataract extraction) can take very little time to complete when performed by skilled gastroenterologists and ophthalmologists. A talented gastroenterologist can easily snake a colonoscope through someone's colon in under fifteen minutes without missing a thing. Should a gastroenterologist be paid any less because he or she is highly skilled and efficient and has good outcomes? Wouldn't you want that in your gastroenterologist? Both procedures also do not involve much pre- or postoperative time from the physician. To use these two simple examples as the basis for drawing broad conclusions about reimbursement formulas for surgical procedures is, at best, unrealistic.

Of course, because I am a surgeon I have my own biases. But the authors of the study are *internal medicine physicians*, not surgeons. I suspect neither one has ever had to drag himself out of bed at two in the morning, in the middle of a cold night, to remove a segment of dead intestine from someone in septic shock and then be awakened from a deep sleep each night for the next three days with phone calls from the patient's nurse. I suspect the authors never spent several hours repairing nickel-size bullet holes in the intestine of someone with hepatitis C, followed by more hours dealing with complications during the patient's hospital stay, only to find out that the reimbursement for all the effort (not to mention potential exposure to hepatitis C, a deadly liver disease) would be zero dollars. I suspect the authors never had to meticulously peel off a cancerous thyroid gland from the vocal cord nerves coursing behind it, in a patient who sings in a church choir, knowing that the slightest hand tremor could damage that nerve and lead to permanent vocal cord paralysis. I suspect the authors never experienced the sheer personal terror of knowing you have less than a minute to blindly wade through a sea of blood after emergently cutting into a distended abdomen in order to gain control of a bleeding ruptured spleen to prevent someone from exsanguinating on the operating room table. Yes, according to the *JAMA* study, surgeons are paid more per time spent for an operation than primary care physicians are paid for wellness office visits. Maybe there is a good reason why.

Performing a surgical procedure pays more than a complicated primary care office visit by a diabetic whose blood sugar levels are out of control. As a result, most competent surgeons make more money than many of their nonsurgical medical colleagues. Still, a lot of surgeons, if you cornered their honesty, will tell you they are not paid *enough* for the expertise they offer patients and the personal price that expertise extracts from them day in and day out. Maybe when the powers that be devised the current reimbursement system for physicians, they took these factors into consideration when deciding to pay surgeons more for their services than some of the other medical specialists. Maybe the fact that it takes five to seven years of long hours and personal sacrifice after medical school to become a qualified surgeon is factored into our reimbursements. Once out of training, it probably takes another five years to truly fine-tune our surgical judgment and skills and build a reputation. Maybe the fact that surgeons are often placed in unique, fluid, and stressful situations where reliance on personal judgment and technical expertise is the only road that leads to a good outcome is part of that equation, too.

On its surface, the reimbursement system in healthcare today is weighted toward rewarding specialists who perform procedures and surgeons who carry out operations. Maybe this setup was designed to attract the best and the brightest to the surgical profession, given the personal sacrifice it takes to become one. Maybe it was designed to make up for the earnings surgeons lose during training, since most do not start full-time employment until they are well into their thirties. If the reimbursement system for surgeons undergoes a drastic change, we need to ask ourselves if there will be enough incentive for quality candidates to commit to the long road one travels to become a surgeon. There is already a shortage of surgeons in this country. Will this shortage worsen as the surgical profession gets squeezed on reimbursement even more? There are more lucrative specialties in medicine that require a shorter time commitment while also yielding a better quality of life than surgery. Dermatology immediately comes to my mind.

Of course, the current reimbursement system can be improved. It can be improved by rewarding the surgeons with consistently good outcomes with better reimbursement and paying less to surgeons whose outcomes are below the norm. Historically, third-party payers have rewarded surgical quantity rather than documented quality; that's the obvious outcome of a fee-for-service system. There is an old saying in private practice: "You eat what you kill," which aptly describes how a surgeon in private practice generates income. He or she needs to be a good hunter. It still applies today.

In private practice, the current fee-for-service system encourages productivity. Critics argue that this system encourages abuse, unnecessary surgery. Why can't surgeons, just like other professionals, be allowed to achieve the American dream if they choose to work hard, sacrifice, and consistently demonstrate good patient outcomes? Why should the medical profession be any different than other service professions in regard to maximizing earning abilities? Some will argue that the altruistic nature of being a physician and delivering care makes the medical profession a unique service industry that should not be "tainted" with the desire to earn more money.

One way to gain some insight into these issues is to examine what physicians, particularly surgeons, earn. In the 2013 Medical Group Management Association (MGMA) Compensation and Production Report, which surveyed more than sixty thousand physician medical care providers, the average specialist's income (including surgeons) was $396,233. The average family doctor and internist earned $220,942 per year. Of the specialists, orthopedic surgeons were at the top of the list, coming in at $563,000 per year. Orthopedic surgeons often find themselves at the top of such lists. I suspect one reason includes the fact that they often operate on a younger, privately insured population, which brings better reimbursement than operating on the Medicare-covered population. Another reason may have to do with the operations they perform, such as total joint replacements, which reimburse well when compared to other operations (starting at anywhere from $1,200 to $1,400 per case). Add to that the fact that many orthopedic surgeons own imaging centers, outpatient surgery centers, or physical therapy clinics, all of which complement the surgical services they provide and all of which generate additional income.

In the report, orthopedic surgeons are followed by gastroenterologists at $521,000 per year and dermatologists at $471,000 per year. General surgeons, like me, were eighth on the list, with average earnings of $367,000 per year. Not bad for the specialty considered the "primary care" of surgery. Neurosurgeons and cardiothoracic surgeons' incomes were not included in the survey. I suspect most in those specialties were not eager to reveal their incomes. Based on my experience, their yearly average incomes usually come in well above those of orthopedic surgeons, partly because of the unique operations they perform and the higher reimbursements attached. Obviously, this list (one of many available to the public) and its figures must be taken with a grain of salt. That said, its numbers resemble what other survey lists have revealed. What this list and others like it do is tell the public what most already know. Physicians who are specially trained to perform procedures and surgeons who are trained to operate earn more money than physicians who are not.

Part of the problem relates to public perception of the medical profession—that they are overpaid and arrogant. Many physicians (especially surgeons) are sensitive to that view. Further fueling the negative perceptions are the occasional "bad apples" who make headlines for performing unnecessary operations on patients solely for financial gain. Worse still, many of these unnecessary operations end badly for people. In my specialty, unethical surgeons can get away with this kind of behavior for some time, if most of their patient outcomes are decent and they are likable individuals. Normally, a critical mass of patient carnage and death has to be reached before these abusers are revealed, lawsuits are filed, and headlines are written.

In some circles, the thinking is "surgeons make enough money!" and they should not have the freedom to work as hard as they choose to make more. Does the public resent the earnings status of surgeons more so than that of other professionals in society? In an article published on Medscape.com, a website for practicing physicians, in May 2010, a psychiatrist quoted an old Russian proverb: "The doctor is an angel when he tenders his cure and a devil when he tenders his bill." Patients want to believe that decisions about their medical care are firmly based in altruistic logic and not influenced by a desire to make money. A person wants to believe that the surgeon is removing his or her gallbladder because it will eliminate pain—not because it pays the bills. For most practicing physicians and surgeons, I believe patient-focused care (not money-focused care) *is* the norm. That should not preclude surgeons being paid a fair wage for their services.

In the aforementioned Medscape.com article, the premise was posed as "Why Aren't Doctors Allowed to Care About Money?" Most doctors do care about money. If they do not, they are at the very least naïve and, at the worst, dinosaurs (or disingenuous). Most doctors, however, care about doing an honest day's work even more than they care about money. Surgeons are a special category of physician when it comes to generating income from their expertise. In a fee-for-service private practice setting, surgeons have the freedom to decide how busy they want to be, which directly affects how much money they earn. Surgeons can operate on as many people as their practice brings them (provided the operations are necessary), or as few as they desire. Most surgeons I know enjoy operating. They enjoy the challenge each operation offers and the immediate benefits a patient receives from their expertise. Of course, they also enjoy the income that operating generates, along with the lifestyle it provides. Most surgeons I know have busy practices. They are busy primarily because of the quality of care they provide. What I find interesting about the mentality of some surgeons in private practice (including me) is how perspective changes over time. As a surgeon, you spend an enormous amount of time and energy getting to the point where you can operate independently. Once they start generating income, most surgeons work as hard as they can for as long as they can to shorten the time to retirement. A surgeon's earning capacity has a finite number of years much like the career of an NFL running back; it's not long before physical, mental, or political factors start to slow him down. Not surprisingly, most surgeons want to take full advantage of those prime years and generate as much income as possible.

In private practice, surgeons learn to become as efficient inside the operating room as their skills will allow. Given the current reimbursement system, efficiency in the operating room has direct consequences for earning power, going home at a decent hour at the end of the day, and quality patient outcomes. A surgeon's efficiency means less time under anesthesia for the patient, always a good thing, and fewer operating room costs. Being "fast" inside the operating room without compromising surgical quality means that both the surgeon and patient benefit. Is this a bad thing? Is it wrong for a fast, technically efficient, safe surgeon to maximize his or her operative caseload and generate more income because of it? I don't think it is.

Over the course of the last ten years, reimbursements for specialist and surgeon services have continuously declined while the cost of running a practice (including malpractice insurance) has increased. Not too long ago, a routine colonoscopy, for example, used to pay roughly $1,200. Now the going rate is anywhere from $300 to $500. In order for gastroenterologists to maintain their income levels in the face of declining reimbursements, they need to increase the number of procedures they do. This scenario plays out in operating rooms across the country as well. Sadly, more and more the delivery of health boils down to a numbers game for the physicians who provide it and the hospitals where it is provided. As reimbursements decline, physicians try to maintain their level of income by working harder, if the work is there. For surgeons, working harder means seeing more patients, working longer hours, and performing more operations. Surgeons generally do not advertise. They do not troll for clients over the airwaves like some in the legal profession do. They do not stand on street corners, handing out self-promotional brochures (some do in the confines of their office). Surgeons generally rely on referrals and their reputations to earn an income, referrals based on financial relationships, employment, and the quality of care they provide.

During the last twenty-five years, surgeons have been broadening their offerings to earn income beyond the operating room. A number of lucrative business opportunities, directly or indirectly, relate to what they were trained to do. An entrepreneurial spirit is a common trait among surgeons, a spirit that leads them into other business ventures and the chance to increase their income. This tendency fits perfectly with their independent outlook, especially for those in private practice. A surgeon working for himself or herself has no employer constraints, no financial conflict-of-interest rules to abide by. The only potential conflict you have to address is your professional oath and personal moral compass. Academic surgeons employed by teaching centers are not as free to take advantage of the business opportunities their skills present to them. There are too many conflict-of-interest regulations in the contracts they sign, too many people to answer to.

One reason many surgeons are in a position to take advantage of potential business opportunities, regardless of the nature of the business, is that they have the capital to do so. Established surgeons have the funds to invest in the up-front expenses without compromising their lifestyles. They are in a position to take financial advantage of the connection they already have with people who need surgery. Another reason is that surgeons generate income not only for themselves but for other entities as well (hospitals, medical device companies).

There is another, seldom mentioned reason surgeons are eager to generate income outside the operating room: burnout. A third of practicing surgeons in the United States today are over age fifty-five. They are getting tired of taking emergency call, frustrated with increasing administrative bureaucracy, and sick of dealing with insurance companies. Frankly, they are getting burned out. National surveys document that close to 50 percent of practicing physicians (it's an even higher number for surgeons) report experiencing burnout symptoms. Many are looking to offset the decline in reimbursements with other cash-based alternatives. And if they can, they want to shorten the road to retirement by earning income outside the operating room.

An example of surgeons taking full advantage of an emerging technology and business opportunity can be found at the genesis of minimally invasive surgery. As soon as Dr. J. Barry McKernan and Dr. William Saye performed the first laparoscopic gallbladder removal on a woman in 1988 at a community hospital outside Nashville, Tennessee, both immediately recognized two things. The first was that laparoscopic technique represented a once-in-a-generation surgical modality that would greatly benefit patients. The second: They had a once-in-a-generation opportunity to make some serious money from inventing this technique. A third surgeon in private practice, Dr. Eddie Joe Reddick, took the business opportunity to new levels after he performed the second laparoscopic operation three months later. As word spread about the feasibility of laparoscopic surgery, surgeons across the country were inundated with requests from patients who wanted to have cholecystectomy (gallbladder removal) done this way. All those surgeons had to go to Nashville, Tennessee, to learn this revolutionary in-demand technique. Drs. McKernan, Saye, and Reddick saw the enormous business opportunity in front of them and took full advantage of it. All three made tens of thousands of dollars charging other surgeons to stand in the operating room and watch them perform a laparoscopic gallbladder removal. After this, weekend training courses were organized for surgeons to come and learn the technique. These courses involved lectures and time in the laboratory. Performing the operation on live pigs under anesthesia was the highlight of the weekend. The demand was enormous. Surgeons were waiting at least six months to get into these courses. At the time, two major surgical device companies wanted to get in on the action and were competing against each other for the three surgeons' attention. All three surgeons made enormous amounts of money from the courses, their celebrity, and their surgical talents. Rumor has it that one of the surgeons also made money by selling the pigs from his farm to the medical device companies who sponsored the pig lab surgeon training courses. As a result of his personal financial gain, Dr. Eddie Joe Reddick left surgery altogether and never looked back. He went on to become a country music singer and songwriter.

Another lucrative market many surgeons are wading into is the cosmetic surgery business. The problem for an unsuspecting public, however, is that most of the surgeons putting up a "cosmetic surgery" shingle over the last five years are *not* board-certified plastic surgeons. This is a relatively new, and potentially dangerous, phenomenon—other surgical specialists such as general surgeons, ENT surgeons, and gynecologic surgeons encroaching on the traditional turf of plastic surgeons. It is becoming more common to see general surgeons taking out gallbladders by day and giving Botox injections or performing liposuction by night. A gynecologist who removed a woman's uterus at the local hospital on Tuesday may be found at his "beauty spa/body shaping clinic" performing a breast augmentation on Wednesday. ENT surgeons are scheduling face-lifts in their offices around the routine tonsillectomies they perform at the hospital.

For some in my profession, the lines separating the surgical specialties no longer exist; the money on the other side is just too enticing. Surgeons are fighting over the price of America's vanity. This phenomenon is being played out mainly in the private practice arena, at community hospitals, surgery centers, and clinics. There are two reasons surgeons not formally trained in plastic surgery are doing this. The first, and most important, is for the money. The second: because they can. They can do it in the confines of their own office, away from any state or federal scrutiny. There are no laws or regulations preventing any physician or surgeon from performing cosmetic surgery on anyone willing to pay. There is no state or federal oversight over this growing industry, no way to monitor patient outcomes. There is no way to verify the competence of the non–plastic surgeon performing cosmetic surgery procedures.

According to the American Society of Plastic Surgery, over $10.4 billion was spent in the United States on plastic surgical procedures in 2011, an increase of 3 percent from the previous year. Over fourteen million plastic surgical procedures were performed that year, with Botox injections topping the list (cost: $1 billion). Breast augmentation was the most common operation, with over 300,000 done in 2011 at a cost of $5,000 to $10,000 a pop. This market is growing, and becoming very popular with surgeons not formally trained in cosmetic surgery, who want a piece of this financial pie. Cosmetic procedures are an all-cash, payment-up-front business, totally eliminating the administrative headaches of the current medical reimbursement system. Surgeons who want to be able (eventually) to quit their day jobs (and night jobs, for that matter) are looking for easier sources of income. The cosmetic surgery business is just that source.

How all this got started is anyone's guess. One of the problems with this trend is the ease with which any physician or surgeon can put up a shingle and solicit business. Gynecologic surgeons venturing into cosmetic surgery already have a built-in market because of the patients in their practice (a fair amount of cosmetic surgery is performed on women, especially to correct the anatomical changes resulting from pregnancy). Gynecologists have the advantage of a female patient base to whom they can market their new skills. As one plastic surgeon, Dr. Joel Aronowitz, a clinical assistant professor of plastic surgery at the University of Southern California, was quoted in a January 2012 *New York Times* article as saying, "A doctor may be good and well trained in his or her specialty, but it takes more than a weekend seminar to achieve mastery in plastic surgery."

For most doctors, though, all it takes is paying a fee for attending a weekend (or weeklong) course and subsequent proctoring by a "qualified" physician. Some private companies are specifically in the business of training non–plastic surgeons in the business of cosmetic surgery. These companies also assist in marketing and promoting the doctor's new business, some of which can be deceiving. Non–plastic surgeons who set up a cosmetic surgery office often promote themselves as "board certified." The problem is they are not board certified in cosmetic surgery, as most people might assume from the advertising. They are no doubt board certified, but it could be in general surgery; that makes the surgeon qualified to remove your appendix but not necessarily to perform your face-lift.

Is this all legal? Oh, yes. Is it ethical? The answer depends on whom you ask. So, buyer beware. The first thing a prospective patient can do is be suspicious of any non–plastic surgeon bearing cosmetic surgery gifts. Any surgeon (or nonsurgeon) doing procedures outside his or her trained specialty should raise a red flag. Also, pay close attention to where the procedures are being done. Most cosmetic surgery performed by surgeons not trained in plastic surgery is done at physician-owned clinics, spas, or offices. It is carried out there because the physicians benefit financially from the procedures and the local hospital would never grant them privileges for cosmetic surgery procedures.

Actually, the trend of physicians and surgeons performing more minor procedures in their offices is growing. It allows them to capture more revenue from the procedures. Surgeons can realize greater reimbursement if they turn their offices into minor operating rooms. They can also add to the reimbursement when imaging, such as ultrasound, is used during the procedure. In these situations, surgeons can bill for the interpretation of the imaging, as well as the procedure itself.

I would also pay attention to the diplomas and certificates on the walls. If there are none at all, be wary. If the certificates state that your surgeon is board certified in general, gynecologic, or ENT surgery, ask about his or her training in *cosmetic* surgery. Do some research online by going to state medical boards to see if the surgeon about to do your liposuction has had any disciplinary action or license suspensions in the past. Some of these new "cosmetic surgeons" may have reincarnated themselves from another surgical life, a life that may have ended poorly. Maybe there are quality reasons why your "cosmetic" surgeon does not practice general or gynecologic surgery anymore. Patients should also try to resist the cheaper prices offered by many of the surgeons who are not board-certified plastic surgeons. Most can undercut the fully trained plastic surgeon's prices because cosmetic surgery is not their primary source of income. Finally, the last thing a prospective patient can do before having that breast augmentation from any board-certified specialist other than a plastic surgeon is to get a second opinion from a real one.

Another rich source of income for physicians and surgeons is ownership in entities they can influence, control, and profit from by directing a patient's care. These businesses include outpatient surgery centers, specialty hospitals, imaging centers, laboratories, and medical device distributorships. Surgeons are in a unique position because some can exert leverage over where they perform surgery. This scenario is a controversial subject because physicians and surgeons walk a fine ethical line when they have a financial stake in a business they can influence. With the trend of declining reimbursements, physicians and surgeons who have ownership stakes in free-standing outpatient entities are under increasing financial pressure to watch that ethical line. Regardless of these concerns, such ownerships are a way for surgeons to take advantage of investment opportunities unique to their skills, which they can control and subsequently profit from. The financial returns can be generous. In 1989, Congress passed what are known as the Stark Laws, named after then congressman Pete Stark. The laws were written to minimize the potential for physicians to profit from referring their Medicare/Medicaid patients to physician-owned services or businesses. Over the years, many exemptions to the original laws have been passed, allowing physicians to earn income from such businesses.

When physicians and surgeons have legal financial stakes in patient-care businesses and profit from them, does it affect medical decision making? Intuitively, you might answer, "How can it not?" Consciously or subconsciously, and despite the best intentions, money talks. In a study published in the journal *Radiology* in September 2013, the authors compared two physician groups and the number of knee MRIs ordered by each. One group had a financial stake in the MRI center and the other did not. After reviewing seven hundred ordered MRIs, the authors discovered that the physicians who owned the MRI scanner had a higher rate of negative exams (33 percent versus

25 percent) than those who had no financial stake, everything else being equal. From this finding, the authors concluded that "doctors with a financial interest in the machines were more likely to order MRIs even when clinical findings suggest they are unnecessary."

Concerns about the influence of surgeon-owned surgery centers or specialty hospitals has been highlighted by the passing of the Affordable Care Act in 2010. Within the bowels of this law are provisions prohibiting the construction of any new surgeon-owned hospital. In addition, the law prohibits expansion of any existing ones if they choose to accept Medicare payments. The reasoning: Such restrictions would help prevent the tendency of surgeons to direct patients for unneeded surgery to facilities where they profit from the surgery itself. Many, including federal lawmakers, feel it is an inherent conflict of interest for surgeons to own the facilities where they can direct their patients to have surgery.

In this country, there are more than five thousand ambulatory surgery centers/specialty hospitals. Most of these are owned by surgeons, many by orthopedic surgeons. All have the ability to direct patients who are referred to them to the facilities they own. According to a May 2013 *Wall Street Journal* article, the American Hospital Directory has stated that "many physician-owned hospitals have enjoyed 20 percent to 35 percent profit margins in recent years (compared to 7 percent for community hospitals as quoted from the American Hospital Association)."

For years, hospitals have felt threatened by the competition of surgeon-owned hospitals. To combat the threat, hospitals have enjoyed state legislative lobbying power to squelch the entrepreneurial spirits of surgeons who wanted to start their own surgery centers or niche hospitals. Even in small communities, hospitals' political power and cash reserves have made them formidable competition. Hospitals have been known to deliberately and falsely stain the reputations of those community surgeons willing to compete against them with their own surgery centers. Hospital administrators and trustees have done this through innuendo, political pressure, and behind-the-scenes financial deals. Yet physician-owned hospitals and surgery centers are getting more positive attention from insurance companies because of their cost-effectiveness, efficiency, patient satisfaction, and good outcomes. For years, it has been a well-kept secret that surgeon-owned surgery centers and specialty hospitals can perform any operation for a lower cost than the local hospital can. Remember the example in Chapter 6 of Mr. Wilkes's laparoscopic hernia repair hospital bill compared to his neighbor's surgery center bill? It can be done cheaper because of the cost efficiency inherent to surgery centers compared to acute care hospitals, plus the fact that many are reimbursed less for the same procedure than the local hospital would be. Health insurance companies are paying serious attention to this cost-saving ability and are rewarding surgeon-owned surgery centers/hospitals with higher reimbursement schedules—all the while saving money compared to the standard reimbursement for a hospital. In addition, under Medicare guidelines, many surgeon-owned surgery centers/hospitals are receiving bonuses for patient satisfaction and quality outcomes, both of which are exceeding many community hospitals' scores.

There are, however, several criticisms of physician-owned surgery centers/hospitals, with the main one centering on the danger of money influencing the medical decision-making process. In a recent Workers Compensation Research Institute study published in *General Surgery News* in March 2013, the authors looked at the referral behavior of Florida-based orthopedic surgeons from 1997 to 2004, before and after they became owners of ambulatory surgery centers. The study concluded that in Florida, orthopedic surgeons who were owners performed seventy-six more operations each year than non-owners. According to these findings, ownership in a surgery center *does* change the way surgeons practice. In an interview regarding the study, the authors stated, "We can't tell if the surgeries were necessary or unnecessary." They also could not state why this behavior change occurred. It can only be left up to the reader to decide why surgeons, once they become owners in an ambulatory surgery center, increased their patient volume. Another study, published in *Archives of Surgery* in 2010, looked at claims data in Idaho over a five-year period for orthopedic surgeon owners and non-owners. The authors confirmed that surgeon owners performed more operations (at their ambulatory surgery centers) than non-owners.

Another criticism leveled at physician-owned surgery centers/specialty hospitals focuses on the decision-making process, or how a surgeon decides whom to operate on and where. The argument was made that physician owners tend to "cherry-pick" their patients based on what insurance companies reimburse. Some studies have supported this argument, specifically one published in the journal *Health Affairs* in May 2008. Here the authors asked the question, "Does physician-ownership affect referral patterns to ambulatory surgery centers?" Data from two metropolitan areas was reviewed, comparing the referring habits of owners to non-owners. The authors found that physicians who owned the surgery centers were more likely to operate on well-insured patients at their facility.

In another study published in *Health Economics* in July 2011, the authors used a sample of Medicare patients from the National Survey of Ambulatory Surgery. They asked whether "the profitability of an outpatient surgery impacts where a physician performs surgery." The study revealed that the operations that reimbursed surgeons (and the facilities they used) more had a greater chance of being done at an ambulatory surgery center. Indirectly, the ambulatory surgery center would benefit more if a complex, higher-reimbursed operation were performed there versus at a hospital. The inference is that surgeons, for their own financial benefit, may bring their better-paying patients to their surgery centers rather than to the local hospital.

The cherry-picking-for-profit argument is valid because physician-owned surgery centers/specialty hospitals are in a position to decide whom to bring in. On the surface, it does make good business sense, if it is legal, to choose the better-paying clients. Life insurance companies cherry-pick to whom they offer life insurance policies. Banks cherry-pick to whom loans are made. Health insurance companies cherry-pick every day when deciding whom to cover and whom to decline, and until the Affordable Care Act, denying coverage because of a preexisting condition was perfectly legal. You could also say that physicians in practice cherry-pick their patients on a daily basis by deciding which health insurance they will accept. When you see a sign in a physician's office that says *Not accepting Medicare or Medicaid*, on what basis do you think that decision was made? It was made solely on the basis of self-interest: cost and reimbursement. How, you might ask, are these surgi-center scenarios any different?

Another business vehicle that allows surgeons to profit from the medical devices they place in patients during surgery is called physician-owned distributorships (PODs). A physician-owned distributorship essentially acts as an intermediary between the medical device manufacturers and the hospitals that purchase the items. PODs often purchase devices (artificial hips, knees, spinal cages, and so on) directly from the manufacturer. They, in turn, market and distribute these devices to hospitals at a marked-up price. The hospitals, in turn, just pass this added cost on to the insurance companies and patients. Many PODs have surgeon investors, the same surgeons who can exert influence on hospitals to purchase from their specific distributorship. Not only do POD surgeons get paid for performing major joint or spine surgery, they also profit from the devices they insert during the surgery. Is this incestuous setup a conflict of interest? It sounds like it to me. The surgeons who own the distributorship have unique leverage with the hospital where they work. They can more easily persuade the hospital's purchasing department to buy from their distributorship (at the expense of the competition), by whispering that they can take their patient business elsewhere. Hospitals, in turn, may be reluctant to play the conflict-of-interest card for fear of losing the operating room business. And there have been situations where the surgeons do not offer full disclosure of their investment in the distributorship when negotiating with the hospital. With such a solid ability to profit twice (fee for the surgery, and profits from the medical device) every time a new artificial joint is placed or a new spinal device inserted, surgeons may be tempted to loosen their indications for surgery, opening the door to unnecessary operations.

On March 26, 2013, the Office of Inspector General (OIG) of the Department of Health and Human Services issued a paper titled "Special Fraud Alert: Physician-Owned Entities." In its conclusion the paper stated: "OIG is concerned about the proliferation of PODs. This Special Fraud Alert reiterates our long-standing position that the opportunity for a referring physician to earn a profit, including through an investment in an entity for which he or she generates business, could constitute illegal remuneration under the anti-kickback statute. OIG views PODs as inherently suspect under the anti-kickback statute."

In a follow-up report to Congress, an OIG study added fuel to the criticism that surgeons who profit from implants they use lead to more (potentially unnecessary) surgery. The study found that approximately 30 percent more spinal surgery was performed at hospitals that bought spinal implants from PODs when compared to those hospitals that did not. Utah senator Orrin Hatch, of the Senate Finance Committee, commented on this report: "My deep-seated skepticism that physician-owned distributors operate in the best interest of patients and save taxpayers money has been confirmed."

Today, there are more and more ways that physicians, especially surgeons, can make money from their expertise. Most are legal. Most are ethical. Some are not. For most practicing surgeons, their only source of income originates from the ethical judgment and expertise they apply when operating on their patients.

After medical school, I decided on a career in surgery primarily because as a surgeon I could immediately make a difference in someone's life with the expertise I would learn. I wanted the opportunity to see the fruits of my labor in the operating room and not have to rely on any other part of the medical profession. I decided to enter one of the most difficult surgical training programs in the country and had the good fortune to succeed in my endeavor to follow my calling. As a practicing surgeon today, I go to work to fix broken people. Every day, I open my office with the intent of improving the quality of my patients' lives.

Some say I am paid too much for what I do. Some say it is hard to justify my income, despite the years of training, sacrifice, and quality outcomes that have brought me to this point. So let me raise the question: *What is a good surgeon worth?* What is a good vascular surgeon worth when he or she is about to clean out your carotid artery (the blood vessel to your brain) in order to prevent you from having a stroke? What are his or her meticulous surgical skills worth to you when the main complication of this operation (at a rate of 3 percent) is a stroke that could leave you paralyzed? Medicare thinks the skills of your vascular surgeon are worth about $1,100 for this difficult operation with potential life-altering consequences. Is that $1,100 enough when the hospital receives nearly ten times that amount for the operation? Is $1,100 enough, knowing that your life could be changed forever after waking up from anesthesia? The National Stroke Association states that the mean lifetime cost of treating stroke is $140,000. This is probably a very conservative number. For only $1,100, competent vascular surgeons are not only saving lives, they are also saving this country's healthcare system a lot of money.

The next time you find yourself on your back, staring at the operating room ceiling, about to be put to sleep for that total hip replacement, brain tumor removal, heart valve replacement, pancreatic cancer resection, or even a simple hernia repair, ask yourself how much a good surgeon is really worth. You might just find the word *priceless* running through your mind as you drift off. My hope is that you never have to think otherwise.

ACKNOWLEDGMENTS

I am again indebted to the individuals who put their trust in me each time I step into the operating room. I remain humbled by and in awe of your humanity. My patients and their families continue to amaze me with their courage, stamina, and hope in the face of personal adversity.

I would like to thank my agent, Don Fehr, of Trident Media Group, for his continued faith in me. I would also like to thank Natalee Rosenstein, of Penguin Random House, along with her assistant, Robin Barletta.

I am extremely grateful for Martha Murphy's friendship, guidance, and editorial assistance from the beginning to the very end of this project.

Others I would like to thank for their inspiration during the writing of this book include the Little Man, the nurses in the operating room (especially Jack) and on Atwood 3, and my office staff.

I would also like to thank my father, John Ruggieri, despite his having left us twelve years ago, for the inspiration to be honest in the face of adversity.

Last but not least, I can never stop thanking my wife, Erin; my three stepsons, Matt, Ryan, and Jacker; and my son, Cody, for all their love and support.

RESOURCES

CHAPTER 1

Arterburn, D., et al. "Introducing Decision Aids at Group Health Was Linked to Sharply Lower Hip and Knee Surgery Rates and Costs." *Health Affairs* 31 (2012): 2094–2104.

Baras, J. D., et al. "MRI and Low Back Pain Care for Medicare Patients." *Health Affairs* 28 (2009): 1133–1140.

Barnato, A. E., et al. "Trends in Inpatient Treatment Intensity among Medicare Beneficiaries at the End of Life." *Health Services Research* 39 (2004): 363–376.

Brox, J. J., et al. "Randomized Clinical Trial of Lumbar Instrumental Fusion and Exercises in Patients with Chronic Low Back Pain and Disc Degeneration." *Spine* 28 (2003): 1913–1921.

Carreyrou, J. "Medicare Records Reveal Troubling Trial of Surgeons." *Wall Street Journal*, March 29, 2011.

Committee on Interstate and Foreign Commerce, House of Representatives. *Cost and Quality of Health Care: Unnecessary Surgery*. Report by the Subcommittee on Oversight and Investigations. U.S. Government Printing Office (1976).

Englund, M., et al. "Incidental Meniscal Findings on Knee MRI." *NEJM* 359 (2008): 1108–1115.

IOM (Institute of Medicine). *Best Care at Lower Cost: The Path to Continuously Learning Health Care in America.* Washington, DC: The National Academies Press, 2013.

Katz, J. N., et al. "Surgery versus Physical Therapy." *NEJM* 368 (2013): 1675–1684.

Kwok, A. C. "The Intensity and Variation of Surgical Care at the End of Life: A Retrospective Cohort Study." *Lancet* 378 (2011): 1408–1413.

Lee, J. "Rethinking Spine Care." *Modern Healthcare*, March 2014.

Liu, W., et al. "Incidental Extraurinary Findings at MDCT Urography in Patients with Hematuria: Prevalence and Impact on Imaging Costs." *AJR* 185 (2005): 1051–1056.

Mancini, G. J., et al. "Nationwide Impact of Laparoscopic Lysis of Adhesions." *J Am Coll Surg* 207 (2008): 520–526.

Moseley, T. B., et al. "A Controlled Trial of Arthroscopic Surgery for Osteoarthritis." *NEJM* 347 (2002): 81–88.

Sheffield, K., et al. "Potentially Inappropriate Screening Colonoscopy in Medicare Patients." *JAMA* 173 (2013): 542–550.

Sihvonen, R., et al. "Arthroscopic Partial Meniscectomy versus Sham Surgery for a Degenerative Meniscal Tear." *NEJM* 369 (2013): 2515–2524.

Sikirica, V., et al. "The Inpatient Burden of Abdominal and Gynecological Adhesiolysis in the US." *BMC Surg* 11 (2011).

Smith-Bindman, R. "Substantial Increase in Rate of Advanced Diagnostic Imaging." *JAMA* 307 (2012): 2434–2435.

Swank, D. J. "Laparoscopic Adhesiolysis in Patients with Chronic Abdominal Pain." *Lancet* 361 (2003): 1247–1251.

Ten Broek, R. P. G., et al. "Adhesiolysis-Related Morbidity in Abdominal Surgery." *Ann Surg* 258 (2013): 98–106.

Waldman, P. "Deaths Linked to Cardiac Stents Rise as Overuse Seen." Bloomberg News, September 26, 2013.

Welch, H. G., et al. *Overdiagnosed: Making People Sick in the Pursuit of Health.* Boston: Beacon Press, 2011.

CHAPTER 2

Decker, S. "In 2011, Nearly One-Third of Physicians Said They Would Not Accept New Medicaid Patients." *Health Affairs* 31 (2012): 1673–1679.

Frangou, C. "Study Reveals Staggering Costs of Ventral Hernia Repair Complication." *Gen Surg News* 41 (2014).

MGMA. "Medical Directorship and On-Call Compensation Survey." 2013.

Muma, D., et al. "U.S. Physician Practices versus Canadians: Spending Nearly Four Times as Much Money Interacting with Payers." *Health Affairs* 30 (2011): 1443–1450.

Neuwahl, S., et al. "The Impact of General Surgeon Supply on the Risk of Appendiceal Rupture in North Carolina." *Ann Surg* 257 (2013): 1170–1175.

Rabin, R. C. "When Doctors Stop Taking Insurance." *New York Times*, October 1, 2012.

CHAPTER 3

Charles, A. G., et al. "The Employed Surgeon." *JAMA Surg* 148 (2013): 323–330.

Cohen, R. "Resident Duty-Hour Limits Linked to Safety, Education Concerns." Reuters, April 3, 2014.

Glenn, B. "Primary Care Physicians Generate More Revenue for Hospitals Than Specialists." *Med Econ*, May 8, 2013.

Goldfine, A. B., et al. "Where Are the Health Care Cost Savings with Bariatric Surgery in Obesity Management?" *JAMA Surg* 149 (2014) 5–6.

Gottlieb, S. "The Doctor Won't See You Now. He's Clocked Out." *Wall Street Journal*, March 14, 2013.

Kocher, R., et al. "Hospitals Race to Employ Physicians—The Logic behind a Money-Losing Proposition." *NEJM* 364 (2011): 1790–1793.

Lee, J. "Rethinking Spine Care." *Modern Healthcare*, March 2014.

Leffell, D. J. "The Doctor's Office as Union Shop." *Wall Street Journal*, January 29, 2013.

Monto, R. R. "Private Practice RIP." *Medscape*, December 2012.

Schauer, P. R., et al. "Bariatric Surgery versus Intensive Medical Therapy for Diabetes—3-Year Outcomes." NEJM.org, March 31, 2014.

Schwartz, S. I., et al. "Effect of the 16-Hour Work Limit on General Surgery Intern Operative Case Volume: A Multi-institutional Study." *JAMA Surg* 148 (2013): 829–833.

CHAPTER 4

Jaheri, P. A., et al. "Trauma Center Downstream Revenue: The Impact of Incremental Patients within a Health System." *J Trauma* 62 (2007): 619–621.

Kocher, R., et al. "Hospitals Race to Employ Physicians—The Logic behind a Money-Losing Proposition." *NEJM* 364 (2011): 1790–1793.

Mathews, A. W., et al. "Health-Care Rivals Battle for Patients in Pittsburgh." *Wall Street Journal*, March 26, 2012.

Miller, P. R., et al. "Acute Care Surgery: Impact on Practice and Economics of Elective Surgeons." *J Am Coll Surg* 214 (2012): 531–538.

Schauer, P. R., et al. "Bariatric Surgery versus Intensive Medical Therapy for Diabetes—3-Year Outcomes." NEJM.org, March 31, 2014.

Weiner, J. P., et al. "Impact of Bariatric Surgery on Health Care Costs of Obese Patients." *JAMA Surg* 148 (2013): 555–561.

CHAPTER 5

Birkmeyer, J. D., et al. "Hospital Quality and the Cost of Inpatient Surgery in the United States." *Ann Surg* 255 (2012): 1–5.

———. "Surgeon Volume and Operative Mortality." *NEJM* 349 (2003): 2117–2127.

———. "Surgical Skill and Complication Rates after Bariatric Surgery." *NEJM* 369 (2013): 1434–1442.

Chen, P. "A Vital Measure: Your Surgeon's Skill." *New York Times*, October 31, 2013.

Eappen, S., et al. "Relationship between Occurrence of Surgical Complications and Hospital Finances." *JAMA* 309 (2013): 1599–1605.

Gottlieb, S. "Medicaid Is Worse Than No Coverage at All." *Wall Street Journal*, March 10, 2011.

Jencks, S. F., et al. "Rehospitalizations among Patients in Medicare." *NEJM* 360 (2009): 1418–1428.

Kassin, M. T., et al. "Risk Factors for 30-Day Readmission among General Surgery Patients." *J Am Coll Surg* 215 (2012): 322–330.

Kazaure, H. S., et al. "Association of Postdischarge Complications with Reoperation and Mortality in General Surgery." *JAMA Surg* 147 (2012): 1000–1007.

Krupka, D. C., et al. "The Impact of Reducing Surgical Complications Suggests Many Will Need Shared Savings Programs with Payers." *Health Affairs* 31 (2012): 2571–2578.

LaPar, D. J., et al. "Primary Payer Status Affects Mortality for Major Surgical Operations." *Ann Surg* 252 (2010): 544–551.

———. "Primary Payer Status Affects Outcomes for Cardiac Valve Operations." *J Am Coll Surg* 212 (2011): 759–767.

Momin, E. N., et al. "Postoperative Mortality after Surgery for Brain Tumors by Patient Insurance Status in the United States." *JAMA Surg* 147 (2012): 1017–1024.

Morris, M., et al. "Results of New Surgical Outcome Study Provide Insight into Reducing Patient Readmission Rates." ACS Clinical Congress, 2012.

Pieper, D. P., et al. "State of Evidence on the Relationship Between High-Volume Hospitals and Outcomes in Surgery." *J Am Coll Surg* 216 (2013): 1015–1025.

Regenbogen, S. E., et al. "Hospital Surgical Volume and Cost of Inpatient Surgery in the Elderly." *J Am Coll Surg* 215 (2012): 758–765.

Rice, S. "Patient Safety Varies Widely Among U.S. Hospitals, Consumer Reports Finds." *Modern Healthcare*, March 2014.

Spencer, C. S., et al. "The Quality of Care Delivered to Patients within the Same Hospital Varies by Insurance Type." *Health Affairs* 32 (2013): 1731–1739.

Tsai, T. C., et al. "Variation in Surgical-Readmission Rates and Quality of Hospital Care." *NEJM* 369 (2013): 1134–1142.

Waisbren, E., et al. "Percent Body Fat and Prediction of Surgical Site Infection." *J Am Coll Surg* 210 (2010): 381–389.

Williams, S. B., et al. "Influence of Surgeons and Hospital Volume on Radical Prostatectomy Costs." *J Urology* 188 (2012): 2198–2204.

CHAPTER 6

Finn, T. "Lack of Pricing Transparency Damages Healthcare's Reputation." *Healthcare Matters*, April 25, 2012.

Hiss, K. "Special Report: Why a Hospital Bill Costs What It Costs." *Reader's Digest*, September 2012.

Hsia, R. Y., et al. "Health Care as a 'Market Good'? Appendicitis as a Case Study." *Arch Intern Med* 172 (2012): 818–819.

Okike, K., et al. "Survey Finds Few Orthopedic Surgeons Know the Costs of the Devices They Implant." *Health Affairs* 33 (2014): 103–109.

Patterson, P. "How Surgery Departments Charge for OR Time." *OR Manager* 27 (2011): 19–23.

Robinson, J. C., et al. "Increases in Consumer Cost Sharing Redirect Patient Volumes and Reduce Hospital Prices for Orthopedic Surgery." *Health Affairs* 32 (2013): 1392–1397.

Rosenthal, J. A., et al. "Availability of Consumer Prices from U.S. Hospitals for a Common Surgical Procedure." *JAMA Intern Med* 173 (2013): 427–432.

Sommers, R., et al. "Focus Groups Highlight That Many Patients Object to Clinicians Focusing on Costs." *Health Affairs* 32 (2013): 338–346.

Tilburt, J. C., et al. "Views of U.S. Physicians about Controlling Health Care Costs." *JAMA* 310 (2013): 380–388.

CHAPTER 7

Camp, M. W., et al. "Patients' Views on Surgeons' Financial Conflicts of Interest." *J Bone Joint Surg* 95 (2013): e9(1–8).

Campbell, E. G., et al. "A National Survey of Physician-Industry Relationships." *NEJM* 356 (2007): 1742–1750.

Feder, B. J. "Artificial Joint Makers Settle Kickback Case." *New York Times*, September 28, 2007.

IOM (Institute of Medicine). *Medical Devices and the Public's Health: The FDA 510(k) Clearance Process at 35 Years.* Washington, DC: The National Academies Press, 2011.

Kessel, A. S., et al. "Distributions of Industry Payments to Massachusetts Physicians." *NEJM* 368 (2013): 2049–2052.

Korenstein, D., et al. "Physician Attitudes toward Industry." *Arch Surg* 145 (2010): 570–577.

Nissen, S. "Physician Groups Welcome Transparency." *Med Econ*, March 25, 2013.

Pearl, R. "Medical Conflicts of Interest Are Dangerous." *Wall Street Journal*, April 24, 2013.

Weaver, C. "Study: Hospitals Overpay for Devices." *Wall Street Journal*, February 3, 2012.

Zuckerman, D. M., et al. "Medical Device Recalls and the FDA Approval Process." *Arch Intern Med* 171 (2011): 1006–1011.

CHAPTER 8

Anderson, J. E., et al. "The First Examination of Outcomes and Trends in Robotic Surgery in the United States." *J Am Coll Surg* 215 (2012): 107–116.

Barbash, G. I., et al. "Factors Associated with Adoption of Robotic Surgical Technology in U.S. Hospitals and Relationship to Radical Prostatectomy Procedure Volume." *Ann Surg* (2014): 1–6.

Beck, M. "Study Raises Doubts over Robotic Surgery." *Wall Street Journal*, February 19, 2013.

Breeden, J. T. "Statement on Robotic Surgery by ACOG President James T. Breeden, MD." American Congress of Obstetricians and Gynecologists, March 14, 2013.

Breitenstein, S., et al. "Robotic-Assisted versus Laparoscopic Cholecystectomy." *Ann Surg* 247 (2008): 987–993.

Juo, Y. Y., et al. "Is Minimally Invasive Colon Resection Better Than Traditional Approaches?: First Comprehensive National Examination with Propensity Score Matching." *JAMA Surg* 149 (2014): 177–184.

Kent, M., et al. "Open, Video-Assisted Thoracic Surgery and Robotic Lobectomy: Review of a National Database." *Ann Thorac Surg* 97 (2014): 236–242.

Langreth, R. "Robot Surgery Damaging Patients Rises with Marketing." Bloomberg News, October 8, 2013.

Liu, J. J., et al. "Perioperative Outcomes of Laparoscopic and Robotic Compared with Open Prostatectomy Using NSQIP Database." *Urology* 82 (2013): 579–583.

Makary, M. *Unaccountable: What Hospitals Won't Tell You and How Transparency Can Revolutionize Health Care.* New York: Bloomsbury Press, 2012.

Martino, M. A., et al. "A Comparison of Quality Outcome Measures in Patients Having a Hysterectomy for Benign Disease: Robotic vs. Nonrobotic Approaches." *Journal of Minimally Invasive Gynecology*, October 28, 2013.

Paraiso, M. F. R., et al. "A Randomized Trial Comparing Conventional and Robotically Assisted Total Laparoscopic Hysterectomy." *Am J Obstet Gynecol* 208 (2013): e1–7.

———. "Robotic-Assisted Laparoscopic Hysterectomy: Optimizing Use of This Technology." *Obstet Gynecol* 122 (2013): 435–436.

Pulvirenti, E., et al. "Increased Rate of Cholecystectomies Performed with Doubtful or No Indications after Laparoscopy Introduction: A Single Center Experience." *BMC Surg* 17 (2013).

Schiavone, M. B., et al. "The Commercialization of Robotic Surgery: Unsubstantiated Marketing of Gynecologic Surgery by Hospitals." *Am J Obstet Gynecol* 207 (2012): e1–7.

"Summary Minutes of the General and Plastic Surgery Devices Panel of the Medical Devices Advisory Committee." U.S. Food and Drug Administration, June 16, 1999.

Tyler, J. A., et al. "Outcomes and Costs Associated with Robotic Colectomy in the Minimally Invasive Era." *Dis Colon Rectum* 56 (2013): 458–466.

Wren, S. M., et al. "Single-Port Robotic Cholecystectomy." *Arch Surg* 146 (2011): 1122–1127.

Wright, J. D., et al. "Robotically Assisted versus Laparoscopic Hysterectomy among Women with Benign Gynecologic Disease." *JAMA* 309 (2013): 689–698.

CHAPTER 9

Berenson, R. A., et al. "Grading a Physician's Value—The Misapplication of Performance Measurement." *NEJM* 369 (2013): 1773–1775.

Boukus, E. R., et al. "A Snapshot of U.S. Physicians: Key Findings from the 2008 Health Tracking Physician Survey." Data Bulletin No. 35, Center for Studying Health System Change, September 2009.

Cassel, C. K., et al. "Assessing Individual Physician Performance: Does Measurement Suppress Mutation?" *JAMA* 307 (2012): 2595–2596.

Cruz, M., et al. "Predicting 10-Year Mortality for Older Adults." *JAMA* 309 (2013): 874–876.

Garvin, P. "Cost of Health Reform." *Boston Globe*, June 26, 2011.

Jha, A. K., et al. "The Long-Term Effect of Premier Pay for Performance on Patient Outcomes." *NEJM* 366 (2012): 1606–1615.

Jost, T. S. "The Independent Payment Advisory Board." *NEJM* 363 (2010): 103–105.

Kowalczyk, L. "Beth Israel Deaconess Settles with U.S. for $5.3M." *Boston Globe*, July 30, 2013.

Lawrence, P., et al. "Professionalism and Caring for Medicaid Patients— The 5% Commitment." *NEJM* 369 (2013): 1775–1777.

Miller, D. C., et al. "Anticipating the Effects of Accountable Care Organizations for Inpatient Surgery." *JAMA Surg* 148 (2013): 549–554.

White, C. E., et al. "When Medicare Cuts Hospital Prices, Seniors Use Less Inpatient Care." *Health Affairs* 32 (2013): 1789–1795.

CHAPTER 10

Baltic, S. "Medicare RUC Responds to Its Critics." *Med Econ*, October 2013.

Carreyrou, J. "Study: Surgery Rate Higher When Implants Purchased from Doctors." *Wall Street Journal*, October 24, 2013.

Gabel, J. R., et al. "Where Do I Send Thee? Does Physician-Ownership Affect Patterns of Ambulatory Surgery Centers?" *Health Affairs* 3 (2008): 165–174.

Hsiao, W., et al. "Estimating Physicians' Work for a Resource-Based Relative Value Scale." *NEJM* 319 (1988): 835–841.

Kane, L. "Why Aren't Doctors Allowed to Care About Money?" *Medscape*, 2010.

Lungren, M. P., et al. "Physician Self-Referral: Frequency of Negative Findings at MR Imaging of the Knee as a Marker of Appropriate Utilization." *Radiology* 269 (2013): 810–815.

Mitchell, J. M., et al. "Effect of Physician Ownership of Specialty Hospitals and Ambulatory Surgery Centers on Frequency of Use of Outpatient Orthopedic Surgery." *Arch Surg* 145 (2010): 732–738.

Mundy, A. "Doc-Owned Hospitals Prepare to Fight." *Wall Street Journal*, May 13, 2013.

Murphy, K. "Ear Doctors Performing Face-Lifts? It Happens." *New York Times*, January 30, 2012.

"Physician Compensation Report: MGMA Survey." *Medscape*, 2013.

Plotzke, M. R., et al. "Does Procedure Profitability Impact Whether an Outpatient Surgery Is Performed at an Ambulatory Surgery Center or Hospital?" *Health Econ* 7 (2011): 817–830.

Sinsky, C. A., et al. "Medicare Payment for Cognitive vs Procedural Care: Minding the Gap." *JAMA Intern Med* 173 (2013): 1733–1737.

"Special Fraud Alert: Physician-Owned Entities." Office of Inspector General, March 26, 2013.

Stern, V. "The Cowboys of Lap Chole." *Gen Surg News* 40 (2013).

Yee, C. "Why Owners of Ambulatory Centers Do More Surgery." Workers Compensation Research Institute Study (WCRI), October 30, 2012.